W0245830

Associative Computing

A Programming Paradigm for Massively Parallel Computers

FRONTIERS OF COMPUTER SCIENCE

Series Editor: Arnold L. Rosenberg
University of Massachusetts
Amherst, Massachusetts

ASSOCIATIVE COMPUTING: A Programming Paradigm for Massively Parallel Computers
Jerry L. Potter

INTRODUCTION TO PARALLEL AND VECTOR SOLUTION OF LINEAR SYSTEMS
James M. Ortega

A Continuation Order Plan is available for this series. A continuation order will bring delivery of each new volume immediately upon publication. Volumes are billed only upon actual shipment. For further information please contact the publisher.

Associative Computing

A Programming Paradigm for Massively Parallel Computers

Jerry L. Potter

Kent State University
Kent, Ohio

Springer Science+Business Media, LLC

Library of Congress Cataloging-in-Publication Data

Potter, Jerry L.
Associative computing : a programming paradigm for massively parallel computers / Jerry L. Potter.
p. cm. -- (Frontiers in computer science)
Includes bibliographical references and index.
ISBN 978-1-4613-6452-8 ISBN 978-1-4615-3300-9 (eBook)
DOI 10.1007/978-1-4615-3300-9
1. Parallel computers--Programming. I. Title. II. Series.
QA76.5.P6354 1992
004'35--dc20 91-40897
CIP

ISBN 978-1-4613-6452-8

Originally published by Plenum Press, New York in 1992
Softcover reprint of the hardcover 1st edition 1992

Preface

Associative processing has been discussed for more than thirty years, but little more than the *a-list* function in Lisp has ever been incorporated into a programming language. The idea of accessing data by its content or meaning instead of an abstract address mapping surely has much to offer in increased programmer productivity. This book is a first step toward unifying associative processing concepts with massively parallel SIMD technology.

This book is intended for students, professionals, and researchers interested in associative processing, content-addressable memories, artificial intelligence, context-sensitive compilation, massively parallel computation, neural networks, and expert systems. The first six chapters have been used successfully for teaching an undergraduate course in SIMD parallel programming at Kent State University. The last four chapters are appropriate for more advanced courses. An associative-computer emulator that executes in a C-Unix environment has been developed as an aid to classroom instruction. Compilers for the Connection Machine and Wavetracer are also available. The software comes with a set of programming exercises, coordinated with the text, which cover all aspects of associative programming. Source-file solutions to the exercises are included with the software. These programs are also used as a test suite to assure that the compiler/emulator is operating properly. A request form for the ASC (associative computing) software can be found inside the back cover of this book.

Chapter 1 introduces and defines some basic terms and concepts of associative computing. In particular, the terms *associative*, *responder*, *word*, *field*, *vector*, *pointer*, and *flag* are defined. The concepts of associative searches, associative triples, associative memories, associative processors, associative computers, and data parallelism are introduced and distinguished. The ability to use associative searching in place of conventional address calculation is briefly discussed. The capability of SIMD computers to perform effective associative retrieval is explained, and the natural mapping of a two-dimensional data structure onto the memory of a one-dimensional SIMD processor is demonstrated. These last two items form the basic rationale for the Single Instruction Tabular Data Associative Computation (SITDAC) model. The model is formally defined and then contrasted briefly with data-parallel, neural networks, relational data bases, list processing, and rule-based systems as models of computation. The affinity among associative programming, natural thought processes, and natural language is discussed. An argument for the simplicity of associative programming as compared with conventional address calculation is presented. The concept of an address function is introduced. Finally, a brief discussion of throughput analysis is given.

Chapter 2 introduces and describes some basic SIMD programming concepts that are important to the SITDAC model. Among them are SIMD flow of control, the classroom model, dynamic memory allocation, massively parallel searching, tabular data arrays, bit-serial arithmetic, numeric searching, responders, responder iteration, data reformatting (corner turning), bucket-brigade communication, data-memory mapping, and data replication.

Chapter 3 describes the search, process, retrieve (SPR) cycle that is the basis of SITDAC programming. The mappings of the SPR cycles onto the basic control statements of ASC are described. Additional ASC statements, including data declarations and I/O, are explained in conjunction with basic associative-programming concepts.

Chapter 4 presents several ASC programs and contrasts them with conventional implementations. This chapter also describes how the associative approach reduces the need for sorting and sort-based data structures such as linked lists, stacks, and queues.

Chapter 5 describes associative data-structure implementation using structure codes. Structure codes allow any logical data structure to be stored in the tabular two-dimensional SITDAC data structure so that they may be searched and processed in parallel.

Chapter 6 describes how recursion can be implemented in ASC. In general, SITDAC associative computing avoids recursion for searching and processing data and instead uses massively parallel searching to find the innermost or terminating level of recursion and then performs the evaluations from the inside out. However, certain functions are elegantly expressed using recursion. This chapter describes recursion both with and without a specialized recursive control statement.

Chapter 7 introduces additional ASC control structures that allow complex pattern searches to be expressed in procedural form. Chapter 8 illustrates how rule-based pattern-matching languages can be compiled into procedural routines using context-sensitive techniques.

Chapter 9 discusses the implementation of a Prolog interpreter in ASC. Associative techniques for unification, and/or tree searching, variable binding, and clause filtering are described. The Prolog interpreter is a significant ASC program.

Chapter 10 proposes a computer design for the SITDAC model. It is based on the classic bit-serial SIMD design but incorporates several specific changes. It includes an I/O stack to provide specialized data-manipulation functions in addition to I/O. It has a byte-serial architecture for data manipulation while maintaining bit-serial manipulation for flag processing. One of the most significant enhancements is the inclusion of a multiple-instruction-stream feature that allows parallel execution of single SIMD programs as well as multiuser and multitasking parallel execution of multiple SIMD programs.

I would like to thank Goodyear Aerospace for the donation to Kent State University of the STARAN computer that enabled much of this research to progress, and the Office of Naval Research, the Supercomputing Research Center, and the state of Ohio for their support over the years. Finally, I would like to thank the reviewers for their helpful comments, corrections, and suggestions.

Jerry L. Potter

Kent, Ohio

Contents

Associative Computing

A Programming Paradigm for Massively Parallel Computers

1

Introduction

Parallelism is often considered the solution to the problem of need for ever more processing power. Critics cite Amdahl's Law—the speed of an algorithm is dominated by its sequential parts—to disparage the potential of massive parallelism. It is often overlooked, however, that the law applies to algorithms, not problems. Indeed, for a given problem, no known procedure can find all applicable algorithms. Thus, while it can be proved that there are inherently serial algorithms or procedures, there is no known proof that any problems are inherently serial.

Given that there are limits to parallelism in a given algorithm, the proper approach to parallelism is to use it in such a way that new classes of parallel algorithms can be developed. Trying to parallelize conventional algorithms designed for optimal performance on a sequential computer surely is of limited value. Whorf (in Whorf and Sapir [1956]) suggests that our system of representation limits our thinking. Parallelism should be used to expand our ability to think by expanding our representational capability. Associative computing is a paradigm for computing that has the potential to allow the development of innovative algorithms that can take direct advantage of massive parallelism.

This book presents the Single Instruction Tabular Data Associative Computing (SITDAC) model developed at the Department of Mathematics and Computer Science of Kent State University and the Supercomputing Research Center of the Institute for Defense Analysis. A major focus of this effort has been the development of the ASC (associative computing language) compiler (Hioe [1986]), emulator, and debugger. ASC embodies associative-computing data-selection and flow-of-control concepts.

ASC was developed from scratch. It was intentionally not an extension of a conventional language such as C, FORTRAN, or Pascal. In keeping with Whorf's concept, using an extension of a sequential language would encourage the programmer to use sequential algorithms and approaches on a parallel-associative computer. A new language encourages computer scientists to develop new algorithms and approaches.

ASC is not intended to be an end in itself. It is meant to be a vehicle for exploring associative computing as an alternative to conventional sequential and parallel programming. There is often a basic confusion between being able to search a sequential data structure in parallel and a parallel data structure. Consider linked lists. Linked lists are an inherently sequential data structure (Harrison and Padua [1984], p. 703). Yet it is commonly felt that, since linked lists can be searched in parallel in $\log n$ time (Hillis and Steele [1986]), they are parallel. But using n processors in parallel to perform sequential searching does not make a sequential data structure parallel. Each processor is still performing a sequential task by itself.

The point is perhaps more easily understood if you consider p processors, say eight, searching n links, say 64. Then, initially, each of the eight processors has eight links to search sequentially. The fact that, when the number of processors equals the number of links, only one link has to be searched per processor and all searches can be done in parallel does not change the basic nature of the data structure.

Indeed, $\log n$ complexity betrays sequentiality. It says in effect that the computation is dominated by the sequential nature of the algorithm and that the sequentiality can be reduced or parallelized to an extent but still requires $\log n$ sequential steps. (This is Amdahl's law at work!). If the algorithm were 100% parallel the computation could be done in constant time with n processors.

Parallel (constant time) algorithms for such tasks as finding the maximum integer in a set have been published for almost thirty years, but they are virtually unknown, due partially to the fact that they are not sequential and therefore not easily expressed in sequential (i.e., C, FORTRAN, or Pascal) languages. One intent of ASC research is to rediscover, expand, and explore these algorithms and to use them to develop parallel alternatives to sequential concepts such as linked lists.

The ASC compiler was designed to produce intermediate code representative of a general model of associative computing. The intermediate code has been compiled to execute on Goodyear Aerospace's STARAN and ASPRO computers and the Thinking Machines Corporation's Connection Machine. Current plans call for the development of versions for the DAP and Wavetracer computers. The emulator executes the intermediate code directly in a Unix/C environment. The interactive debugger operates in an X-windows environment.*

1.1. SITDAC Terminology

The terminology introduced in this section is intended to reflect that used in the literature. However, these terms are not standardized and concepts may vary slightly from those presented here.

*The ASC emulator and compilers are available for a nominal distribution fee. An order form appears at the end of the preface.

In computer science, the term *associative* is used to describe the technique of accessing or identifying an entire datum from a body of data by specifying any portion of it. Associative searching is a form of pattern matching. The term "associative" is normally used when the pattern matching involved is implemented as a primitive operation in hardware or software for a predefined data structure. Pattern recognition usually refers to situations in which the user must write his own routines to do matching using his own data structures.

For example, the term *associative memories* (or *content-addressable* memories) is used for hardware memories designed to retrieve an entire memory word when a subset of its bits, usually organized into fields, is specified. Since pattern matching is involved, any number of words may match the search pattern. Every word that matches is called a *responder*. Some mainframe computers use associative memories for internal-memory address translation. However, they are expensive and relatively limited in their capability. Thus they are not normally used as general-purpose computing devices.

At the software level, more complex associative mechanisms have been implemented that allow the storage and retrieval of triples of data. It has been found useful in artificial intelligence to organize data into *associative triples* of object, attribute, and value in the form (object, attribute, value), e.g., (table, color, red). As described later, the Lisp programming language includes associative data storage and retrieval operations on associative triples as basic functions.

Because of the cost in time and hardware, more-complex associative data structures are rarely implemented. However, the SITDAC model is viable because it uses a two-dimensional tabular data structure that can be efficiently searched and processed using massively parallel SIMD computers. It is important to realize that basic associative selection and retrieval can, in principle, be applied not only to simple data structures such as words, triples, and tables but to any arbitrary data organization including records, tuples, trees, graphs, and user-defined data structures. The only restrictions are the search time and the hardware costs of the implementation.

Because of the historical origin of associative devices as memories, the term *word* is used to refer to the basic unit of memory that holds a datum, even though it may be thousands of bits long instead of the 32 or 64 bits in a traditional memory word. Similarly, the term *field* is used to specify the logical subdivision of a word into sequences of bits. Fields in associative computing may be from one bit to hundreds of bits long. Thus an associative field may be much larger than a conventional memory word. Logically, however, a field in an associative memory and a word in a conventional memory are equivalent in that each is the basic logical unit of storage in its respective device.

In the above paragraph, "field" is used to specify a subdivision of a word. More accurately, in the SITDAC model, a field specification applies to all of the words in the memory, as shown in Fig. 1-1. Thus a field is parallel. That is, a field in general contains many data items of the same type, one item per word. Since the data items in a field form a one-dimensional column of data, a field may

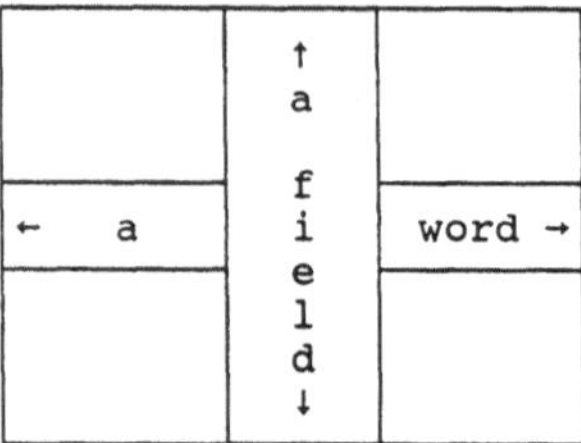

Figure 1-1. Fields and words.

occasionally be referred to as a vector. However, there are several distinct differences. First, the term *vector* refers basically to a logical data structure and implies that the data items are ordered and contiguous. A field is basically a memory-organization term. No ordering of items is implied and, since not all words in the memory are necessarily active, the data items are not necessarily stored contiguously. Finally, the use of the term "vector" in normal computer-science parlance suggests that the data may be processed by special-purpose pipelined hardware called vector processors. The fields in an associative computer, in contrast, are processed in parallel in one operation with physically parallel, not pipelined, hardware.

The discussion so far has centered on associative memories and the associative retrieval of data. Associative retrieval techniques are not new to data-base management. The term *associative processing* is frequently used to extend the concept of associative memories into a more general computational environment, in which special-purpose hardware is used to search and process large data bases. In this context, associative processing generally refers to the tasks necessary to perform a complex data search and retrieval and may include calculations as well as searching. However, computationally intensive tasks such as image convolution, fast Fourier transforms, and matrix multiplication are not normally included in the concept of associative processing, nor are non-numerical tasks such as compilation or software management (i.e., operating systems).

For the purposes of this book, *associative computing* will mean a method or formalism for expressing the entire range of conventional procedural computations using associative techniques to specify operands wherever feasible. This definition is intended to include associative processing, computationally intensive tasks, and non-numerical computation. More specifically, "associative computing" will refer to the SITDAC model of associative computing introduced in section 1.2.

The reader should be aware that the distinction between associative processing and associative computing as established here is by no means universal and that in many papers in the literature the terms are used interchangeably. However, the distinction is an important feature of the research into associative computation, and therefore the terms are used here with the specific meanings noted above.

However, the terms "processing" and "computing" without the modifier "associative" are used interchangeably.

One intent of associative computing is to supplement the address-calculation techniques of traditional von Neumann computation with associative data specification. The most basic function of a compiler or assembler is to convert symbolic names and labels into addresses. This requires that addresses be assigned at compile time. As a result, memory is allocated statically to accommodate the anticipated worst-case data demands.

An alternative to address calculation is searching. Searching can be performed at run time to find data. It is not widely used as a mode of operation in conventional computers due to its slow execution on sequential architectures. In associative computing, however, *associative searching* of one field of the entire array is accomplished in parallel in one step. Thus, run-time associative searching is an alternative to compile-time address calculation. Most modern languages have techniques for dynamic run-time memory allocation. These techniques use pointers and often result in complex address expressions such as those shown in Fig. 1-2. One intent of associative searching is to eliminate or reduce the address-computation portion of a program and thus to make programming simpler.

Frequently, one or more association entries may respond to an associative search. It is often desirable to remember which items responded. Logical fields can be set to indicate the status of the responders. These fields are called *flags*.

In normal conventional computation it is not uncommon for a pointer to point to an array of records. In associative computation, it is not uncommon for a flag field to flag several responders. Thus flags and pointers are logically similar in that they are both used to identify data that are to be processed. It is not uncommon to intermix the terminology in casual conversations, especially if the conversers are more familiar with conventional programming than with associative programming. In particular, it is often said that flag vectors point to association entries. In an attempt to avoid confusion, the term *pointer* will be used exclusively to refer to address pointers. "Flag" and "flagged" will be used in reference to association responder marking. Thus, the preferred wording for "The busy/idle vector points to the busy words in memory" is "The busy/idle field flags the busy words in memory."

In conventional address-calculation computation, if many data items are to be processed by a common operation, the normal procedure is to write a loop and process each item sequentially. In massively parallel computation, these loops are replaced by a single iteration on the operation, which is executed in parallel on all

```
(*(*((*(workers+i)).kids+j)).name).last

((((workers+i)->kids+j))->name)->last
```

Figure 1-2. Complex address expressions.

data items. This type of parallelism is known as *data parallelism*. Data-parallel computation is an independent field of study with considerable ongoing research in algorithms and languages (Siegel *et al.* [1983], Gallopoulos [1985], Reeves [1985], White [1985], Hillis and Steele [1986], Rose and Steele [1987], and Johnsson and Mather [1989] to name just a few). In associative computing, the use of associative searching allows all operands to be identified and processed in parallel using data parallelism. It is not the intent of associative computing to duplicate data-parallel research. In most instances, computations which require only indexing and nearest-neighbor computations can be performed in the SITDAC model with little or no modification. That is, it is assumed that the data parallelism of massively parallel computers is subsumed by associative computation and that any new techniques that may be developed can be easily added to the ASC language. Only algorithms that rely heavily on parallel pointer following are excluded. As a result, data-parallel algorithms are not stressed in this book. Instead, predominantly non-numerical applications are explored.

1.2. The SITDAC Model

This selection formally defines the SITDAC model. But, first, the selection of a bit-serial, single-instruction, multiple-data architecture as the basis for an associative computer model and the selection of the file as the basic data structure are explained. Then the synergy between these two decisions is described. After the SITDAC model is defined, each aspect of the model is explained.

1.2.1. The Basic Associative Computer

Many massively parallel computers are bit-serial, single-instruction, multiple-data (SIMD) computers. A very large, relatively cheap associative memory can be modeled using a SIMD computer simply by searching the various fields of the association entries and flagging the responders. In actuality, the result is not an associative memory, since the responders are not retrieved but simply flagged, but it is in fact an associative computer since all of the flagged responders can be processed in parallel, each by its own processing element. The SIMD architecture is widely accepted as the basic architecture for associative computers and processors. In fact, Duncan [1990] classifies associative processors as a subclass of SIMD processors.

Associative SIMD processors are much cheaper than associative memories of comparable size. In a true associative memory, every bit of memory has comparator logic associated with it. In a SIMD processor, all of the bits of a word share the common comparator logic in the word's processing element (PE). So, although the sharing means that the associative search will take slightly longer in a SIMD processor than in an associative memory, it is still fast (on the order of a microsecond for a 32-bit field at 20 nsec per instruction), it is constant regardless of the number of words taking part in the search, and the hardware is orders of magnitude cheaper. For example, for a SIMD processor with 64K bits per word, the sharing of the PE means that the hardware cost for the comparison logic is approximately 64K times less.

When small memory sizes are used, content-addressable memories (cam) are inefficient because of the large percentage of a word's bits needed to distinguish it from the other words in the memory and the extra hardware required to perform the content match in parallel. However, when very large, efficient content-addressable or associative arrays of cells are built using conventional memories and conventional hardware shared by all bits in a cell, the result is a practical form of data selection. For example, as shown in Table 1-1, if a cam is 32 bits wide and 1024 words deep, since 1024 words require 10 bits of address, 10/32 or over 31% of each word (in bits) is needed to select a responder. However, a content-addressable array of 1024 cells with 8K bits per cell needs only 10/8192 or 0.12% to uniquely identify a cell.

Not all SIMD designs are well suited to associative computation. For example, after an associative search, instead of simple data-parallel computation, it may be desirable to process the responders individually or in groups or to detect the absence of all responders. These situations are most economically handled by special-purpose hardware. Such hardware efficiently identifies each responder in turn and provides for the efficient transfer of the responder's data to the program-control portion of the machine for additional processing. The STARAN SIMD computers built by Goodyear Aerospace had such special-purpose hardware and were accordingly frequently referred to as associative computers.

In summary, the hardware features which distinguish an associative computer from SIMD computers and associative processors are

1. massively parallel searching achieved by active memory logic so that searching can be used as an alternative to addressing,
2. tightly coupled control via a responder/no responder signal which can be tested in constant time for the effective use of parallel-search feedback in program flow control,

Table 1-1. Percentage of Memory Used for Addressing

Number of bits per word	Number of words in memory			
	1024	2048	32768	65536
32	31.25	34.37	46.87	50.00
64	15.62	17.18	23.43	25.00
1K	0.97	1.07	1.46	1.56
8K	0.12	0.13	0.18	0.19
32K	0.00030	0.00034	0.00460	0.00049
64K	0.00015	0.00017	0.00023	0.00024

3. resolution hardware which can select an individual responder from a set of many in unit time,
4. an efficient array-to-sequential control-data path that allows the transfer of data from the selected responder to the sequential control in constant time, and
5. an efficient sequential control-to-array data path that allows the broadcast of data to all array processors in parallel in constant time.

1.2.2. The Basic Tabular Data Structure

As stated earlier, the general concept of associative retrieval can be applied to any style of data structure. A common data structure in computer science is the data file consisting of a number of identical records. If a prototype of this data structure is diagramed as in Fig. 1-3, it is easy to recognize it as equivalent to a conventional table of data. That is, the columns of the table are the fields of the records and the rows of the table are the individual record entries in the file. A data structure of this form will be called an *association*. The rows of the association will be called *entries*. In an association, the individual values of the association fields for a given entry are said to be associated with one another. So, for example, in Fig. 1-4, red, large, and fast are associated with one another in the Buick entry, while blue, small, and fast are associated with one another in the Ford entry.

As illustrated in Figs. 1-3, 1-4, and 1-5, a file may be interpreted as an association which maps directly onto the two-dimensional memory of an associative computer. In the remainder of this book, whenever an association is depicted, the natural mapping of the association to the two-dimensional memory is understood. That is, an illustration of an association such as Fig. 1-4 is equivalent to the illustration of Fig. 1-5.

1.2.3. The Combined Architecture and Data Structure

Because of the natural fit of a file into a SIMD memory, the ability of a SIMD processor to emulate an associative memory, and the existence of SIMD processors as viable, commercially available parallel computers, the specific associa-

Color	Size	Speed	Object
red	large	fast	Buick
red	large	slow	Chevy
blue	small	slow	Toyota
blue	small	fast	Ford
red	small	fast	Lamborghini

Figure 1-3. A data file.

Attributes			
Color	Size	Speed	Object
red	large	fast	Buick
red	large	slow	Chevy
blue	small	slow	Toyota
blue	small	fast	Ford
red	small	fast	Lamborghini

Figure 1-4. An association.

tive model of computation proposed here is based on a two-dimensional tabular associative data structure and a (bit serial) SIMD processor.

The selection of the tabular data organization and the bit-serial SIMD architecture as the basic components of the associative model described is based on purely practical considerations and is in no way intended to limit or confine the general concept of associativity. As described above, the general concept of associative computing has many interesting facets and possible realizations using different assumptions of how data is organized and hardware is configured. One of the primary reasons for the selection of the SITDAC model was the availability of existing computers with architectures close in design to the architecture desired. This allows associative concepts and techniques to be explored and developed in a real-time environment on existing, economically practical hardware.

For example, ASC, the associative computing language based on SITDAC, was implemented on the Connection Machine (CM) since it is a widely known, currently available, bit-serial SIMD computer, even though it is not an associative computer. That is, the CM's design is not intended specifically for associative computing and, indeed, it lacks hardware support for the very basic associative-

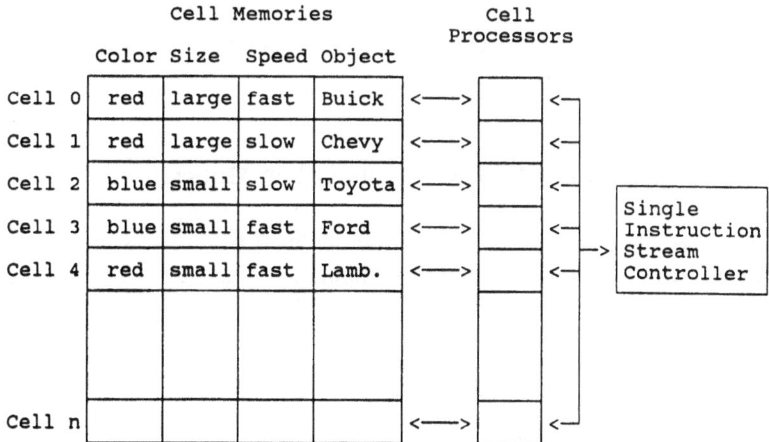

Figure 1-5. An association in an associative processor.

computing functions such as one-step responder identification and data retrieval. In addition, its system-support software is nonassociative in that some functions such as minimum and maximum value are implemented using the hypercube interconnection network in preference to the faster associative routines described in Falkoff [1962]. Nevertheless, it provides many of the capabilities needed by an associative computer and is a good system for the development of associative programming techniques.

1.2.4. The Formal Model

The SITDAC model consists of

1. a cellular memory,
2. an exclusive read/write capability,
3. a restricted concurrent-read capability, and
4. a restricted number of instruction streams.

A cellular memory means that the memory is organized into memory cells. Each cell has its own word of memory and PE (see Fig. 1-6). Only one memory location in a cell may be accessed at a time, but all cells may be accessed in parallel. The exclusive read/write capability means that any given memory cell can be accessed by only one processor at a time. However, the concurrent-read restriction means that one location from one memory word from a single memory cell may be read by all processors at a time. This restriction is essentially equivalent to reading a single cell and performing a global broadcast of the retrieved data.

The restriction on the number of instruction streams requires, in essence, a SIMD mode of operation. The restriction is that the number of instruction streams must be much smaller than the number of cells. For example, an associative computer with 64K cells may have from 8 to 16 instruction streams. Chapter 10 outlines how the multiple instruction streams can be used for parallel-associative SIMD program execution.

1.3. SITDAC versus Other Models

The associative model of computation defined here differs in a number of significant ways from other models of computation that use massive parallelism.

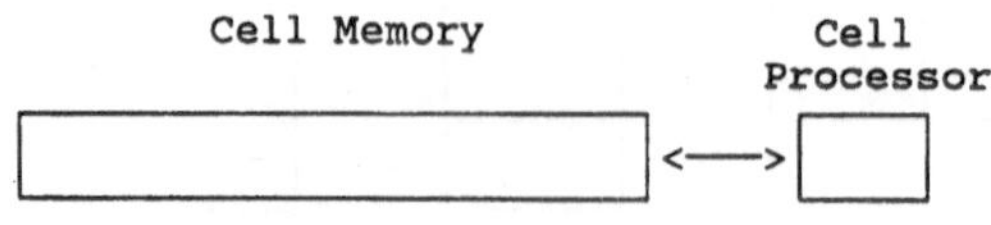

Figure 1-6. An associative cell.

The other models (data parallelism, neural nets, relational data bases, symbolic computation, and rule-based languages), are much too complex to discuss in detail. As a consequence, just the major differences between them and associative computing are stated. The fact that the advantages of the other models are not listed is not to be interpreted as implying that they are deficient. The intent is only to illustrate that associative-computation models are different from these other models and are deserving of their own research and development.

1.3.1. Data Parallel

The data-parallel approach used by many SIMD researchers is a straightforward extension of conventional von Neumann programming, which in essence simply replaces sequential DO loops with parallel expressions. Thinking Machines Corporation's documentation (Thinking Machines Corp. [1986]) emphasizes that "no new language features need to be introduced in order to perform parallel control flow, inter-processor communication and memory allocation" (p. 39). On the other hand, the intent of associative computation is to explore new programming techniques with the hope of simplifying programming. Thus, the ASC language described later specifically introduces new language-control structures based on associative retrieval concepts the intent of which is to simplify the overall programming task. The data-parallel approach to SIMD parallelism (except for parallel pointer following) is subsumed by the SITDAC model and is supported by ASC.

1.3.2. Relational Data Base

Another model that may be considered close to associative computation is (relational) data-base management. But, as explained above, associative computation includes general-purpose computation as well as computationally intensive tasks. The procedural nature of associative computing makes convolution and other computationally intensive tasks simple to specify, as well as noncomputational tasks such as depth-first tree searches. These computations are somewhat awkward to express in traditional data-base-management languages.

The intent in most interactive data-base applications is to find (or isolate) one or more items from a large number of items. The data-base search process is fundamental. In a data-base search, the queries are initially "ill formed" and the process is intended to refine the query until the desired item(s) are found. In associative searching, the search is precisely defined and the actions to be taken are explicitly stated, whether

1. all responders are to be processed in parallel
2. the responders are to be processed iteratively one at a time, or
3. there are no responders.

Associative searching would be an appropriate primitive for implementing a relational data base on an associative computer.

1.3.3. Neural Networks

Associative computing differs from the use of neural networks in two ways. First, neural networks evolved out of a model of the mind at the subconscious neural-cell level into the present self-organizing computational model. Associative computing, however, evolved from a model of the human mind at the linguistic/conscious level. In particular, it models the ability of the mind to recall many facts about objects or situations once they have been described. All of the information associated with the identified items can be processed in parallel and/or retrieved for further processing.

Second, while associative programming is procedural, neural networks are not. With current technology, neural networks of a few hundred thousand physical nodes are possible. A network of millions of nodes can be obtained by emulating one thousand virtual nodes per physical node by time sharing. At these levels of neural simulation, programming in the conventional sense is not possible. The individual nodes may contain software, but it is a general purpose "neuron" emulation program function that is identical at each node except for local weights and parameters. Some neural nets are structured into several levels. Different levels of nodes may have different program functions. Neural nets of this design must be trained in the same manner as hardware pattern-recognition devices.

In associative computation, the programmer explicitly declares the desired logical associations, thus establishing at compile time all conscious data relationships. In neural nets, these relationships must be either determined at the onset by setting weights and/or parameters or learned by a process that may take perhaps several thousands of run-time examples to learn. Associative programs, being procedural, can be readily modified, yet the flexibility and spontaneity of "neural" learning is maintained, at a much higher level, since the system can be programmed to modify associations dynamically at run time. This allows the establishment of "new neural links" in the associations which can be searched using massive parallelism. In addition, the slower mental processes such as "thinking" can be modeled by extracting information from identified associations to search for related associations.

1.3.4. Symbolic Programming

List-based symbolic programming languages such as Prolog and Lisp are used frequently for non-numerical tasks. The computational model of Lisp and Prolog is based on the nested Lisp list data structure (i.e., *s*-expressions). This data structure is inherently sequential. That is, the primitive CAR, CDR, and CONS operations defined on the data structure are designed to efficiently tear lists apart and link them together in a sequential computer environment. Whether Lisp can be implemented efficiently on a massively parallel computer is not in question. The point is that the basic thought processes that go into Lisp programming are based on inherently sequential techniques. In associative computing, the intent is to incorporate the more natural two-dimensional tabular data structure in place of nested lists and to facilitate the expression of natural parallel operations on this data structure using associative techniques.

1.3.5. Rule-Based Languages

Associative computing shares the pattern-matching concept with rule-based languages such as OPS5 (Forgy [1981]). However, unlike rule-based languages, associative computing is procedural. Thus the flow of control-data structures (so-called secret-messaging, Pasik [1988]) required by rule-based languages and added to the problem's data base are not needed. The associative data configurations are predominately pure data. There are very few control or administrative data structures, the major exception being flag fields. Another difference is the inclusion of data-parallel expressions in associative computing. Most versions of rule-based languages do not address data parallelism.

1.4. Hardware Ramifications of SITDAC

The SITDAC model of computing assumes one processor per data object (i.e., record or association item) and is well suited for the requirements of VLSI design, massive parallelism, and the elimination of the classic memory–CPU bottleneck.

As VLSI technology develops, allowing more and more components on a chip, all interconnection networks such as the two-dimensional grid illustrated in Fig. 1-7 require more and more edge space for chip-to-chip communication. The

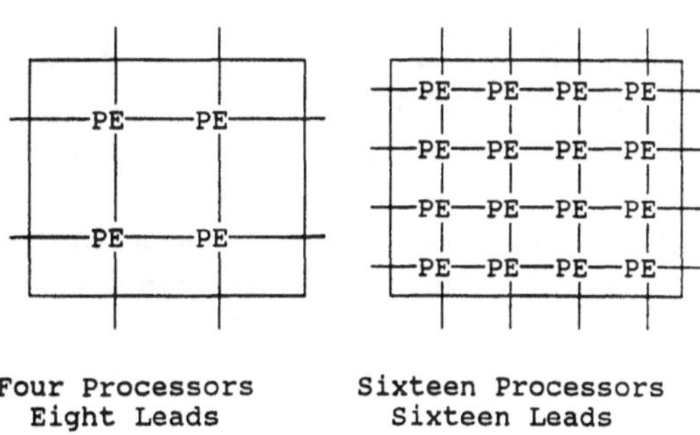

Figure 1-7. Increasing edge demands of VLSI.

associative model of computation, however, does not rely on any particular interconnection network. Chapter 10 describes a conceptual design that requires only a constant number of edge leads regardless of the packing density of associative cells.

The associative model assumes only simple processors; as a result, many can be packed on a chip. Current SIMD designs put 8, 16, 32, on up to 256 processors on a single chip. With these densities, computers with 2K, 16K, and 64K processors have been built. Associative computing is one approach to using these massively parallel computers effectively.

Memory bandwidth is a significant factor in computational throughput. Stone [1975] says, "If we must choose a single, simple parameter of performance, memory bandwidth is a good choice" (p. 530). It should be added that the measure should be data-memory bandwidth, since instruction fetches *per se* do not process data. One way of increasing bandwidth is to increase the size of the memory, the CPU, and the memory-CPU bus. In effect, a SIMD computer with 64K processors has a bus width of 64K bits. Even at a nominal rate of 100 nsec per instruction, volumes of up to 82 Gbytes of data can be delivered to the processors in 1 sec.

In associative computing, data records are processed *in situ*. A data object is referenced by describing it (its contents), not by naming it (its address). As a result, the necessity to move data from memory to a CPU is eliminated and the need to move data from one processor to the next is reduced, thus in turn reducing the impact of interconnection networks. Interconnection networks can take up from 25 to 30% of the available space on a PE chip.

The common memory aspect of many models of computation make them distinctly different from associative computers. As mentioned previously, the SITDAC model assumes a tightly coupled architecture with distributed memory and processors. While it is true that other models can simulate associative computing by time sharing, the frame of mind used for associative computing versus sequential computing is as different as watching TV is from going to the movies.

In order for effective computation to take place, instructions and data must come together at a common location. In conventional computing that place is the central processing unit. In associative computing, this conjunction takes place in each individual memory cell. Similarly, in order for communication to take place, the message (a newsreel, for example) and recipient must come together at a common location. For movies, that location is a theater. For TV, the location is the living room of any home.

The purpose and effect of both situations is the same. But in one, the product (TV program or instruction) is delivered to every user using relatively modest equipment (TV set or processor), while in the other, the users must go, one at a time in this example, to a central location with much more-complex equipment. The logistics involved in getting everyone to a theater to see his or her choice of film are vastly different from the logistics of everyone staying at home and watching what he or she wants on TV, even though the same effects can be achieved by time-sharing the theater and using buses for mass transit.

1.5. SITDAC Algorithms

The logistical differences between TV and the movies make the user's perception and utilization of them quite different, even though they can both deliver the same product. The analogy applies to associative computation versus conventional (sequential) and parallel computation. They all deliver the same product, yet their utilization is vastly different. Associative computing makes use of massive parallelism in a new way. The intent is to provide an easier, more natural programming environment and achieve fast, efficient computation.

Associative computing leads to the development of new classes of algorithms by literally adding a new dimension to computing. A conventional computer has a zero-dimensional CPU and a one-dimensional memory. An associative computer has at least a one-dimensional CPU and a two-dimensional memory. It is important to realize that the dimensionality of the CPU is dependent on the functional capability of the instruction set, not simply the physical layout of the PEs or interconnection network. For example, as mentioned at the end of section 1.2.1, the instruction set must include instructions which

1. query all processors in parallel,
2. select one or more of the processors in one step, and
3. provide for constant time communication between the array and control processor.

The constant-time, one-step criterion is crucial since these same functions can be performed in multiple steps on other types of computers.

Because of the one-dimensional CPU in associative computers, one-dimensional data structures such as strings, expressions, and lists can be accessed and processed in parallel, i.e., in unit time (see Reed [1985]). This allows new approaches, algorithms, and techniques such as context-sensitive parsing to be developed, as described in Chapter 8.

1.6. History

The history of associative computing is a mixture of several forces. First, we will review the logical models of associative processing. Then we will give a short history of SIMD processors and their programming languages, followed by a short description of associative processing in data-base management.

The focus of this section is on the logical models of associativity because SITDAC is an extension of these models. The history of SIMD processors and computers is provided to give a complete background. However, by and large these machines have been used traditionally for image processing, numerically intensive computations, and data-base management (associative processing). Associative computing as embodied in the SITDAC model was never a focus of any of these machines.

1.6.1. Logical Associative Model

The concept of associativity has been present in computer science for many years. (For example, see Jacks [1971] or Findler [1979].) The most prevalent realization of associativity is associative triples in artificial intelligence. The standard definition of an association is an ordered triple. Many similar definitions for associations have been formulated (e.g., Simon and Newell [1970] and Savitt *et al.* [1967]). The concept has also been used in programming languages such as Lisp.

Two of the most powerful features of Lisp are the properties list and a-list. For example, the value of an object's attribute, or property, can be obtained by the **get** function, assuming the data has been entered with a **putprop**. Figure 1-8 illustrates how these functions work.

The association functions are underused, however, for two reasons. First, they are implemented using linked lists, and when there are perhaps 1000 items (i.e., 100 lists with 10 items apiece or 10 lists with 100 items apiece), retrieval and update become quite slow.

The second reason is that the **putprop** and **get** functions are associative features in an otherwise list-based language. That is, the essence of Lisp is list processing and functional programming. The associative ideas were never fully developed as a mode of computation. For example, as shown in Fig. 1-8, the attribute and value can not be used to retrieve the associated object as would be the case in a completely associative memory.

Kohonen [1978], realizing the limitations of attribute value pairs, rejected the standard definitions of associativity in favor of a more general definition. He proposed a model of association in which a collection of triples forms an associative memory and an entire triple is retrieved when any portion of it is used

```
Establish the database
   (putprop 'Jane 'Sam 'father)
   (putprop 'Jerry 'Elmer 'father)

Query the database
   (get 'Jane 'father) --> Sam
   (get 'Jerry 'father) --> Elmer

Illegal query (i.e., not supported by Lisp)
   (getobj 'Sam 'Father)
```

Figure 1-8. Lisp associations.

to query the memory. Figure 1-9 gives an example of associative retrieval. (In Fig. 1-9, and elsewhere in this book, the $ character is used to denote the match-all operator, similar to the * or wild-card character used in many operating systems. In ASC, $ is used to refer to all responders in parallel.)

The SITDAC model of associative computing expands on Kohonen's model of an associative memory. Triples of data have been replaced by associations of any number of items (i.e., data records). An arbitrary number of different kinds of associations may be stored in memory. Thus in the general associative model outlined in section 1.2, sets of collections of items form an associative memory and an entire data object (an association entry) is selected when any subset of its items is used to query the memory.

In the generalized association concept, the shape of the object is important also. That is, several data entries may respond to the associative search for specific items, but only those that also agree with the shape of the search pattern are true responders, as illustrated in Fig. 1-10. In Fig. 1-10, two quite different queries are formed using a search for any object modified by blue. In Fig. 1-10a, blue is a color and modifies the object "table" directly. In Fig. 1-10b, blue is an abstract term for a state of mind and can modify the object Joe only indirectly. The structure of the search pattern is essential for retrieving the appropriate responders.

In addition to extending the definition of an association, the concept of associative memory can be extended to associative computing. In associative computing, each association has its own dedicated processing unit. Thus, when an association is successfully matched or responds to a search, it is not retrieved and processed by a central processing unit, but is processed in place by its dedicated processor. Consequently, all operations performed on the responders to an associative search are executed in parallel. Figure 1-11 illustrates the basic search and process phases of computation in an associative computer.

```
Given Associative Memory

  OBJECT  ATTRIBUTE  VALUE
  table     color    blue
  table     size     big
  chair     size     small
  table   location   at_window
  chair    color     red

Query
   (table color $)
 produces
   (table color blue)

Query
   ($ location $)
 produces
   (table location at_window)
```

Figure 1-9. Associative retrieval.

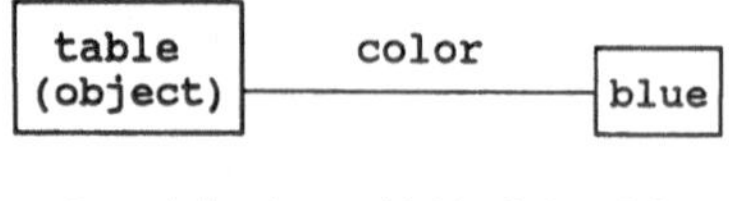

a - An object modified by blue
("object" $ blue)

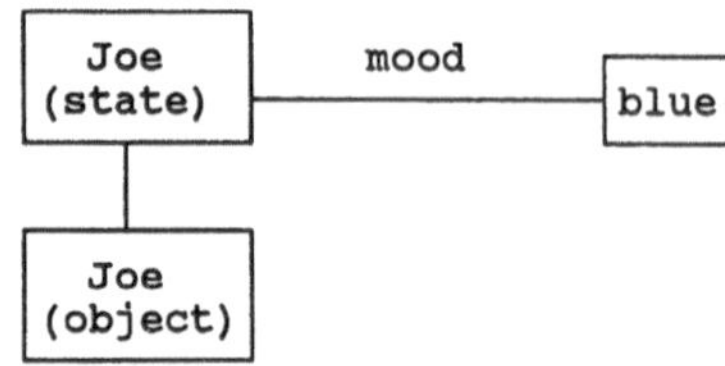

b - An object with a blue mood
("object" $ ($ $ blue))

Figure 1-10. Two objects modified by blue.

1.6.2. SIMD Processors

The Illiac IV computer developed at the University of Illinois in the 1960s is one of the first SIMD computers built (Barnes *et al.* [1968]). It was designed for solving partial differential equations and for matrix manipulation and was used for scientific applications. In the late 1960s Goodyear Aerospace, under contract to the U.S. Air Force, explored associative memories. The concept of using bit-serial SIMD parallelism and special-purpose hardware to identify, select, and retrieve

```
Given Associative Memory

     OBJECT  ATTRIBUTE  VALUE
     table     color    blue
     table     size     big
     chair     size     small
     lamp      size     big
     chair     color    red

SEARCH:    Query ($ size big)

PROCESS:   Action VALUE=SMALL


Result

     OBJECT  ATTRIBUTE  VALUE
     table     color    blue
     table     size     small
     chair     size     small
     lamp      size     small
     chair     color    red
```

Figure 1-11. Search and process phases of associative computing.

data from responders to achieve associative computation evolved out of this research and resulted in the STARAN associative computer (Batcher [1976]). This early design work concentrated on hardware and is largely documented in Foster [1976]. Although assembly-level associative routines were developed, there was no effort to explore associative computing as a general-purpose, high-level mode of computation. An airborne version of the STARAN, called ASPRO, is currently being manufactured for the U.S. Navy by the Defense Systems Division of Loral.

In recent years, a number of SIMD machines have been designed and built that can be used to support associative computing although they were not designed specifically to do so. Among these are the Massively Parallel Processor built by Goodyear Aerospace for NASA and the Connection Machine built by the Thinking Machines Corporation. The Distributed Array Processor (DAP) was a contemporary of the STARAN developed in England as an add-on processor for ICL computers. An updated version of the DAP, which can be hosted by several different machines, is being sold by Active Memory Technology. Lately, two new machines have been introduced, MasPar and Wavetracer.

1.6.3. Associative Processors

During this same period, a number of exploratory associative processors designed specifically for data-base management were proposed and developed. Among these are RELACS (Berra and Oliver [1979]), RAP (Schuster *et al.* [1979]), CASSM (Heaty *et al.* [1972]), and more recently ASP (Lea [1985]). A number of associative languages were also developed (Savitt *et al.* [1967], Findler [1967], and Feldman and Rovner [1969], for example). These languages were predominantly set-oriented data-base languages, not procedural, general-purpose computing languages. Hsiao [1983] discusses the use of associative memory for data base machines; also see (Thurber [1975]) for a survey of the earlier associative processors.

1.7. The Nature of SITDAC Programming

One of the tenets of the SITDAC model is that associative programming is easier than conventional programming. That is, for a given problem, the associative data structures are simpler, the associative code is shorter, and as a result associative programming is more cost effective than conventional programming (i.e., the programs are easier to debug and the programmers are more productive). Chapter 4 presents several problems and their algorithms to illustrate this point.

Programming languages should be easy to write and read. Mathematical or functional languages are designed to be precise and powerful. However, like mathematical papers, programs once written in mathematical notation can be difficult to understand and nearly impossible to modify or maintain. A program is not only a message between the programmer and the computer. It is also a message to other programmers. It is essential that the message be intelligible with a minimum of effort to all who want to read it. The point here is that English-speaking programmers are expert at speaking and understanding English. It should be possible to capitalize on this expertise, especially when associative computing is an efficient mode of computation and shares many qualities with natural language. It is hoped that the similarities among associative programming, human thought processes, and natural language will result in a more usable language.

This section describes several similarities between associative programming and mental processes as reflected in their communicable form—natural language (English in particular). The intent is to illustrate similarities that make SITDAC programming easy to assimilate and use, not to propose a theory of human thought processes or natural language. In no way is the precision or detail required by conventional programming problems hindered or interfered with by these similarities. Among the items to be discussed are

1. the tendency to describe objects and name verbs in natural language and to describe data items and name operations in associative programming,
2. the similarity between the singular–plural and scalar–parallel dualities,
3. the reference to identified items by pronouns,
4. the syntax of English and the flow of a command sequence in SITDAC programming, and
5. the tendency for people to search mathematical expressions and other complex representations (such as Lisp lists) for an innermost kernel and then analyze or evaluate them from the inside out.

1.7.1. Describing Objects

As described earlier, attribute–value pairs have been used in artificial intelligence to capture some of the descriptive power of natural language. Thus any natural-language descriptor (e.g., adjective or adverb) can be used to describe an object or action by converting it to the attribute–value form as shown in Fig. 1-12.

Attribute–value pairs can be associated with objects to capture meaning. For example, "the large, fast red car" can be represented as a graph or semantic

```
Descriptor  Attribute
            Value pair

 red        (color red)
 fast       (speed fast)
 large      (size large)
```

Figure 1-12. Attribute–value pairs.

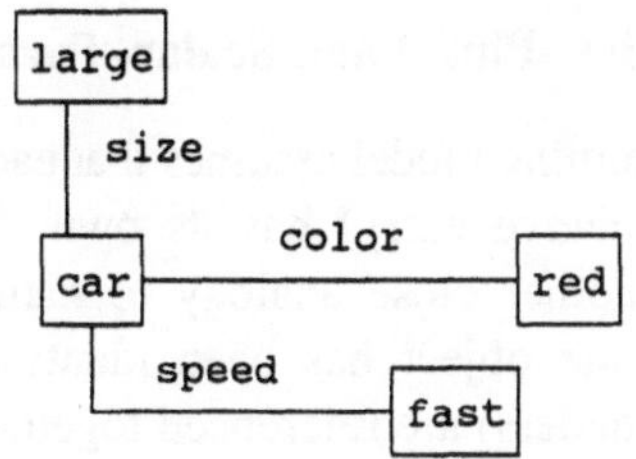

Figure 1-13. A semantic representation.

network (Quillian [1968]), as shown in Fig. 1-13. Note that in Fig 1-13, the attribute takes the form of an edge label and the value is a node. The contents of the semantic representation can be expressed in "computer readable form" as associative triples of the form (object attribute value), e.g., (car size large), (car speed fast), and (car color red).

If there are many cars, all sharing the same set of attributes, it is economical to organize the data into a tabular form as was shown in Fig. 1-4. The attribute values in a row are associated with the named object. An important feature of the components of the association of Fig. 1-4 is that, collectively, they form a set of attributes that uniquely identifies each entry. That is, there is one and only one entry in the association for every used car on the lot. The uniqueness feature of an association can be used to describe the individual entries in the association. Thus the attribute–value pairs (color red), (size small) describe and uniquely identify the Lamborghini.

If (color red) and (size small) are used to search for entries, the association is being manipulated as if it were a content-addressable memory. That is, when an association is searched by an attribute–value description such as "(color red) AND (size small)," the entire association of entries in all of the responding rows is activated. This method of content-addressable activation can be effectively used for computation because new information is retrieved on every successful search. For example, searching for (color red) AND (size small) will activate the entry which also contains (speed fast) and (object Lamborghini).

This process is analogous to the process of description and identification used in natural language. For example, a potential customer of the used-car lot could use the descriptors red and small to identify uniquely the car he is interested in. Having done so, he is now able to extract from the salesman additional information such as its potential speed and its make.

The associative search process is similar to but should not be confused with searching a data base. In SITDAC computing, knowledge of the desired data allows precise descriptions to be generated so that only specific items are identified.

1.7.2. The Singular–Plural and Scalar–Parallel Dichotomies

The SITDAC programming model assumes that each word of the associative memory (i.e., each associative entry) has its own dedicated processor. This arrangement results in another close analogy to natural language. In natural language, if more than one object has been identified by a description, all identified objects (or responders) are referenced together. Thus "wash the large, red cars" means that all of the objects (i.e., cars) that fit the description are to be washed. In the SITDAC model, since each memory has its own processor, all responders to a descriptive search are processed in parallel. And just as the singular–plural dichotomy of natural language is signified by the presence or absence of an *s*, the scalar/parallel dichotomy of associative computing is signified by the presence or absence of a $ (as will be explained in more detail later).

1.7.3. Pronouns

Once the responders are identified in natural language, they may be referred to by pronouns such as *he*, *it*, or *them*. If the responders from two or more similar searches are referred to, they must be identified by name. In SITDAC programming the last set of responders generated may be referred to by the pronoun *them*. This avoids the need to repeatedly specify the same search in separate control structures. *Them* is especially useful during debugging when the programmer wants to display the results of the last search. If the responders from two or more searches are active, they must be referred to by explicitly named flag fields. There is a close similarity between pronoun reference in English and flag-field reference in SITDAC programming.

Possessive pronouns also have a counterpart in associative programming. Thus after the search "the fast red," the phrases "its size" and "their sizes" refer to the "size" attribute of the responders. In associative programming, these phrases would be written as size[xx] and size[$], where *xx* is a parallel index variable and $ is the parallel responder marker.

1.7.4. Flow of Control

In natural language, communication is initiated by identifying the object(s) of discussion as distinct from all other possible objects by giving an adequately unique description. For example, "the large red (car)" uniquely describes and thus identifies Buick from all other cars on the lot. This step is similar in form and function to the first phase of an associative computing cycle.

For example, an associative cycle begins with a search phase such as

size[$] .eq. large .and. color[$] .eq. red

The primary differences between the associative form and the natural-language form of a description are the presence of

1. the attribute names *color* and *size* and
2. the logical connective AND.

In natural language, the attribute names and the relation AND are understood. Since most modern programming languages allow domains to be declared—i.e., size {large, small} and color {red, blue, green, black}—the link between the value and its domain name can be clearly established. As a result, the above associative search could be abbreviated to "large red" if a sequence of values were understood to be implicitly ANDed just as in natural language.

The SITDAC programming "pronouns" are used in the second or process phase of the associative search, process, retrieve cycle. The process phase specifies all of the operations to be performed on the responders in parallel. The position of the process phase after the search phase follows natural language in that in a conditional command, the conditions are given first and then the actions: for example, "If there are dirty dishes, wash them."

The third and last phase of an associative SPR cycle is the retrieval phase. In the retrieval phase, values of the current cycle are retrieved so that they ay be used as parameters in subsequent cycles. This allows multiple cycles to be chained together into effective programming structures. The natural-language counterpart of the chaining together of cycles is the progression of a discussion from the general to the specific. So, for example, once the top-level responders to (color red) and (size large) have been identified, certain attributes of the objects may be retrieved (e.g., fuel requirements, service requirements) to initiate more detailed discussions. In general, these discussions may be further refined several more times.

The article in natural language can be given an interpretation in SITDAC programming. The definite article, *the*, can be considered a keyword to initiate an associative search. There may be one or more responders. The indefinite article (*a* or *an*) also initiates a search, but if more than one cell responds, *a* (*an*) indicates that an arbitrary single responder should be selected.

1.7.5. Inside-Out Evaluation

We are taught to evaluate expressions such as those shown in Fig. 1-14 from the inside out. That is, we search the expression for the highest-priority operator (the nested addition in this case) and then reduce it to a simpler expression as shown. This simpler expression is searched and processed in the same way. The process is repeated until the answer is derived. In many sequential implementations, this problem would require recursion and parsing to discover the structure of the data.

```
4+(3+2)*5 = 4+(5)*5 = 4+25 = 29
```

Figure 1-14. Inside-out Evaluation.

Since associative computing allows massive searching to be performed in parallel, a compiler written using associative programming techniques can search the statements and expressions of an entire program and generate the appropriate intermediate code in a process similar to the above (Asthagiri and Potter [1991]). This approach eliminates the need for recursion and/or first-in, last-out stacks used by parsers written in conventional languages and allows code with near-optimal register utilization to be generated directly without the need for a separate optimization pass.

Inside-out evaluation is a new programming technique made possible by the SITDAC model. It is very powerful, yet easy to use because of its similarity to natural (or at least prelearned) thought processes. This approach reduces the need for recursion.

1.8. Reduced Programming Complexity

The purpose of this section is to present one reason why associative programs are simpler than conventional programs. The explanation depends on the analysis and breakdown of a program into its procedural and addressing component (or addressing function). The components of the addressing function are described and the potential for confusion because of the use of one notation for two purposes is described. Finally, the simpler associative-programming approach is explained by showing that portions of the address function are not needed in associative programming.

The simple nature of associative programming can be best understood by analyzing the fundamental components of a program. When a program is viewed as a message between a programmer and a computer, as illustrated in Fig. 1-15, it contains two basic types of information. First, the program directs the computer in the procedural execution of the fundamental steps of the algorithm. Second, the program embodies the positional identification information of the data structure by fetching and delivering to the central processing unit the data from the appropriate memory location at the appropriate time. That is, if the algorithm is calculating hospital-insurance premiums based on age, the program must deliver the age datum, not the blood pressure datum, to the CPU. In conventional computers, the datum in memory is selected or identified by an address. Consequently, the data-delivery task involving the mapping relationships mentioned above can be modeled by an addressing-function component of the program. Thus, the structure of the data provides identification information. For example, in the record shown in

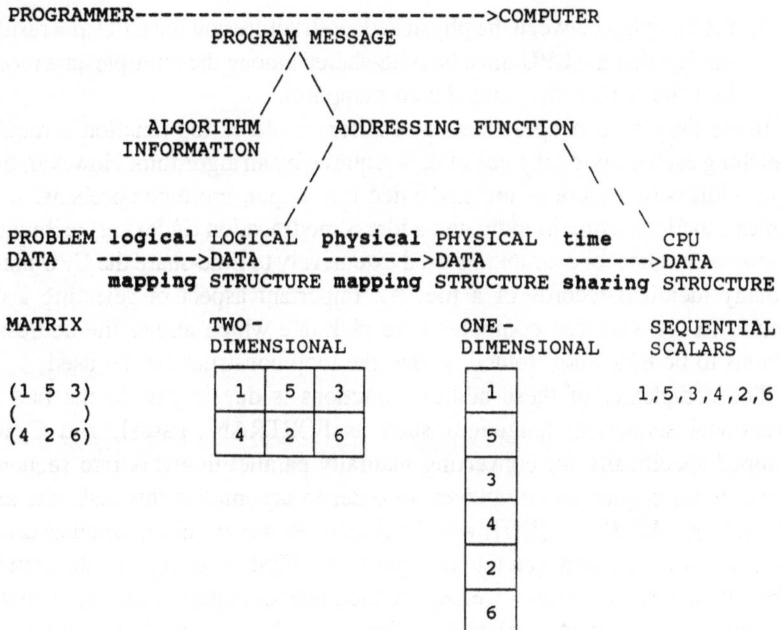

Figure 1-15. A conventional program message.

Fig. 1-16 the number 50 can be recognized as the AGE attribute of the patient JONES not by any inherent property of its own, but by the fact that it is in the second (AGE) position of the record. Many modern languages mask this addressing mechanism as a data structure, allowing the programmer to name the various addresses. This treatment acknowledges that it is easier for programmers to deal with a symbolic label, which is a form of a description, for a data item than a numerical address.

The addressing function of every program is influenced by three factors:

1. the mapping between the problem data and the logical data structure (called the logical mapping),
2. the mapping between the logical data structure and the physical data structure in the computer memory (called the physical mapping), and

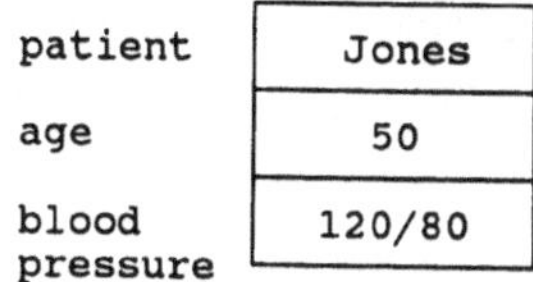

Figure 1-16. A simple data structure.

3. the mapping between the physical data structure and the CPU as a result of the fact that the CPU must be time-shared among the multiple data records in a file (called the time-shared mapping).

In the simplest conceptualization, a different addressing function is required for fetching each individual piece of data required by an algorithm. However, these simple addressing functions are combined into larger, more comprehensive and complex functions using looping and address modification (indexing) techniques. The loop construct, for example, is used extensively to time-share the CPU among the many identical records of a file. An important aspect of selecting a data structure for a sequential computer is to pick one which allows the addressing functions to be efficiently folded so that the loop construct can be used.

The complexity of these address functions is due in part to the fact that conventional sequential languages such as FORTRAN, Pascal, and C were developed specifically for converting naturally parallel thoughts into sequential commands for sequential computers. In order to accomplish this task, the array notation (e.g., A(I,J) or A[I][J]) was developed. However, this notation as used in most conventional languages has two purposes. First, it is used as the standard mathematical matrix notation, i.e. $\mathbf{A}_{I,J,}$ to facilitate the expression of mathematical equations. Second, it is used to serialize parallel thoughts. For example, the thought "Copy the *B*s onto the *A*s" is programmed as

```
for(i=0; i<10; i++) A[i]=b[i];
```

instead of

```
A[$] = B[$];
```

Complex index expressions are due largely to this latter use in loop constructs. The use of one notation for two entirely unrelated purposes greatly increases the confusion of programming in conventional languages.

SITDAC computers reduce the complexity of addressing functions without recursion and without limiting the logical data structure; thus they are easier to program than conventional computers. First, since every association entry has its own dedicated processor, the need for a time-sharing factor in the address function is eliminated. Second, the physical mapping component of the address function is replaced by parallel (associative) searching. Finally, as described in section 5.2, the logical mapping relationships are stored associatively as structure codes with the data elements, eliminating the need for run-time address calculations.

For example, in Fig. 1-17, the logical portion of the address function consisting of the matrix row and column indices are stored with the data elements. Since the data structure codes are dependent only on the logical mapping, the programming task is reduced to

1. directing the computer in the sequential execution of the fundamental steps of the algorithm and
2. the manipulation of the logical data structure codes.

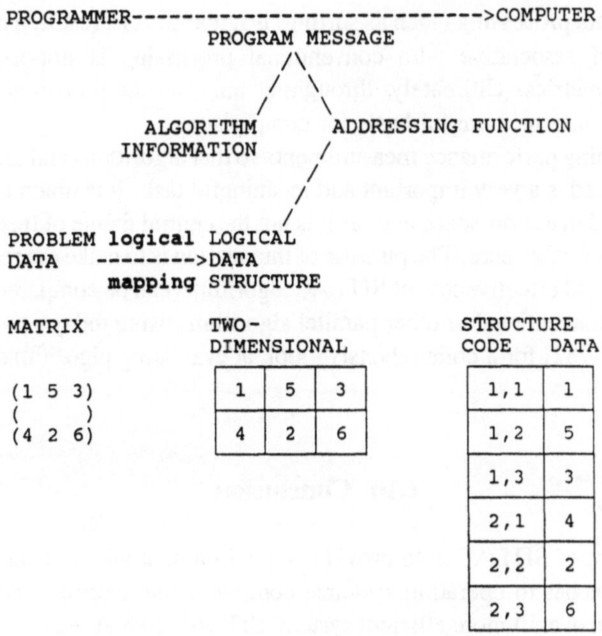

Figure 1-17. An associative program message.

The artifacts of time-sharing the CPU and the physical sequential organization of memory are eliminated.

1.9. Throughput Analysis

The intent of this section is to illustrate the difficulty of comparing results from two different machines. In this case, not only are the machines different, but their basic architectures are quite distinct. Moreover, the algorithms chosen for the problem may be quite different. Finally, the real question is what parameters should be measured.

One of the arguments against associative and SIMD computing is the perceived low utilization of the PEs. However, the throughput of a computer system can be meaningfully measured only in total. That is, only the useful computation of the system should be measured. The overhead of the operating system, compilers, and debuggers, must all be factored in if one is to say that algorithm *A* on machine *X* is superior to algorithm *B* on machine *Y*. Unfortunately, due to historical factors, it is customary to measure one of the cheapest components (i.e., the computer's CPU) in a computer installation in the crudest way (i.e., basic operations). The cost of the most expensive component (the programmer) is ignored. The cost of complex compiler operations is ignored. The cost of preliminary data processing (such as sorting) is ignored. As a result, a meaningful comparison of associative with conventional processing is impossible using conventional metrics. Ultimately, throughput analysis for problems, not algorithms, is the only meaningful basis for comparison.

Determining performance measurements so that algorithms and architectures can be compared is a very important and meaningful task. It is much too difficult to be addressed in a short space and, as it is not the central theme of this book, it is not considered further here. The purpose of this section is to make the reader aware that the speed and effectiveness of SITDAC algorithms can be compared only very crudely with conventional or other parallel algorithms using today's metrics. (See Siegel *et al.* [1982] for a comprehensive look at evaluating algorithms on SIMD machines.)

1.10. Conclusion

The intent of SITDAC is to provide an environment where straightforward, simpler approaches to operating systems, compilers and algorithm development can result in an overall more efficient system. SITDAC computing is easy because of the many similarities to natural language. These similarities are due in large part to parallel-associative searching. Associative searching replaces the address-mapping mechanism of conventional, mathematically based languages.

The SITDAC model of computing extends the concepts of attribute–value pairs and content-addressable memories and combines them into a single cohesive approach. The components of an association are used to describe and thus uniquely identify one or more entries in an association. When an entry is identified, its entire set of component values is available for retrieval and/or further computation.

2

Basic Concepts of Associative Programming

This chapter introduces many concepts essential to understanding SITDAC programming and the remaining chapters of this book. Chapter 1 explained that bit-serial SIMD computers share many properties with SITDAC associative computers. As a result, they also share many programming techniques. However, since SIMD computers are not widely known, this chapter will discuss several basic concepts that facilitate the programming of associative and SIMD computers. The first concept is SIMD parallelism; section 2.1 describes the execution of conditional statements. Section 2.2, on flow of control, describes more complex conditional-execution sequences. The classroom model described in section 2.3 describes a design aid based on a familiar situation: Many associative-programming situations can be directly mapped onto a teacher as the sequential control and students as individual associative cells.

Memory allocation or, more accurately, cell allocation, which is very simple and efficient in SITDAC programming, is discussed in section 2.4. Section 2.5 explains massive data-parallel searching using the classroom model and shows that associative searching is an alternative to pointers for accessing data. Section 2.6 establishes the special relationship of tabular data arrays in SITDAC programming. A SITDAC computer does not have to be bit serial. However, many SIMD computers are. Consequently, section 2.7 describes bit-serial arithmetic and shows that it is an approach already known by everyone.

Section 2.8 introduces the most important basic concept in this book. It describes how the responder hardware identified in Chapter 1 as distinguishing an associative computer from associative and SIMD processors is used to develop powerful associative searching routines. Section 2.9 describes how the step/find hardware is used for iteration.

Section 2.10 is on corner turning. Corner turning is simply the data reorganization required to convert conventional sequential data files into a format suitable for bit-serial computation. Bucket-brigade communication (section 2.11) describes a learning aid that facilitates the understanding of grid-interconnection network communications. Section 2.12 describes the rationale for mapping multidimensional data onto multidimensional memories. Section 2.13 describes how data can be duplicated in parallel arrays for little additional overhead, a process that may allow considerably more parallelism. Section 2.14 reviews this chapter.

2.1. SIMD Parallelism

This section describes how statements are executed conditionally in a SIMD environment. The SITDAC model for associative computing assumes a basic SIMD flow of control. That is, a single instruction stream is always broadcast to all of the parallel processors. Each processor has its own mask bit which it can set to 1 (*execute* or TRUE) or 0 (*ignore* or FALSE) based on the results of local computation. The mask bits are used to determine which processors execute the instruction stream and which processors ignore it. The instruction stream may also contain global set commands, which are executed by the processors regardless of the state of the mask bit.

This situation can be likened to a TV station broadcasting programs to all of the homes in an area. The TV on–off switch corresponds to the mask bit. Each person in a home (which represents the information content of a cell) determines whether or not to turn on the switch and watch the TV. There are other broadcast signals, such as a severe-weather siren, that are heard by everyone regardless of the position of the TV on–off switch and that demand that everyone turn on the TV if it is not already on and pay attention to the forthcoming message.

The conditional execution of a parallel **if** statement illustrates the use of the mask bit. In general, all parts of an **if** statement must be broadcast in the instruction stream since there is a high probability that both true and false results are present in the parallel data. So, for example, as illustrated in Fig. 2-1, a typical **if**-statement instruction sequence would be

- Set all mask bits.
- Broadcast code to calculate the **if** condition.
- Set the individual cell mask bit to
  - TRUE if the local condition is true.
  - FALSE otherwise.
- Broadcast code for the TRUE or **then** portion of the **if** statement.
- Complement the mask bits; i.e.,
  - if the condition was true, set the mask bit to FALSE.
  - if the condition was false, set the mask bit to TRUE.
- Broadcast code for the FALSE or **else** portion of the **if** statement.

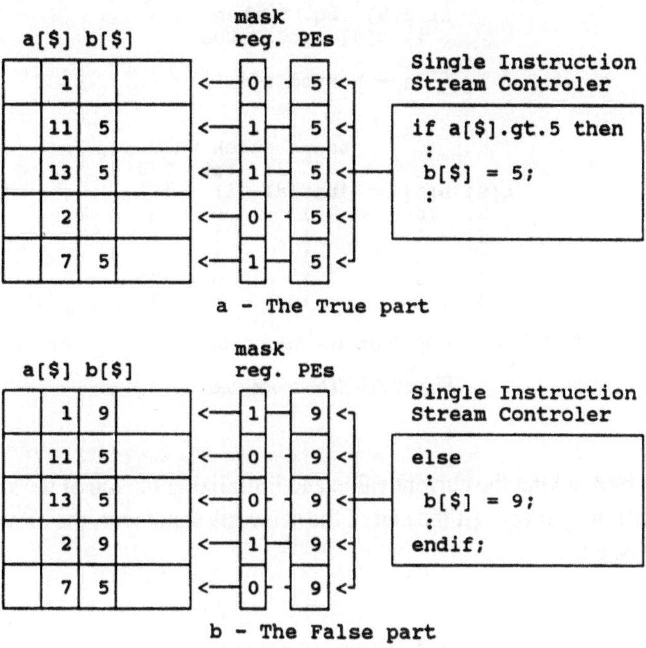

Figure 2-1. A parallel **if**.

In general, in SIMD programming, there is always the concept of each cell having a local mask bit which controls which cells execute which instructions. Logically, when the mask bits are viewed collectively, they form a mask field 1 bit wide. Physically, when the individual mask bits in the cell processors are viewed collectively, they form a single mask register with as many bits as the machine has processors. This mask field or register is easily accessible to the assembly-language programmer, and at this programming level, flow of control is effected by generating, saving, and restoring the mask field. Much of the facility of high-level SIMD languages is the automatic administration of the mask register in a manner which appears logical and natural to the programmer.

One approach is to administer the mask register as a stack. In this approach, every parallel operation is restricted by the scope of the bit field at the top of the scope stack. When a program starts, the top of the stack is set to all 1s (TRUE). When a parallel **if** statement is executed, the result of the **if** condition is ANDed with the top of the scope stack and then pushed onto the stack. As a result, nested **ifs** as shown in Fig. 2-2a are automatically ANDed. Thus, in Fig. 2-2b, the result of the second **if** statement is TRUE (1) only where both a [$] .eq. 5, and b[$] .gt. 7.

When the end of an **if** statement is encountered, the top scope is popped off the stack and the new top of the stack is established as the new scope.

A second statement such as **setscope** is needed to allow the scope stack to be

```
if a[$] .eq. 5 then
  if b[$] .gt. 7 then
```

a - Nested ifs

a[$]	b[$]	scope stack values initial	1st if	2nd if
3	10	1	0	0
5	8	1	1	1
5	6	1	1	0
4	3	1	0	0
5	9	1	1	1

b - Effect on Scope Stack

Figure 2-2. The scope stack.

overridden by stacking the current value and initializing the top of the stack to any specified activity pattern. At the end of the **setscope** statement, the previous scope is re-established.

2.2. Flow of Control

Section 2.1 described the basic SIMD concept of using masks to control which sections of code are executed. This section describes more-complex situations which use both masking and conventional branching to control the flow of a SITDAC program.

Parallel **ifs**, described in sections 2.1 and 3.7, can be nested to any level to achieve a very powerful form of flow of control. However, there are situations which require more-direct control over the contents of the mask register. Consider a problem in which the individual association entries may be in any one of four states. This is analogous to a situation requiring a case statement in conventional languages. If four bit flags are allocated, one for each of the states, then the instructions pertaining to state *n* will be executed by the appropriate cells if the mask register is initialized to bit flag *n* prior to their broadcast. Figure 2-3 illustrates the situation where edges *ab*, *cd*, *ef*, and *gh* are in states 1, 2, 2, and 4, respectively. No edges are in state 3.

As the program progresses, the contents of the state bit flags are updated to

node1	node2	state 1	2	3	4
a	b	1	0	0	0
c	d	0	1	0	0
e	f	0	1	0	0
g	h	0	0	0	1

Figure 2-3. The use of bit fields.

reflect the current state of the algorithm. The state flags themselves can be initialized and updated by being specified as the left-hand side of a logical parallel-assignment statement.

The use of state flags allows the programmer to control when and how the flags are updated. A parallel **if** or **setscope** statement can be used with a state bit flag to set the mask register to the desired state. The parallel **if** will AND the state bit flag with the contents of the current mask register. The **setscope** statement overwrites the present contents of the mask register with the bit flag regardless of the mask register's contents. Both statements save the old mask register before writing the new mask and restore the mask register to its original state at the end of the statement.

The use of bit flags to record the various states of association entries is an efficient, fundamental mode of operation in parallel associative and SIMD computing. By recording all associative cells that are to be treated alike in a logical parallel bit flag, parallel execution of the appropriate code is achieved by simply moving the bit flag to the mask register before the instruction sequence is broadcast.

In the above sequence, flow of control is achieved not by branching but by executing the entire sequence of code and setting the scope so that the appropriate PEs execute the appropriate code.

A more-traditional flow-of-control concept is based on the number of responders to a search. In particular, an associative computer must be able to test for a responders/no-responders condition and then branch as a result. For example, a common scenario would be to search for a specific set of association entries, then test to see if there were any responders. If there are, the responders are processed. If not, a branch is executed, skipping the responder processing code. Strictly speaking, this branch is not necessary; since the mask register would be set to all 0s, the code could be broadcast and ignored. However, faster execution is achieved by branching. In other situations, the branch might go to a section of code that issues a warning that expected results were not present.

Finally, traditional, scalar-**if**-statement flow of control is possible where a false scalar result causes the program to branch around the *then* portion of the statement. Generally, scalar **ifs** are used in the initialization portion of the code. Rarely are they used in the body of a SITDAC program. In fact, their use may be considered a measure of the quality of a SITDAC program. As a rule of thumb, if the main body of a program contains more than a few scalar **ifs**, either the design of the program is not making full use of the available parallelism or the algorithm is not suited for associative computing.

2.3. The Classroom Model

A conventional classroom models the fundamental modes of SITDAC computation and provides a valuable aid for SITDAC program design. For example, the chairs in the room represent the processors, since they can be full (active) or empty (idle). And while the chairs may be numbered and placed in a specific configuration, the configuration does not determine which student sits where.

The students, of course, represent the knowledge, or data, in the model. The student plus his or her chair represents a cell. The model assumes there are more chairs than students. If this is not true, the situation is rectified; that is, more chairs are brought in or the class is divided into two sections.

Each student is an element of an association. An association is a logical organization of the students based on some common interest. Any number of associations may be present in the room.

The teacher represents the associative program and controls all the activity in the room. When work is to be done, it is initiated by the teacher. A typical exchange might be for the teacher to identify a subset of students by describing them and commanding them to identify themselves as responders, as in "Students from Ohio: Raise your hands." Every student hears the command. Each searches his memory for the location of his residence. Those from Ohio respond to the instruction; the remainder "turn off" (i.e., clear their mask bits) and ignore the subsequent sequence.

Once the students have responded, the teacher may address them all together (i.e., in parallel) or one at a time (iteratively). When processed in parallel, the action is identical for all responders. After all of the responding students have been processed, the nonresponders may be addressed and become the responders for an **else** action that also may be executed in parallel or iteratively. This sequence of actions is achieved in SITDAC programming by using a parallel **if** statement as described in section 3.7.

When the action the teacher wants to take is to be tailored to each student's needs (i.e., as determined by the auxiliary data in the association entry), the students are processed iteratively. That is, one of the responders is selected at random. Specific facts are then elicited from the student selected. These facts can be broadcast to all of the students or given to just one or two or retained by the teacher for later use. The querying of the student may be interrupted with other parallel and iterative types of commands. Finally, when the first student has been processed, he or she is told to put his or her hand down, and a new student is selected from the remaining responders. This procedure continues until all responders have been processed. This sequence of actions can be invoked with a SITDAC associative **for** or **while** statement, described in section 3.8.

Occasionally, when the teacher asks a question, there are no responders. If this case is unexpected, a completely different set of directions may be needed. For example, when the teacher asks the students to turn in their homework and no one responds, they may be given an extension, instead of the teacher collecting and grading the homework. This capability is provided by adding an *else-not-any* (**elsenany**) option to many of the SITDAC associative statements.

2.4. Memory Allocation

In modern programming languages the desire for dynamic memory allocation has resulted in the development of techniques for the manipulation and use of run-time data structures. Most of these techniques use pointers. Associative computing provides an alternative programming approach to the use of pointers. For example, consider the conventional data structure shown in Fig. 2-4. In conventional address programming, address expressions such as are shown in Fig. 2-5 are required to access the data. These expressions can be quite long, complex, and difficult to read. In addition, pointer arithmetic or array index

```
struct workers
  { char *first;
    struct depend *kids;
    int id;
    int ssn;
  };

struct depend
  { int age;
    int mid;
    struct moniker *name;
  };

struct moniker
  { char *first;
    char *middle;
    char *last;
  };

struct workers *emp;
```

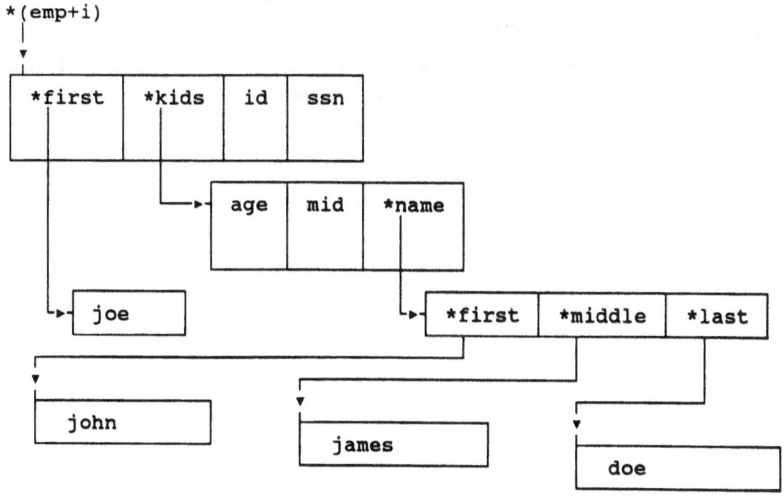

*(emp+i)
*first
*kids
id
ssn
age
mid
*name
joe
*first
*middle
*last
john
james
doe

Figure 2-4. A complex data structure.

```
(*(*((*(emp+i)).kids+j)).name).first

((((emp+i)->kids+j))->name)->first
```

Figure 2-5. Reference to a complex data structure.

manipulation must be performed in conjunction with loop iteration to assure that all items in the data structures are processed.

In contrast, in associative SITDAC computation, all of the data is stored in tabular arrays as shown in Fig. 2-6a. The path through the "data structure" is implemented by associative control structures. Since the items sought are actually data instead of pointers, the innermost resultant code in Fig. 2-6b is simpler. The examples shown here use ASC statements described in Chapter 3. The intent here is only to show the simpler statement structure. An explanation of general memory allocation and release is given later in this section.

One argument often used against the tabular storage of data is the large amount of wasted memory due to replicated data (fields name, ssn, and id in Fig. 2-6a). As in any situation, there are tradeoffs. First, run-time memory allocation is simple and efficient in SITDAC programming. No memory is wasted by declaring excessively large static arrays. Second, the overhead in wasted memory is roughly the same for both dynamic systems, since in conventional schemes there is considerable memory overhead for pointer storage. For example, a comparison shows that five of the eight data fields in Fig. 2-6 contain unique data. Therefore, $\frac{5}{8}$ would be a very crude estimate of its efficiency. Note that the equivalent pointer data structure of Fig. 2-4 has a total of 15 cells, seven of which are pointers, and thus has a rating of $\frac{8}{15}$. Both are about sixty percent efficient, but the SITDAC structure has fewer total cells. The administrative data structures, busy/idle maps (e.g., bi[$]) in SITDAC programming and heap administration in conventional programming, are ignored in both cases. Of course this is just an illustrative example to point out that conventional memory allocation wastes space, too. The

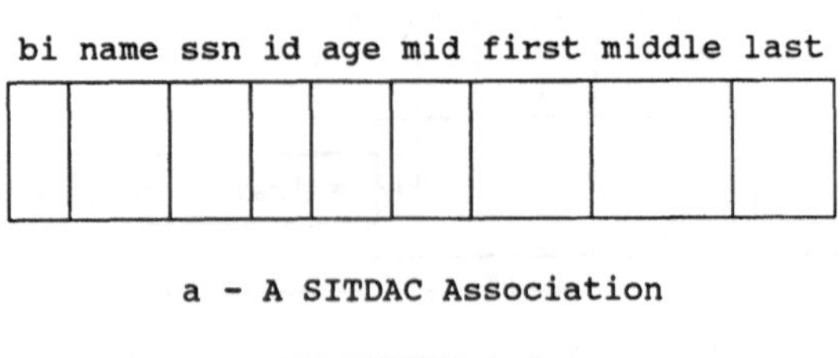

a - A SITDAC Association

```
for xx in "joe" .eq. name[$]
   first[xx]
```

b - A SITDAC Reference

Figure 2-6. A SITDAC association.

actual tradeoff between the two approaches depends on the number of dependents per employee (in our example) and many other factors and is too complex for further analysis here. (However, a more detailed discussion is given in Chapter 4 for the programming examples described there.) Finally, memory is cheap. Efficient utilization of memory is not of prime importance. The ease of allocating, releasing, and accessing memory produces a good tradeoff of programmer productivity for computer memory.

Fig. 2-7 compares the number of statements (which are a form of overhead) required to allocate, access, and release the memory for the data structures of Figs. 2-4 and 2-6. The code required to access the data structures is shown in Fig. 2-7c and d. While a hash function would perform the job of the conventional access function more efficiently, it is considerably more complex to implement when the code necessary to detect and resolve collisions is considered.

Note that in an address expression for Joe's *j*th child, there is no meaningful relationship between Joe and his *j*th child. That is, any of Joe's children could be his *j*th, depending on how the data is ordered, by age, medical id (mid), etc.

```
emp = calloc(emp_size, sizeof(struct workers));
(emp+i)->kids =
   calloc(kids_size, sizeof(struct depend));
(((emp+i)->kids+j))->name->first =
   calloc(name_size, size of(char));
```

a - Conventional Memory Allocation

```
allocate xx in bi[$];
   :
endallocate;
```

b - SITDAC Memory Allocation

```
for(i=0; i<emp_size; i++)
  if(strcmp((emp+i)->name,"joe") == 0)  break;
```

c - Conventional Memory Access

```
if "joe" .eq. name[$] then
```

d - SITDAC Memory Access

```
free((( emp+i)->kids+j))->name->first)
free((emp+i)->kids)
free(emp)
```

e - Conventional Memory Release

```
release bi[$] from bi[$];
```

f - SITDAC Memory Release

Figure 2-7. Code comparison for pointer vs. associative memory allocation.

However, the equivalent associative statement clearly establishes the desired relationship. Thus

for xx in "joe" .eq. name [$] .and. mindex(age[$])

references Joe's youngest (minimum age—the **mindex** function is explained in section 2.8) child, while

for xx in "joe" .eq. name [$] .and. mindex(mid[$])

references Joe's child with the lowest mid. Of course, if the order of accessing the children is not important, the simple statement

for xx in "joe" .eq. name[$]

is sufficient.

To recapitulate, the SITDAC model assumes that every association entry has its own dedicated processor. The memory that holds the association and its processor are collectively called a data cell. Memory is allocated by assigning data cells to the associations as needed.

Each association has a logical parallel variable with the same name as the association, which acts as a busy/idle map. If a bit of the association variable is 1 (*on* or *active*), the corresponding data cell is active and is in the association. If the bit is 0 (*off* of *idle*), the data cell is not in the association.

There is a global busy/idle map variable which contains a 0 if the data cell is active in any association and a 1 otherwise. When memory is allocated, the first idle cell bit in the global busy/idle map variable is selected. This bit is set to active in the global busy/idle map and the association variable. As a result, the association variables are mutually exclusive and are covered by the compliment of global busy/idle map.

Figure 2-8 shows a hypothetical memory-allocation map, dal[$], before and after a new entry is allocated. Note that there are "holes" in the allocation map. They are due to the release of entries in an order different from that in which they were allocated. Holes are of no concern. The first idle cell is allocated no matter where it is. As a result, association entries are not necessarily contiguous or in order. This is quite acceptable in SITDAC programming since association entries are accessed and processed in parallel by their contents, not by their physical location in memory. That is, an association entry may be in any associative cell, and it can still be found in one step by searching.

The format of the cell memories varies, depending on the association to which each belongs. Obviously, the configuration of the memory must agree with the association specification. This agreement is accomplished by the use of the association busy/idle variable as a mask. For example, in

if dal[$] .and. "condition" then

the responders to the "condition" are restricted to the dal association, all of whose entries have the same format.

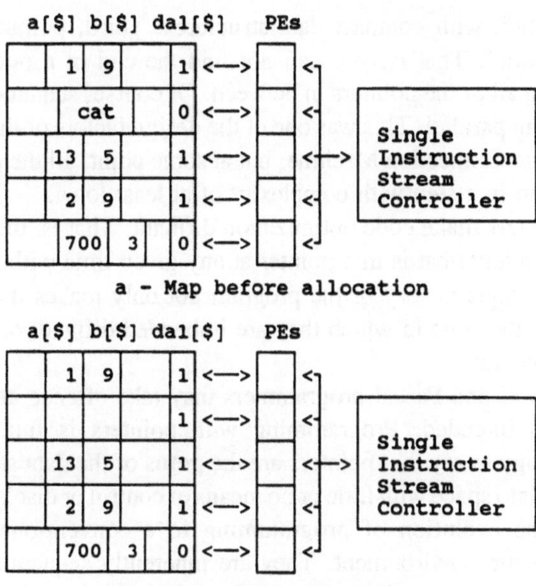

Figure 2-8. Memory association map.

Thus, the associative programmer can control the scope of his parallel statements by using the association busy/idle masks. Moreover, he may combine them in any way which makes sense and, in particular, the compliment of the global busy/idle mask, which is equivalent to the inclusive OR of all of the association busy/idle masks, can be used to select all active cells.

2.5. Massive Parallel Searching

As the classroom model indicates, the typical mode of SITDAC operation is to broadcast the description of the desired responders to all of the association elements. This allows all processors to be searched in parallel. In the SITDAC model, searching is preferable to sorting and/or pointing.

In the classroom model all chairs are identical and equally accessible. A teacher who wishes to locate specific students quickly might expend time and effort to sort them alphabetically. However, upon reflection, the teacher will realize that the alphabetical ordering process requires time and effort which is not necessary, since any given student or set of students can be found in one broadcast command as fast or faster than by scanning down an ordered sequence of chairs.

Pointers are not emphasized in SITDAC programming for a number of reasons. First, they are addressing constructs closely tied to the basic index-register architecture of conventional computers, and as such are the antithesis of SITDAC searching. Second, pointers are difficult to use and understand, especially in connection with complex data structures. Third, pointer following is inherently sequential. That is, you can not find the end of a pointer sequence without following all of the pointers in between. Of course, sequences of pointers may be followed in parallel. This was one of the design factors of the interconnection network in the Connection Machine, but at some point, all the paths followed must be linked up in a step with complexity of at least $\log n$.

Finally, pointers make code optimization difficult. That is, the property that there is no way to tell what is in a pointer at any given time without completely analyzing the previous history of the program not only makes them difficult to debug but makes the code in which they are imbedded difficult or impossible to optimize automatically.

While many C and Pascal programmers may take offence at the following remark, none is intended: Programming with pointers is fun, but it is an appropriate analogy to say that pointers are the **goto**s of the data structures. That is, they point off into space with little or no means of control or discipline. They are an artifact of the evolution of programming in a conventional, sequential-computer-architecture environment. They are inherently sequential. And while they are very useful in certain situations, they are hard to deal with and to understand. During the evolution of programming languages, structured programming techniques were developed, reducing the need for **goto**s. As languages and programming techniques evolve further, new approaches, such as massively parallel searching, will be developed to reduce the need for pointers.

As was seen in Fig. 2-4, the use of pointers adds addressing data and structure to the problem's data and structure that serves no direct purpose in solving the problem. In contrast, SITDAC data structures contain only problem data, and in most cases, the desired data can be extracted from the tabular data structure using massive parallel searching as fast or even faster than by following pointers. In Chapter 4, a minimal spanning-tree algorithm is used to illustrate the differences between using pointers and linked lists in conventional approaches on the one hand and parallel searching in associative computing on the other. In Chapter 5, the ease of working with data directly instead of pointers, linked lists, stacks, and queues is illustrated.

Massively parallel searching is a fundamental concept of associative computing. Accordingly, in the remainder of this text, unless it is explicitly stated otherwise, the term *searching* always means massively parallel searching whose time complexity is constant. Frequently, "massively parallel" is used with searching to emphasize the constant-time complexity aspect of associative computing.

2.6. Tabular Arrays

An important aspect of all programming tasks is the mapping of the data onto the computational model. One of the advantages of SITDAC programming is that the data maps onto the hardware in an easy-to-comprehend, two-dimensional tabular format. An ASC associative declaration statement is in essence the definition of a tabular data organization that might be used for program documentation or for communicating algorithms to other programmers.

The association statement establishes the column labels of the table. Since the SITDAC model assumes there are enough cells for all data, there is no need to specify the number of association entries or rows in the table. They are dynamically allocated at run time. Thus, the column labels contain a $ index variable to indicate that the size of the first (column) dimension is variable and to remind the user of the parallel (plural) aspect of the variable.

Entries are made in an ASC association at run time by either a read statement or an assignment inside a memory-allocation statement. For example, whenever a **read** statement is executed, the number of rows input is determined and the appropriate number of association entries are allocated in the specified association variable (see Fig. 2-9).

An ASC **allocate** statement and parallel index variables are used if information from two or more associations is to be combined into a new association entry. As illustrated in Fig. 2-10, the index variables *xx*, *yy*, and *zz* flag the association entries involved in the process. The *xx* and *yy* indices flag entries in associations I and II that will be used to create the *zz* entry in association III. The **allocate** statement obtains an idle entry in the specified association and uses the *zz* index variable to flag it.

2.7. Bit-Serial Arithmetic

The massive parallelism in an associative computer is obtained by processing entire columns of the association in parallel. This can be achieved by using bit-serial arithmetic in many simple PEs instead of word-serial arithmetic in a few complex CPUs. Figure 2-11 shows an arithmetic operation on three columns, a [$],

```
Input file
     0  17   9
     3   2   6
     8   1  22

Read statement
     read a[$] b[$] c[$] in d[$];

Resultant array memory
   a[$]b[$]c[$] d[$]
```

	a[$]	b[$]	c[$]		d[$]	
	0	17	9		1	
	3	2	6		1	
	8	1	22		1	
					0	
					:	

Figure 2-9. An ASC **read** statement.

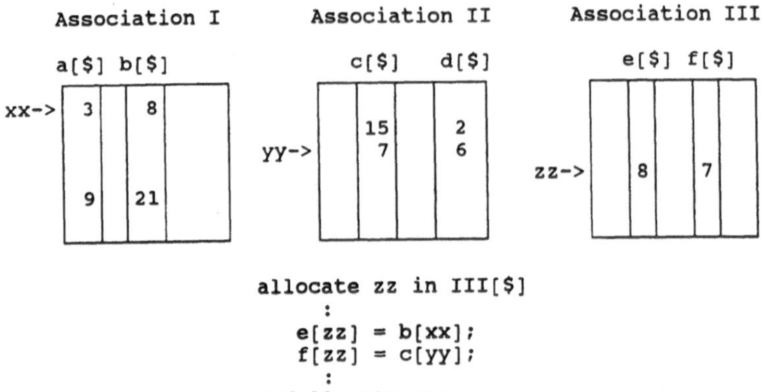

Figure 2-10. ASC association generation.

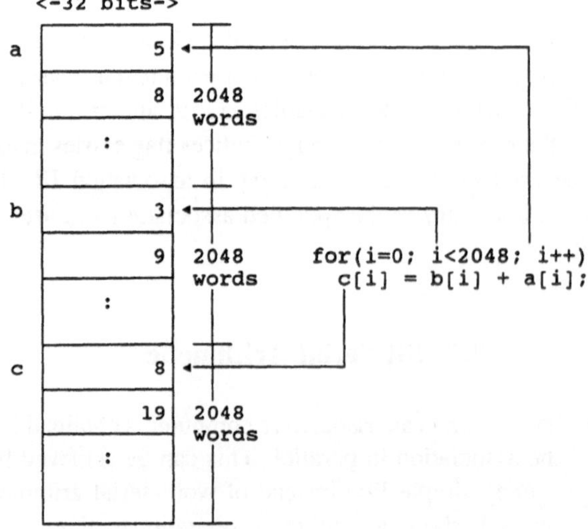

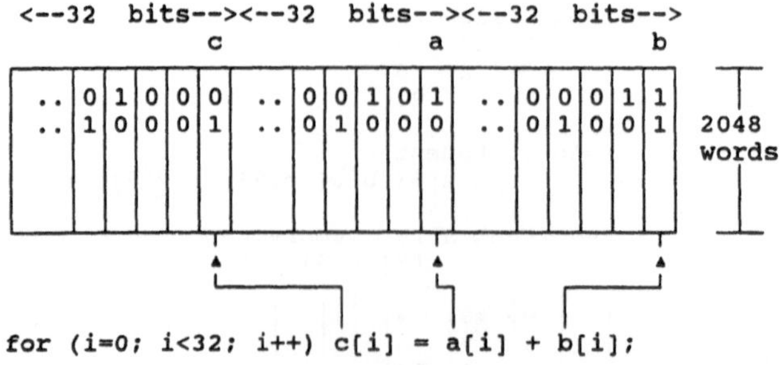

Figure 2-11. Word- and bit-slice organizations.

b[$], and c[$], of an association with K(2048) entries. In a conventional computer (Fig. 2-11a), all of the 32 bits in each of the words would be fetched and processed (i.e., added) and the resultant word stored in bit-parallel, word-serial fashion. This process would be repeated K times (in a loop) to process all of the entries in the association columns.

In a bit-serial computer (Fig. 2-11b), the least significant bits of all of the K words are fetched, processed, and stored in word-parallel, bit-serial fashion. If the process is addition and only 2 bits per word are being added, the result is 1 bit of the sum and 1 bit of carry. The sum bits of the K words are stored in the result column, and the carry bits are saved in the processors so they can be added to the next bits processed. This process is repeated (in a loop) 32 times to process all of the columns.

One way of remembering the bit-serial process is to imagine a classroom of K students. Each student is to add two 32-digit numbers. The classroom teacher tells the students to add the rightmost digits. They do so, placing the sum digit in the rightmost position of the result and placing the carry (if any) over the next-rightmost digit of the addends. The teacher then instructs them to add the next-rightmost digit, and so on. Obviously, bit-serial addition is addition as we learned it in grammar school, except that binary instead of decimal numbers are being added.

2.7.1. Bit-Serial Addition

More specifically, Fig. 2-12 shows a generic PE. It contains an X and a Y bit register. Table 2-1 shows that exclusive OR is equivalent to summing 2 bits and that a logical AND calculates the carry from the sum of 2 bits. These equivalences are used in the algorithm shown in Fig. 2-13. This algorithm also uses the fact that, when the carry is included, the addition of two numbers is actually the addition of three numbers and can be organized into two additions of two numbers, as in

partial sum = first addend + carry in
final sum = second addend + partial sum.

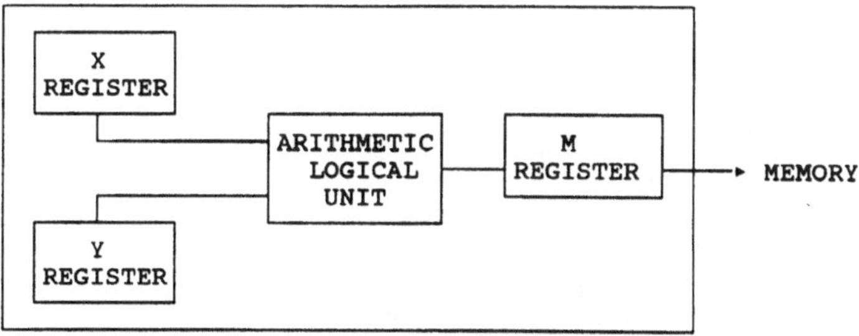

Figure 2-12. A simplified processing element.

Table 2-1. The Sum of Two Bits

A	B	A+B	AANDB	AXORB
0	0	0	0	0
0	1	1	0	1
1	0	1	0	1
1	1	10	1	0

The pseudo-code in Fig. 2-13 is an approximation of triple-address intermediate code, or quadruples. For binary operators, the first two arguments are operands and the third is the result or destination. For unary operators, the first argument is the operand, the second is the result.

The first "addition" in Fig. 2-13 is the addition of the carry from the previous bit slice to the bit slice from the first addend. This addition produces a carry, which is saved in the *X* register, and a partial sum bit, saved in the *Y* register. The second addition adds the second addend bit to the partial sum, producing the carry-out bit slice and a sum bit slice. The sum bit slice is stored in memory and the carry is saved in the *X* register and then moved to the *Y* register at the top of the loop in preparation for the addition of the next bit slice.

The carryout from the second addition is computed by (X^Y)B(I) + X (where ^ is the exclusive OR operator, the addition sign means logical OR, and multiplication means logical AND). Thus, X^Y is the sum of the sum and the carry from the first addition. The formula states that a carryout will occur whenever there is a 1 in either the carry or the sum of the first addition, if there is also a 1 in the second bit slice, *B(I)*. This will not give the correct result only when there is a carryin from

```
                 ADD   A,B,C

CLEAR  X
FOR I = 31,0,-1
  MOV     X,Y
  CLEAR  X
; ADD FIRST ADDEND BIT TO CARRY
  AND     A(I),Y,X
  XOR     A(I),Y,Y
; ADD SECOND ADDEND BIT
  AND     B(I),Y,TEMP
  OR      TEMP,X,X
  XOR     B(I),Y,Y
; SAVE SUM
  STORE  Y,C(I)
ENDFOR

A(I) fetches bit I of addend A.
The bits are numbered from
left(bit 0) to right (bit 31).
```

Figure 2-13. Bit-serial addition.

the previous bit slice and there is a 1 in the first addend bit slice but there is not a 1 in the second. In this situation, the carry from the first addition will be set, so it is sufficient to OR it in giving (X^Y)B(I) + X. This expression can be reduced to YB(I) + X, which is the sequence shown in Fig. 2-13. The first instruction after the ";ADD SECOND ADDEND BIT" comment calculates the AND of the first sum and second addend bit slice. The result is ORed with the first carry and saved in the *X* register as the second carry.

Figure 2-13 shows the total bit-serial addition routine as eight instructions; however, it is possible to combine some of the operations so that as few as four instructions and no temporaries are needed. Figure 2-14 shows the truth table for the addition shown in Fig. 2-13.

2.7.2. Bit-Serial Subtraction

Bit-serial subtraction is achieved by algebraic addition. That is, the field to be subtracted is complemented and then added. The complementation can be carried out when the bit slice is read just before the addition so that the arguments need to be read only once.

If two's-complement arithmetic is to be used, complementation and addition may seem to be impossible since it requires a 1 to be added in after the complementation. However, recall that addition has a provision for adding in the carry bit which is initialized to 0. If it is initialized to 1, the complementation, add-1 and addition processes can be carried out all at once, as shown in Fig. 2-15.

2.7.3. Bit-Serial Multiplication

Bit-serial multiplication is achieved by repeated adds. Again the algorithm is the same as that used in elementary school. To review, each digit in the multiplier is

Y_1	A(I)	B(I)	X_1	Y_2	TEMP	X_2	Y_3
0	0	0	0	0	0	0	0
0	0	1	0	0	0	0	1
0	1	0	0	1	0	0	1
0	1	1	0	1	1	1	0
1	0	0	0	1	0	0	1
1	0	1	0	1	1	1	0
1	1	0	1	0	0	1	0
1	1	1	1	0	0	1	1

```
Y1    - carry_in
X1    - A(I)carry_in  = A(I)Y1
Y2    - A(I)^carry_in = A(I)^Y1
TEMP  - B(I)(A(I)^carry_in) = B(I)Y2
X2    - B(I)(A(I)^carry_in)+A(I)carry_in = TEMP+X1 = carry_out
Y3    - B(I)^(A(I)^carry_in) = B(I)^(A(I)^Y1) = B(I)^Y2 = sum
```

Figure 2-14. Truth table for bit-serial addition.

```
SUB   A,B,C

SET     X
FOR I = 31,0,-1
  MOV     X,Y
  CLEAR   X
; ADD FIRST ADDEND BIT TO CARRY
  AND     A(I),Y,X
  XOR     A(I),Y,Y
; SUB SECOND ADDEND BIT
  NOTAND  B(I),Y,TEMP
  OR      TEMP,X,X
  NOTXOR  B(I),Y,Y
; SAVE SUM
  STORE   Y,C(I)
ENDFOR

A(I) fetches bit I of addendA.
The bits are numbered from
left(bit 0) to right (bit 31).
```

Figure 2-15. Bit-serial subtraction.

processed from right to left. A partial result is formed by multiplying the multiplicand by the current digit of the multiplier, shifting the result left by an amount equal to the position of the multiplier digit, and adding the result to the previous partial result.

Fortunately, the multiplication table for binary multiplication is trivial since the multiplier bit can only be a 0 or a 1. A 0 multiplier requires no action, and a 1 multiplier is simply addition. The algorithm for bit-serial multiplication is outlined in Fig. 2-16.

```
product = 0
for each bit in multiplier (right to left)
    if bit is one, add multiplicand to product
    shift multiplicand left one bit

Example:
  Multiply 01101 by 01010
```

	multiplier	multiplicand	cumulative product
bit 0	0101[0]	01101	0000
bit 1	010[1]0	011010	011010
bit 2	01[0]10	0110100	011010
bit 3	0[1]010	01101000	10000010
bit 4	[0]1010	011010000	10000010

Figure 2-16. Bit-serial multiplication.

2.7.4. Bit-Serial Division

Bit-serial division is also an elementary-school algorithm. The only complication is determining where to position the divisor for subtraction. This is done mentally in the grade-school algorithm by multiplying the divisor by a digit and testing whether it is less than the leftmost portion of the dividend. Again this process is quite simple because of the use of binary arithmetic. That is, the only multiple of the divisor that needs to be tested is the divisor itself (i.e., its multiple by 1). The test is achieved by subtracting the divisor from the dividend and then testing for a negative result. (See Fig. 2-17 for an outline of the algorithm and an

```
1.  Calculate the difference in the sizes of the dividend
    and divisor; save in delta.

2.  Make the divisor the same number of bits as the
    dividend by adding zeros to the right.

3.  For delta+1 times,
    3.1  subtract divisor.
    3.2  if positive, put a 1 in next bit of quotient,
              update dividend with difference.
    3.3  if negative, put a 0 in next bit of quotient.
    3.4  decrement to point to next bit of quotient.
    3.5  shift divisor right one bit.

Example:
    Divide 10010111 by 101

        STEP DIVIDEND     DIVISOR        TEST       QUOTIENT
        1.    10010111    00000101     delta = 8 - 3 = 5
        2.    10010111    10100000
        3.1   10010111 -  10100000 -> 1111110111
        3.3                                          0
        3.4                                           ↑
        3.5               01010000
        3.1   10010111 -  01010000 -> 0001000111
        3.2   01000111                               01
        3.4                                            ↑
        3.5               00101000
        3.1   01000111 -  00101000 -> 0000011111
        3.2   00011111                               011
        3.4                                             ↑
        3.5               00010100
        3.1   00011111 -  00010100 -> 0000001011
        3.2   00001011                               0111
        3.4                                              ↑
        3.5               00001010
        3.1   00001011 -  00001010 -> 0000000001
        3.2   00000001                               01111
        3.4                                               ↑
        3.5               00000101
        3.1   00000001 -  00000101 -> 1111111100
        3.3                                          011110
        3.5   00000001
                  ↑
             REMAINDER
```

Figure 2-17. Bit-serial division.

example.) The numbers to the left in the example specify the step of the algorithm that has just been executed.

2.8. Responders and Numeric Searching

The responder/no-responder signal of the associative computer, also known as the sum–or signal in some SIMD processors, gives it a very powerful search capability. That is, the controller is able to query the entire array of processors with only one instruction. This instruction allows numeric search functions such as maximum-, minimum-, next-higher-, and next-lower-value and other numeric search functions to be efficiently implemented (Falkoff [1962], Foster [1976], Hwang and Briggs [1984]).

2.8.1. The Numeric Searching Functions

Consider the maximum-value function. This function searches all entries in a field in parallel for the largest value. The general idea behind the algorithm is to use bit slices as masks for the maximum value. Figure 2-18 shows that if two entries are otherwise equal, the entry with a 1 in any given bit slice is the larger. The algorithm proceeds from the most significant bit to the least. It initially assumes that all entries are maximal and therefore sets the **maxdex** (maximum index) variable to all 1s. As each bit slice is processed, it is ANDed with **maxdex**. Those entries which are still flagged by **maxdex** are the largest of the entries initially flagged by **maxdex**.

At any point in the process, the entries flagged by **maxdex** contain the common largest value in the field to the left of the current bit. This situation is illustrated in Fig. 2-19. After processing the fourth bit (i.e., bit 3), the second, fourth, and fifth entries are tied for the largest value of 1011 in bits 0 to 3, as shown in the boxes.

Clearly, if one entry contained all 1s, it would be flagged as the maximum entry, since the algorithm essentially ANDs all of its ones from left to right. Any entry with a 0 at any bit position would be eliminated, since ANDing the 0 would clear the **maxdex** flag. Obviously, in general, the maximum value of a field will not be all 1s. But the maximum value of a field will have a 1 at every bit position

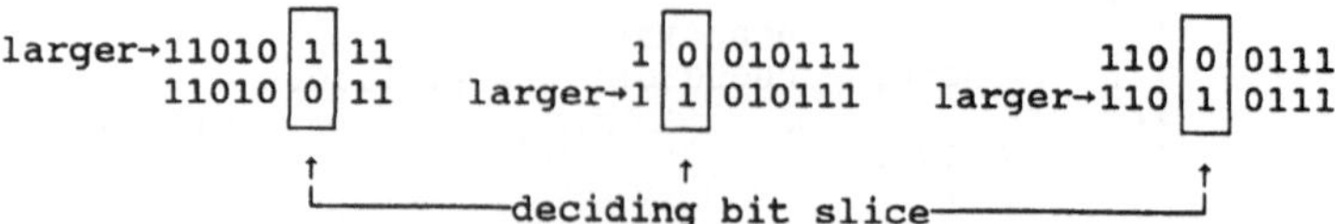

Figure 2-18. The maximum of two otherwise equal entries.

```
maxdex*  | bit slice
012345   | 0123 4567
---------+----------
1000000  | 0011 0011
1111111  |[1011]1001
1110000  | 1001 1111
1111100  |[1011]0010
1111111  |[1011]1000

*initially and                equivalent maximal
 after processing bit   [  ] = entries after
 slice 0-5.                   processing bit 3
```

Figure 2-19. Equal maximal values.

where a decision about which of several numbers is larger has to be made (a decision point), or it would not be the maximum.

The decision points are those bit slices that, when ANDed with the current maximum values, do not annihilate them. That is, at least one new maximum value remains. Thus the algorithm depends on the detection of responders to determine decision points so that **maxdex** is updated only if there are responders. If there are no responders at a bit position, then all current entries with the maximum value have the same bit value and remain tied even though that bit value is 0. For example, when bit slice 4 in Fig. 2-19 is ANDed with **maxdex** there will be two responders and **maxdex** will be updated to flag just them. However, when bit slice 5 is processed, the result is all 0s and **maxdex** is not modified. This same condition occurred earlier at bit slice 1. Figure 2-20 gives the algorithm for the maximum-

```
SET MAXDEX
FOR I = 0,31,1
   AND    A(I),MAXDEX,Y ;Y<-M .AND. A(I)
   BNR    Y,CONTINUE    ;BRANCH IF NO RESPONDERS IN Y
   MOVE   Y,MAXDEX
ENDFOR
```

a - Maximum Field Index

```
SET MINDEX
FOR I = 0,31,1
   NOT    A(I),X
   AND    X,MINDEX,Y          ;Y<-M .AND. .NOT. A(I)
   BNR    Y,CONTINUE          ;BRANCH IF NO RESPONDERS IN Y
   MOVE   Y,MINDEX
ENDFOR
```

b - Minimum Field Index

Figure 2-20. Maxdex and **mindex**.

field and minimum-field index functions. Note that the BNR (*b*ranch if *no* *r*esponders) instruction is the realization of the responders/no-responders query.

The maximum and minimum search functions are very powerful for general-purpose situations. There are additional functions that are very powerful for working with structure codes. Structure codes allow the SITDAC search capability to be used for complex searching and pattern matching. Structure codes for trees, for example, encode the path from the root of the tree to a given node. When structure codes are associated with data at the nodes of a tree, the structure of a pattern as well as its data content can be searched for. Structure codes are discussed in detail in Chapter 5. Here it is necessary only to understand that the structure codes represent the ordering of the associated data elements.

Consider the problem of searching structure codes for neighboring nodes. For example, the problem may be to find, given a flagged node, the node that is its nearest right neighbor. The right neighbor nodes are any nodes to the right of the flagged node when the structure is displayed as a tree.

As shown in Fig. 2-21, all right neighbor nodes have structure codes greater than the structure code of the flagged node. The nearest right neighbor is the right neighbor with the minimal code. Obviously a nearest right neighbor can be found by using two searches, one to find all right neighbors and another to find the minimal one. The nearest left neighbor can be defined and found analogously. Thus the direct approach to find the nearest left and right neighbors requires four searches. However, the logic from all four searches can be combined into just one.

The **sibdex** (sibling index) or nearest-neighbors algorithm is shown in Figs. 2-22 and 2-23. The key to understanding the **sibdex** algorithm is to realize that almost all codes start with a 0 in the leftmost bit (structure codes are unsigned numbers) and that the codes can be divided into three categories:

1. those less than the flagged node,
2. those greater than the flagged node, and
3. those equal to the flagged node.

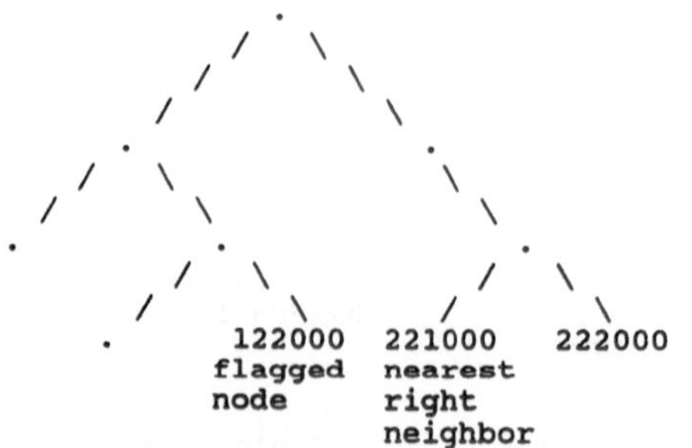

Figure 2-21. Neighboring nodes on a tree.

```
LOAD C,FLAGGED
SET  AVAIL
CLEAR  NXTDEX, NXTSLT, PRVDEX, PRVSLT
 ;FIRST LOOP
FOR I = 0,31,1
     BBS  I,GOTONE          ;EXIT LOOP ON FIRST ONE IN CODE
     NOT  A(I),X            ;GENERATE COMPLEMENT BITS
     AND  A(I),AVAIL,Y      ;BITS NUMBERED LEFT(0) TO RIGHT(31)
     BNR  Y,LP1             ;BRANCH IF NO RESPONDERS IN Y
      MOVE Y,NXTDEX         ;ESTABLISH NEW MINIMAL NXTDEX
      MOVE Y,NXTSLT         ;ESTABLISH NEW MINIMAL NXTSLT
      BR   LP2
     ;UPDATE MINIMAL NXTDEX AND NXTSLT
LP1: MOVE NXTDEX,NXTSLT
     AND  X,NXTDEX,NXTDEX ;NXTDEX <- NXTDEX .AND. .NOT. A(I)
     ;UPDATE AVAIL
LP2: AND  X,AVAIL,AVAIL
ENDFOR

GOTONE:   ;ESTABLISH EQUAL, PRVDEX AND UPDATE NXTDEX
     AND  A(I),AVAIL,EQUAL
     NOT  A(I),X
     AND  X,AVAIL,PRVDEX
     AND  X,NXTDEX,Y
     BNR  Y,LP3
      MOVE NXTDEX,NXTSLT
      MOVE X,NXTDEX
LP3:
```

Figure 2-22. Nearest-neighbors algorithm.

These categories can be established only after a 0 and a 1 from the flagged node code have been detected.

If the flagged code starts with a 0, then all codes with a 0 in their left-most bit are less than or equal to the flagged code. Those with 1s are greater. This condition is true for all the leading 0 in the flagged code. The first **for** loop of Fig. 2-22 performs this function. The variable *avail* keeps track of the codes which are not larger than the flagged code. The BBS (*b*ranch *b*it *s*et) instruction interrogates the bits of the flagged code loaded into the C register by the first instruction. The bit interrogated is specified by the variable I. Thus the bit of the flagged code and the bit slice of the field (*A*(*I*)) are synchronized by the index variable *I*. When the first 1 in the flagged code is detected, *avail* is divided into two categories: lesser codes (**prvdex**—previous index) and equal codes.

Before the first 1 is detected, the greater codes (**nxtdex**—next index) must be treated in a special way. The goal is to find the least greater code (nearest right neighbor), so that a **mindex** search is performed as the initial bits of the codes are processed. However, when a flagged *avail* code (whose initial portion is all 0s) has a 1, it is less than all of the greater codes and greater than the flagged code (which is still a 0), so all previous greater codes are discarded in favor of the new codes. This logic occurs after the first BNR instruction in the first loop. The no-responder portion (i.e., the target of the BNR Y,LP1 jump) contains the logic for the minimum search.

```
;SECOND LOOP
FOR J = I+1,31,1
     BBS  J,DOONE            ;BRANCH IF BIT J IS A ONE
     AND  PRVDEX,A(J),Y      ;FLAGGED BIT IS ZERO
     BNR  Y,LZ1              ;BRANCH IF NO RESPONDERS IN Y
       MOVE PRVDEX,PRVSLT
       MOVE Y,PRVDEX
LZ1: AND  EQUAL,A(J),Y
     NOT  A(J),X
     BNR  Y,LZ2
      MOVE Y,NXTDEX
      BR   LZ3
LZ2: AND  NXTDEX,X,Y
     BNR  Y,LZ3
      MOVE NXTDEX,NXTSLT
      MOVE Y,NXTDEX
LZ3: AND  EQUAL,X,EQUAL
     BR   EF1

DOONE:                       FLAGGED BIT IS ONE
     NOT  A(J),X
     AND  NXTDEX,X,Y
     BNR  Y,LO1
      MOVE NXTDEX,NXTSLT
      MOVE Y,NXTDEX
LO1: AND  X,EQUAL,Y
     BNR  Y,2
      MOVE Y,PRVDEX
      BR  LO3
LO2: AND PRVDEX,A(J),Y
     BNR  Y,3
      MOVE PRVDEX,PRVSLT
      MOVE Y,PRVDEX
LO3: AND  EQUAL,A(J),EQUAL

EF1:
ENDFOR
```

Figure 2-23. Nearest-neighbors algorithm, cont.

Figure 2-24 illustrates the result of the algorithm. When I = 1, codes 40 and 60 are detected as larger than 01, the flagged code. When I = 2, a minimum search is performed on 40 and 60, and code 40 is determined to be smaller, as indicated by the value of the *n* flag shown at the bottom of the figure. When I = 3, an *avail* code is discovered with a 1, so the current **nxtdex** flag is discarded and reinitialized as shown.

When the first 1 in the flagged code is detected, the first loop of Fig. 2-22 is exited and the three categories are established and updated. The second loop, shown in Fig. 2-23, is divided into two portions depending on the value of the currently flagged code bit.

Consider the processing when the flagged bit is 0. If **prvdex** is nonzero and is not annihilated by the bit slice, it is updated to its new value. The equal entries whose bits are 1s are put in the **nxtdex** category. Those with 0s remain in the equal category.

Contrarily, when the flagged bit is a 1, if **nxtdex** is not annihilated by the

```
GIVEN:
              I= 0123
flagged --> 00000001 (01)
            01000000 (40)
            01100000 (60)
            00010000 (10)

RESULT FOR:
  b=bit slice
  n=nxtdex
  a=avail

WHEN:
  I=0  I=1  I=2  I=3
  bna  bna  bna  bna
  011  001  001  001
  011  110  010  000
  011  110  100  000
  011  001  001  110
```

Figure 2-24. The result of **sibdex**.

complement of the bit slice, it is updated to its new value. Those equal entries with a 1 bit remain in the equal category. Those with 0s are put in the **prvdex** category. If the flagged bit is 0, then, as explained above, the right-neighbors flags (i.e., **prvdex**) will not be modified by any value in the equal category, and so they are updated using the conventional maximum-fields algorithm. However, if there are any equal values with 1, the right neighbors are discarded and replaced by the equal values for the same reason as described for the first loop.

The **sibdex** algorithm is an extension of the associative computing algorithms first reported by Falkoff [1962]. **Sibdex** is a very powerful function and takes the same order of time as **mindex** and **maxdex**. As will be shown in Chapter 5, **sibdex** allows expressions to be parsed in a straightforward and natural manner by finding the highest-priority operator in the expression, marking it as the flagged node, running **sibdex** to find the operands, and then reducing the operation, replacing the three nodes with the result node, and then repeating the entire process until all operators have been processed.

2.8.2. Numeric-Searching Complexity Analysis

Key to the performance of many of the associative programs using structure codes (described in Chapter 5) is the efficient execution of the numeric-search functions. The conventional wisdom is that, while algorithms to find the maximum value of a field with n numbers execute in constant time on machines with n^2 processors, the fastest parallel time for such functions on a practical machine is $\Theta(\log n)$. Yet, the numeric search functions have been reported for almost thirty years, and real machines which can execute these functions have been produced for almost twenty years. The purpose of this section is to develop the argument that the numeric search functions execute in constant time.

Obviously, from the search algorithm descriptions in section 2.8.1, these functions must in the worst case look at every bit slice in a field. Since a number, N, requires $\lceil \log N \rceil$ bits to store it, strictly speaking from Fig. 2-20, the search routines execute in approximately $3 \log N$ time. This time is a function of the size of the field, not the number of integers searched. In fact, since there is an associative cell for every integer, the time for searching is independent of the number of integers searched and is therefore constant.

However, this time must be compared with the time required for the execution of a maximum integer search algorithm on a sequential computer and a non-associative SIMD. If n is the number of integers, then $n - 1$ comparisons are required to find the largest or smallest integer (Baase [1978], p. 41) on a conventional sequential computer.

The amount of time required to find the maximum integers in a nonassociative SIMD search is $\Theta(\log n)$ by using a parallel version of the tournament method in which two adjacent processors compare their values. The winners are compared, and so on, as illustrated in Fig. 2-25.

Further comparison of the times $3 \log N$, $\Theta(n - 1)$, and $\Theta(\log n)$ requires a finer-grained analysis. The associative numeric searching routines take approximately $3 \log N$ instructions. Assuming a 32-bit field (i.e., $N = 2^{32} - 1$), the execution time is 96 instructions. Assuming the same sophistication of hardware, approximately three instructions are required for a compare in a sequential computer, so that $\Theta(n - 1)$ is actually about $3n - 3$ instructions. Figure 2-26

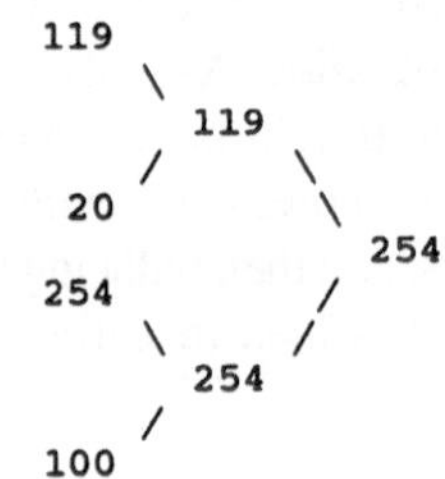

a - The Tournament Method

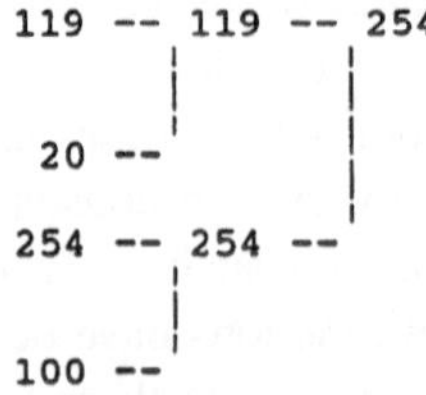

b - Tournament on a Grid

Figure 2-25. Tournament searching.

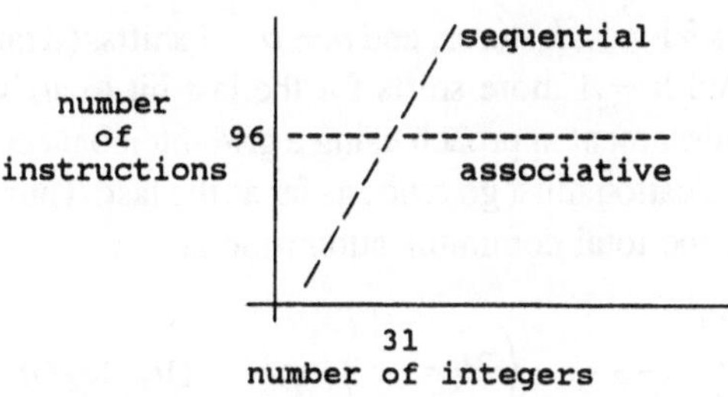

Figure 2-26. Time comparison.

graphs these two functions and shows the crossover at $n = 31$. That is, for $n < 31$, sequential searching is faster; for $n > 31$ associative searching is faster. Bear in mind that this analysis is biased in favor of the sequential machine because of the 32-bit-field assumption. That is, if only 31 numbers are to be searched, it is highly probable that they will fit into a field less than 32 bits wide. In the best case, they would require only a five-bit field, which could be searched associatively in 15 instructions versus the 93 required by a sequential computer. (As an aside, note that the graph of Fig. 2-26 is typical of SIMD computer throughput diagrams. It is flat—that is, constant throughout the entire range of computation under the assumption of one cell for every datum.)

The $3 \log N$ associative time must also be compared with the $\Theta(\log n)$ time for the parallel tournament approach. Again, a 32-bit field is assumed. However, it is important to realize that the $\Theta(\log n)$ time includes interprocessor communication. That is, one step of the comparison consists of transmitting the integer from one processor to its neighbor and then comparing them.

In an effort to generate a concrete example, this discussion assumes a nearest-neighbor grid interconnection network. Other networks will produce different times. However, the reader is cautioned against assuming that a network with a dimension of $n^{1/2}$ will produce better actual results, since such networks frequently require a relatively large address calculation overhead. Of course a specialized binary fan-in circuit for p processors would produce the best results of approximately $\log p$ time, which would be constant for $n < p$.

In a grid interconnection network, communication time is a function of the distance moved and the length of the field. Basically, one unit of time is required for every PE on the path of communication. Thus to move 1 bit three PEs requires three instructions plus the instruction to load and store the result. The sequence is: *load shift shift shift store*.

If multiple bits are being shifted and the intermediate PEs are not transmitting their own data, the loading and shifting can be intermingled to assure that the shift operation is operating at maximum efficiency. That is, the sequence *LHLHLHS-LHSHSHS*. where *L* is load, *H* is shift, and *S* is store, will move 4 bits along by three PEs in 14 instructions. The formula for b bits and p PEs is $3b + p - 1$

instructions. It takes b loads, b stores, and $p + b - 1$ shifts. (It takes p shifts for the first bit to arrive and $b - 1$ more shifts for the last bit to arrive.)

In a parallel tournament approach using a grid interconnection network, each succeeding communication must go twice as far as the last. Thus if b is the number of bits in the field, the total communication time is

$$\sum_{p=1}^{\log n} (3b + p - 1) = \left(3b - \frac{3}{2}\right) \log n + (1/2) \log^2 n.$$

At each stage of the process, the comparison requires $8b$ instructions. A move is also needed to assure that all of the winners are in the same field for the next round, requiring another $2b$ instructions. Log n comparisons are required for a total of $10b \log n$ instructions for comparison. The total time, then, is

$$\left(13b - \frac{3}{2}\right) \log n + (1/2) \log^2 n$$

instructions.

If n is a reasonable number, say 512, then this routine takes 3771 instructions, which is almost 40 times slower than the associative searching techniques. In summary, Table 2-2 shows that the execution time for an associative search is constant and small compared to most other general approaches. For example, at the modest point of 256 integers in a 32-bit field, the associative search is approximately an order of magnitude faster than either of the other approaches. This relatively high speed and the fact that this routine is faster than a parallel bit-serial add give justification to the claim that the associative search functions execute in constant time.

2.8.3. The Bit-Serial Requirement

The SITDAC model does not rely on bit-serial computation *per se*. That is, massively parallel searching could be done nibble serial, byte serial, or word serial, and of course the ASC source program would not change. However, the associative numeric search functions, i.e., **maxval**, **minval**, **maxdex**, **mindex**, **prvdex**, **nxtdex**, and **sibdex** require bit-serial computation for efficient operation. The key to these functions is

1. the use of the binary digits as the mask register and
2. the ability to detect responders/no responders in one instruction.

Any other implementation such as nibble serial would require log n steps because the nibbles must be communicated to neighboring PEs to be compared in a parallel tournament manner. As a result, even in the best case, the associative search function would no longer execute in constant time but in log n time. Thus a bit-serial design has a considerable advantage over other designs. The ultimate associative computer design would include a bit-serial operation mode for the

Table 2-2. Maximum Field Speeds

	Size of Field								
	8 bits			16 bits			32 bits		
Number of numbers	assoc[a]	seq[b]	log n[c]	assoc	seq	log n	assoc	seq	log n
4	24	9	207	48	9	415	96	9	831
32	24	93	525	48	93	1045	96	93	2085
256	24	765	852	48	765	1684	96	765	3348
512	24	1533	963	48	1533	1899	96	1533	3771
64K	24	196605	1768	48	196605	3384	96	196605	6760

[a]assoc: associative numeric search
[b]seq: sequential tournament
[c]log n: parallel tournament

associative numeric search routines and byte or word serial mode for arithmetic computation and comparisons.

2.9. Responder Iteration

As mentioned in section 1.3.4, the formal SITDAC model assumes the existence of special-purpose hardware that allows it to identify and select (or find) a responding cell in one step. This capability is essential to associative iteration. That is, the basic mode of looping in the SITDAC model is to

1. perform a parallel search to identify a set of responders,
2. use the find hardware to select a cell to be processed,
3. execute the body of the iteration referencing the selected cell,
4. update the responders by clearing the bit associated with the selected cell, and
5. repeat until all responders have been processed.

Processing in the body may include reading from, writing to, and modifying the contents of the selected cell as well as performing all other types of parallel operations.

Note that responder iteration performs the same function as **do**, **for**, or **while** loops in conventional languages, but it is implemented quite differently. First, the cells in the memory are organized randomly as explained by the classroom model (section 2.3). Thus there is no need to determine the order in which the responders will be processed. If certain cells must be processed prior to others, this order is achieved by specifying in the parallel search the attributes that distinguish the cells that must be processed first. Within the set of cells so selected, the cells are processed iteratively in arbitrary order.

Second, the extent of iteration is dynamic. That is, with some sets of data, many cells may respond and be processed; with other sets no cells or very few cells may respond. It is completely run-time data dependent. Moreover, new data cells may be added and old ones deleted in any order at any time with no need to sort or otherwise reorganize the data.

Third, there is no concept of an index for data ordering or control iteration in this mode of operation. As a result, the multiple use of indices for mathematical notation such as their use in vectors and matrices and as an organizational counter for ordering the processing of the elements of data structures is avoided.

Section 3.8 describes the ASC **for** and **while** statements which use the resolution hardware and embody the associative responder iteration concept. Chapter 10 gives more details on the operation of the special-purpose resolution hardware.

2.10. Corner Turning

Corner turning is the term used for the type of data reorganization required for converting conventionally organized, row-oriented data into a form that can be used on column-oriented machines. Figure 2-11 illustrated that conventional computers access data a row of bits at a time whereas column-oriented bit-serial computers access data a column of bits at a time. Since the world is dominated by conventional computers and the peripherals that support them, almost all data has to be converted from row-oriented to column-oriented on input to a SIMD or SITDAC computer and converted from column-oriented to row-oriented on output.

The corner-turning process can be envisioned as a platoon *m* soldiers men wide and *n* deep, marching north onto a parade ground. When the platoon is in the center of the parade ground, the sergeant orders the soldiers to right face and march off going east, forming a platoon *n* soldiers wide and *m* deep. In effect, the platoon has turned a 90° corner.

Perhaps the best example of the need for corner turning with computer equipment is to imagine printing an association of data on a conventional printer. Consider an association of three fields. When the first field or column of data is processed in parallel in the computer and is sent to the printer for output, the printer will print the data in a row format as illustrated in Fig. 2-27.

```
An association          The printer output
of three fields          of three fields

  a  1  10                  a  b  c d
  b  5  20                  1  5  8 6
  c  8  19                 10 20 19 3
  d  6   3
```

Figure 2-27. Association output without corner turning.

needs (a row at a time), all of the data must be corner-turned using a two-dimensional buffer array. Thus the column-oriented computer must write data into the buffer a column at a time, as for example in

```
for (j=0; j<no_of_cols; j++)
    {column[$] = field[$,j];
     for (i=0; i<no_of_rows; i++)
        buffer[i][j] = column[i];}
```

The data can then be retrieved a row at a time for the printer, as follows:

```
for (i=0; i<no_of_rows; i++)
    {for (j=0; j<no_of_cols; j++)
        row[j] = buffer [i][j];
     print row [$];}
```

There is a fundamental difference between the above example and actual corner turning. In the above code, the items being turned are complete logical entities; i.e., each entity is an individual datum. In corner turning, however, subentities (i.e., bits) are turned. The difference can be illustrated by the difference between reversing the words in a sentence and reversing the letters in the words. The processes are similar, but as shown below, the results are quite different:

Backwards is sentence this.
Siht ecnetnes si sdrawkcab.

The need for corner turning is present in every SIMD design. Of special interest are the bit-serial SIMD architectures which dominate current massively parallel computers. The "normal" bit-parallel, word-serial organization is shown in Fig. 2-28a. The word-parallel, bit-serial organization required by bit-serial SIMD and associative computers is shown in Fig. 2-28b. Figure 2-28c shows how the organizations align. All bit-serial computers have special-purpose hardware to

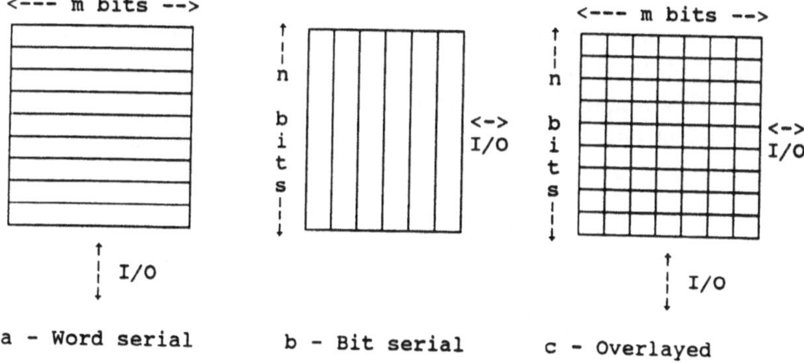

Figure 2-28. Corner turning.

the organizations align. All bit-serial computers have special-purpose hardware to facilitate this reorganization. Of course, there are many alternative approaches to corner turning. A typical operation to convert from a word-serial organization to bit-serial is to read n (e.g., 2048) words of m (e.g., 32) bits from the conventional computer via a word-serial access path, then write m (i.e., 32) bit slices of n (i.e., 2048) bits via a bit-serial path. The operation is reversed to convert bit-serial data to word-serial.

2.11. Bucket-Brigade Communication

In any parallel machine, the communication mode(s) are fundamental. Associative and SIMD computers are synchronous. Thus when one processor is told to fetch data from the right, they all do. This requires that all processors simultaneously fetch data from the right and give data to the left. In effect a "bucket brigade" is formed with bits instead of buckets being passed down the line of processors (see Fig. 2-29).

In bit-serial SIMDs, the X and Y bits of the PEs, illustrated in Fig. 2-12, are often organized into X and Y registers; thus, this movement can be achieved by a shift. However, logically it is different from a shift, in that in a shift all of the bits belong to the same datum. Here every bit is from a different datum.

The bucket brigade provides communication along one dimension. Within that dimension, the bucket brigade may at any one time be passing bits to the left or to the right, but not both. Imagine a number of bucket brigades packed on top of one another—in essence creating a two-dimensional array. Then in addition to left and right, buckets may be passed up and down. Thus a two-dimensional mesh-interconnection network has four directions of communication, which correspond to the four directions on a map. Consequently, this kind of grid is often called a NEWS (north, east, west, south) grid. Some SIMD computers have grids that allow communication in eight directions (north, northeast, east, southeast, south, southwest, west, and northwest).

The exact communication capabilities of different machines varies greatly. Some may have only a one-dimensional grid while others may have up to a six-dimensional grid. In addition, other interprocessor communication networks may be available. However, the bucket-brigade or grid type of communication is one of the most efficient types of interprocessor communication available for short to moderate distances since

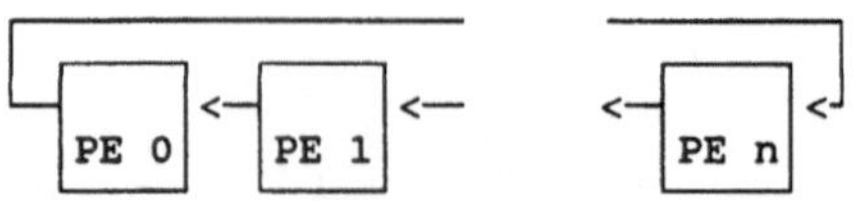

Figure 2-29. Bucket-brigade communication.

1. no address calculations are required and
2. all processors act in synchronism, passing data and receiving data in parallel.

Grid communication can be an order of magnitude or more faster than more general address-directed communication schemes.

2.12. Data Mapping

When analyzing the communication capabilities of a machine, the processors's data memory can be viewed as a set of virtual dimensions, just as in a conventional sequential computer. Moreover, these intraprocessor communication paths are often much more efficient than interprocessor communication. If the interprocessor communication hardware can support from one to six dimensions and the processors' memories can be viewed as even more virtual dimensions, how should the two-dimensional tabular data association arrays of the SITDAC model be mapped onto such architectures?

In general, the tabular associative data structure may be mapped onto

1. a two-dimensional memory with a one-dimensional array of processors, as shown in Fig. 2-30a, or
2. a two-dimensional array of processors as shown in Fig. 2-30b.

When an association is mapped onto the computer configuration of Fig. 2-30a, the highly efficient intraprocessor communication path is used during all parallel intraassociation computation. And, since every association entry is guaranteed its own dedicated processor, bit fields in the cell's memory can be used as flags for the entire association entry.

There are, of course, some situations which call for a multidimensional data structures within an association. The efficiency of the computation often depends on the orientation of these data structures. Assume, for example, that a two-

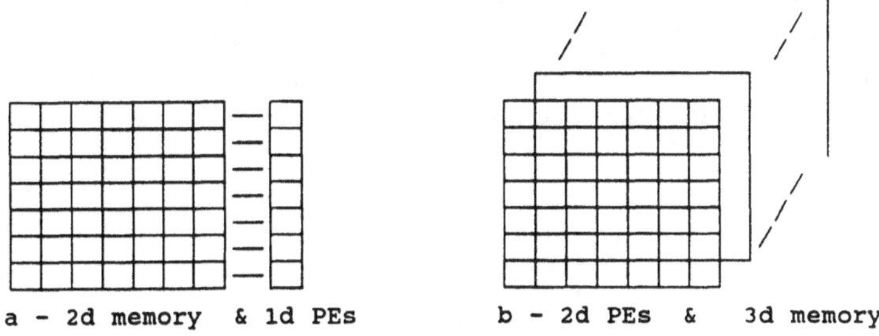

Figure 2-30. Association to hardware mappings.

dimensional matrix is a member of an association. The programmer should be able to specify that the matrix be mapped onto a two-dimensional communication grid (supported by the hardware) by specifying two parallel, variable-length dimensions (i.e., image[$,$]) or that it be mapped onto a two-dimensional memory grid by specifying one parallel variable and one fixed-length dimension (i.e., image [$,512] or image[512,$]).

When given a matrix whose size is considerably smaller than the array size (i.e., the number of PEs) of the SIMD computer, it is often advantageous to replicate the data to achieve maximum parallelism. In these situations, the rule of thumb is that the longest dimension of the array should be aligned with the intraprocessor communication path. This is true even in situations where the cost of replication may be somewhat higher using this organization. This organization gains from the high utilization of the intraprocessor path. It also gains from being able to replicate more copies in memory and thus achieve more medium-level parallelism.

2.13. Data Replication

The question often arises of efficient utilization of all of the memory cells in associative and SIMD computers. That is, if the machine has 64K cells, but the "inherent" parallelism uses only 512 cells, the remaining 63.5K cells are idle, resulting in a utilization of only $\frac{1}{128}$ of the machine. In these situations replication is often beneficial.

There are basically three different levels of parallelism at which replication is useful. These will be called fine-grain or data-level parallelism, medium-grain or association-level parallelism, and coarse-grain or algorithm-level prallelism. The intent here is to illustrate a programming technique. There is no reason why replication cannot be used at other levels of parallelism as well.

As an example, consider multiplication of the matrix and the vector shown in Fig. 2-31. As written, there appears to be no parallelism. But a few moments of analysis reveals that all of the elements in the first column of that matrix are multiplied by 4, those in the second by 10, and those in the third by 8.

The use of the rule of thumb of section 2.12 to maximize intraprocessor communication suggests that the vector data should be replicated and aligned as shown in Fig. 2-32. Now the *n*th column of the matrix can be multiplied in parallel by the *n*th column of the replicated vector, producing a field of partial products of

```
( 3 5 7 )     ( 4 )
( 8 2 1 )  *  (10 )
( 0 1 0 )     ( 8 )
```

Figure 2-31. Matrix–vector multiplication.

```
( 3 5 7 )     ( 4 10 8 )
( 8 2 1 ) * ( 4 10 8 )
( 0 1 0 )     ( 4 10 8 )
```

Figure 2-32. Fine-grain replication.

the output vector. Note that the partial products can also be summed in parallel to form the output-vector components. In total, the problem has been reduced from nine sequential multiplications and six additions to three parallel multiplications and two parallel additions, achieving a speedup of a factor of 3. This is an example of fine-grain replication used to achieve additional parallelism.

Figure 2-33 shows that the same approach can be used at a medium-grain level when two entire matrices are to be multiplied. The first matrix is replicated once for every row. The columns of the second matrix are replicated as individual vectors. As a result, 27 sequential multiplications and 18 sequential additions are reduced to three parallel multiplications and two parallel additions.

Finally, Fig. 2-34 illustrates coarse-grain parallelism. This level of parallelism can be used even for inherently sequential algorithms. As shown, the associative program is to execute an algorithm for 64K separate cases in parallel. The only requirement for using this kind of parallelism is the need to execute the algorithm or a portion of it 64K times. It could be argued that if you don't need your algorithm executed 64K times, you don't need (massive) SIMD parallelism.

At first glance, replicating portions of the data may appear to be expensive. However, the replication frequently can be achieved with minimal overhead by using masks and broadcasting the data on initial loading to all processors that require it. That is, in many SIMD computers and the SITDAC design given in Chapter 10, it costs little more on an initial load to send the data to all cells than it does to send it to just one cell.

```
            ( 3 5 7 )     ( 4 3 7 )
            ( 8 2 1 ) * (10 6 6 )
            ( 0 1 0 )     ( 8 9 2 )

( 3 5 7 )     ( 4 10 8 )->(118)
( 8 2 1 ) * ( 4 10 8 )->(060)---+
( 0 1 0 )     ( 4 10 8 )->(010)   |
                                  v
( 3 5 7 )     ( 3  6 9 )->(102)   (118 102 065)
( 8 2 1 ) * ( 3  6 9 )->(045)-->(060 045 070)
( 0 1 0 )     ( 3  6 9 )->(006)   (010 006 006)
                                              ^
( 3 5 7 )     ( 7  6 2 )->(065)              |
( 8 2 1 ) * ( 7  6 2 )->(070)--------------+
( 0 1 0 )     ( 7  6 2 )->(006)
```

Figure 2-33. Medium-grain replication.

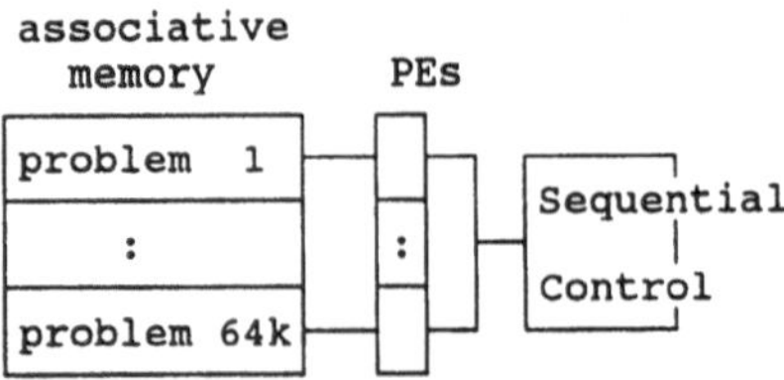

Figure 2-34. Coarse-grain parallelism.

2.13.1. Data Replication during Input

SITDAC associative and SIMD computers may have several I/O paths. The SITDAC architecture proposed in Chapter 10 has a high-speed I/O stack. The use of the stack to perform data replication is described there. The other types and styles of high-speed I/O used by other SIMD computers are too varied to discuss here. However, every associative and SIMD computer has an I/O data path from the outside peripherals through the host or sequential control to the parallel array. This is the broadcast data path. The broadcast path and the masking capability of the PEs allow for data replication in the array with virtually no increase in overhead. Figure 2-35 shows that by setting the mask register to a specific pattern and then broadcasting the data from the sequential control, the data replication pattern of Fig. 2-32 can be produced. Figures 2-36 and 2-37 illustrate that the more complex pattern of replication shown in Fig. 2-33 can be formed by establishing a pattern in the mask register and broadcasting a portion of the data and then shifting the mask pattern before broadcasting the next set of common data. Complex patterns of replicated data can be generated in this manner.

2.13.2. Data Replication during Computation

The discussion in section 2.4 illustrated that when using SITDAC tabular associations, it is not uncommon for a value to be replicated several times. This

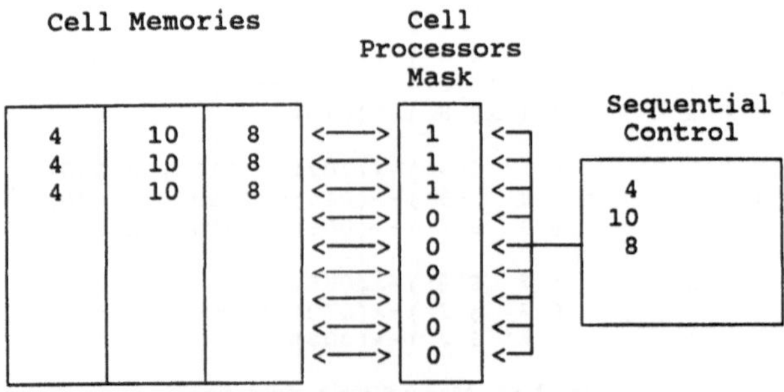

Figure 2-35. Simple data replication.

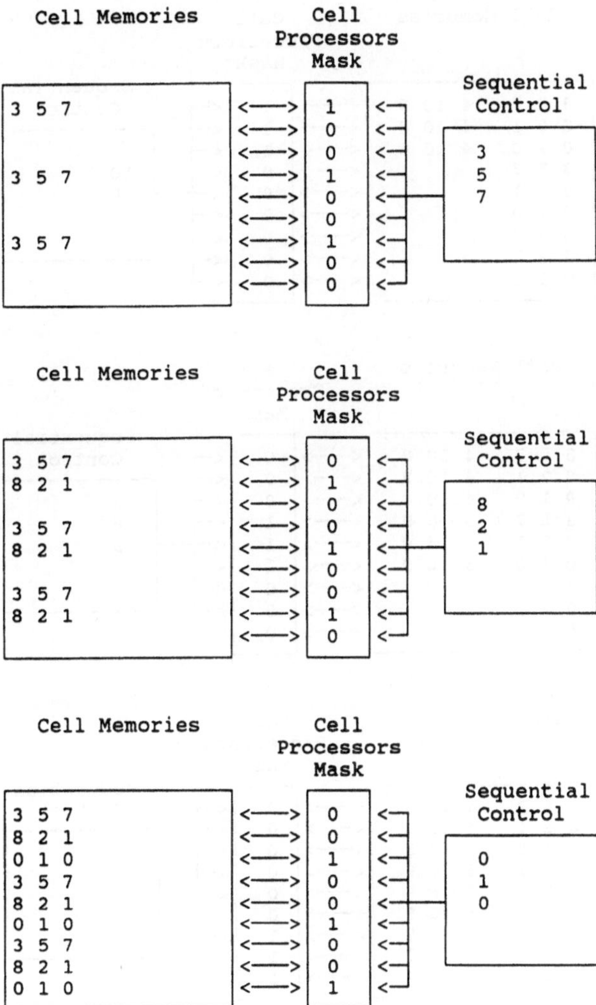

Figure 2-36. Complex data replication.

section describes a technique for generating replicated data structures which costs no more than generating the unreplicated data structures in the first place.

Assume that the data base of Fig. 2-4 is being converted from a sequential-machine format to the SITDAC tabular format. The major problem is that, in general, there is no way of knowing how many records follow the header. As a result, the number of entries required in the association is unknown.

One solution is to preload all replicated data so that when an association entry is allocated, the replicated data is already present and only the specified data items need to be inserted. The only additional overhead incurred with this technique is

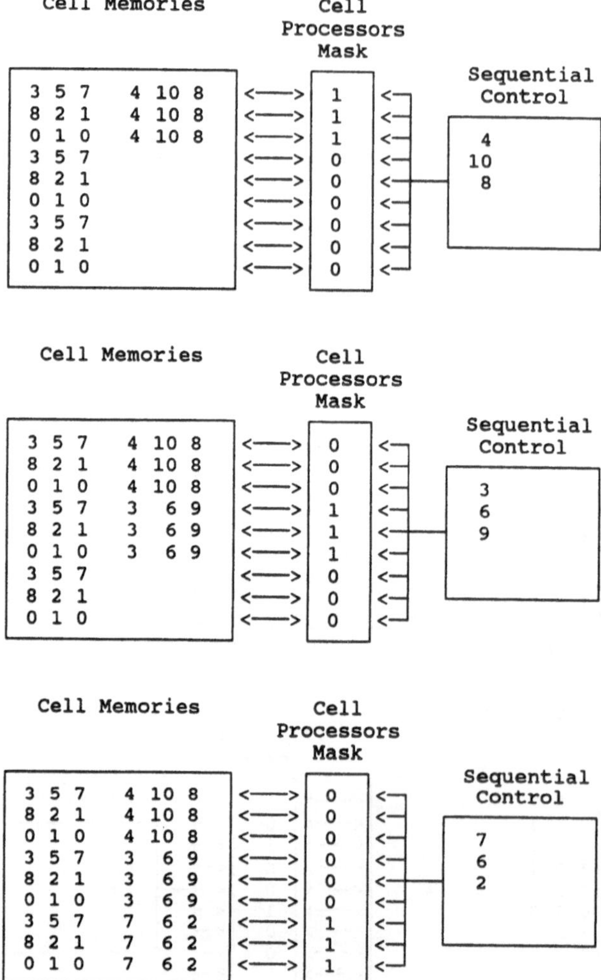

Figure 2-37. Complex data replication, cont.

the cost of restoring the unused entries to the initial state when the process is finished.

Figures 2-38, 2-39, and 2-40 illustrate the process. In the current example, the replicated name Joe, his ssn, and his id are stored in the *unallocated* cells of the parallel array, as shown in Fig. 2-38. Then, as the record for each of Joe's dependents is processed, an idle cell is allocated and the unique data items inserted, as shown in Fig. 2-39. When all of the repeating records have been processed, the unallocated portion of the parallel array is cleared (see Fig. 2-40).

bi	name	ssn	id	age	mid	first	middle	last
0	joe	187	47					
0	joe	187	47					
0	joe	187	47					
0	joe	187	47					
0	joe	187	47					
0	joe	187	47					

Figure 2-38. Prereplicated data.

bi	name	ssn	id	age	mid	first	middle	last
1	joe	187	47	10	374	jim	tuska	doe
1	joe	187	47	13	943	john	waras	doe
1	joe	187	47	19	001	harry	james	doe
0	joe	187	47					
0	joe	187	47					
0	joe	187	47					

Figure 2-39. Preloaded data after allocating three cells.

bi	name	ssn	id	age	mid	first	middle	last
1	joe	187	47	10	374	jim	tuska	doe
1	joe	187	47	13	943	john	waras	doe
1	joe	187	47	19	001	harry	james	doe
0								
0								
0								

Figure 2-40. Restored idle cells.

2.14. Conclusion

In this chapter, some of the basic concepts of SIMD and SITDAC associative programming were introduced. The intent of this chapter is to show that these concepts are simple and straightforward in the hope that, once they are understood, they will facilitate the comprehension of SITDAC paradigms. In later chapters, algorithms will be given for several problems. In many instances, the solutions are as easy as or easier than conventional sequential or conventional parallel multiprocessor solutions. The purpose of this chapter is to introduce SIMD parallelism, the classroom model, dynamic associative-memory allocation, massively parallel searching, two-dimensional associative data structures, bit-serial arithmetic, corner turning, bucket-brigade communication, and data replication so that the reader may better understand basic SITDAC programming. Of special significance to SITDAC programming are the numeric searching and the responder-iteration concepts.

3

An Associative Model of Computation

This chapter formally defines a specific associative model of computation based on the SITDAC model and provides a conceptual realization of this model, the associative computing (ASC) language. An associative processor has a cellular memory that is partitioned into cells each consisting of a processor and its memory. The memory in a cell is sufficiently large to hold one or more association entries plus any required data for the operating system and/or other utilities. The cell processors are dedicated to operating on the data in their cells. At any one time, only one cell may be read, resulting in the equivalent of a global broadcast capability. The fundamental mode of operation is SIMD. That is, if more than one instruction stream is present, they are all executing in SIMD mode, each on its own subset of memory cells.

The next two sections describe the associative model of computation—first informally, using the classroom model, and then more formally, explaining the search, process, retrieve cycle. Subsequent sections of this chapter describe the ASC statements that embody the various forms of associative computation. However, first there are two sections on data organization and one section on memory allocation, which enable the later discussions to be more specific and accurate. A major purpose of this chapter is to illustrate how the search, process, and retrieve phases of the associative computing cycle are incorporated into programming statements. The syntax and examples of the ASC statements given are accurate for those who are primarily interested in learning the use and syntax of the ASC statements. Chapter 4 gives examples of how to implement some standard tasks in ASC.

The SITDAC model is based on SIMD parallelism and therefore subsumes all of the basic concepts of SIMD programming discussed in Chapter 2, including data parallelism. However, since data-parallel techniques have been and are being addressed in detail in many other places (see Hillis and Steele [1986], for example), and their implementation in ASC is straightforward, as shown briefly in Chapter 4, the thrust of this book is associative computation, not data parallelism.

3.1. The SITDAC Model of Computation

There are two fundamental modes of computation in the SITDAC model. The first is completely parallel and consists of a parallel search followed by a parallel action. For example, using the classroom model, the parallel search is effected by the teacher's query–command, "If your score is between 90 and 100, raise your hand." The parallel action might be "If your hand is raised, give yourself a grade of A." After a brief period, both the teacher and the students become familiar enough with the mode of operation that the explicit commands "raise your hand" and "if you hand is raised" are not necessary. The sequence simply becomes, "If your score is between 90 and 100, give yourself an A." or

```
if 90 .lt. score [$] .and. score [$] .le. 100 then grade [$] = A;
endif;
```

The second mode of operation is a parallel search followed by an iterative action. The search might be, "If you have a grade of A." The action might be, "Give me your name." Obviously, this can not be done in parallel, since the teacher would receive the names of all responders at once and they would become jumbled and incomprehensible. The teacher must iterate on the students who have their hands raised.

The teacher points to a responding student (the selection is completely arbitrary). Having selected a student, the action "Give me your name" is now successful, since only the selected student responds. The teacher records a name and grade, tells the student to put his or her hand down, and then selects another student and repeats the operation. This continues until all responders have been processed.

These two fundamental modes of SITDAC computation form the basis of ASC programming and are implemented using a parallel-associative **if** and an iterative-associative **for** statement.

These two fundamental modes of associative computation have many auxiliary forms, however, most obvious is the addition of an **else** portion to the associative **if**, but other situations may be modeled also. For example, the query

```
if 90 .lt. score [$] .and. score [$] .le. 100 then
```

may have no responders.

Two alternatives are possible. First, the situation was anticipated and is normal, so the **else** auxiliary form mentioned above is used. The **then** portion is executed with no responders (essentially a no-op); then the **else** portion, if present, is executed. The second alternative is more subtle. It occurs when the lack of responders to the query is anticipated but is not considered normal. In such a situation, an **else-not-any** responders action is desired. In the discussion here, the determination that no student received an A may cause the teacher to repeat the material for the entire class. The ASC statements given later cover the most useful auxiliary forms of associative computation.

More formally, the associative computing model consists of a basic cycle of three phases: search, process, retrieve. The specification of the values of a subgrouping of the items of an association constitutes a pattern used in the search phase of the cycle. The associations that respond to the search phase are called the *active associations* or *responders*. The process phase consists of a sequence of operations executed by the cell processors dedicated to the active associations. The retrieve phase consists of retrieving the values of specific items of the active associations so that they can be used in subsequent cycles.

If any one cycle, the process and/or the retrieve phase may be omitted. Consequently a sequence of cycles might consist of *search*, *retrieve*, *search*, *process* or *search*, *process*, *search*, *process*. The control statements of the ASC language are mapped onto one or more SPR (*s*earch, *p*rocess, *r*etrieve) cycles.

The SPR cycle is an associative process because, during the search phase, the entire data records are selected on the basis of their contents. That is, not only are the searched items selected, but also all of the other items associated with them by being in the same entry. Which items are grouped together into associations is declared explicitly by the **associate** statement (see section 3.5).

3.2. Cycle Nesting

The basic SPR cycle can be made quite complex by allowing nested cycles in the process and retrieve phases. When this occurs, the group of association entries that can participate in the nested cycles is restricted to the active entries of the nesting cycle.

Cycles can be nested to any arbitrary number of levels. The scope of a group of active associations extends across all phases and subphases of a cycle. As each new level of nesting is entered, the active associations are further restricted by the search phase on that level, producing a new subgroup of active associations.

When a level of nesting is exited, the group of active associations is restored to the state it was in at the time the level was entered. At the top level, all of the associations in the program are in the active group. Figure 3-1 illustrates the nesting of cycles.

All ASC statements are constrained by the active associations, or responders, of the statements in which they are nested. Only the **if** or **setscope** statement can establish a new active association group. Parallel **if**s refine the set of responders. **Setscope**s completely redefine it. That is, at times it is desirable to process an

```
        search,  process ..................process, retrieve
           /                                     \
         search, process ...........process, retrieve
                  /                             \
                   search, process, retrieve
```

Figure 3-1. Nested cycles.

association other than the current active responders. The **setscope** statement described in section 3.14 can be used for this purpose.

3.3. Items and Expressions

The ASC model allows both scalar and parallel items. (A parallel item in ASC is realized as a parallel field in the SITDAC model.) Items in ASC correspond to variables and arrays in conventional programming languages. Consequently, the terms are used interchangeably. A $ index in a parallel item refers to all of the items in the active association entries. A specific item from an individual association entry can be referenced by an index variable that flags the location of the association entry. Thus, level [$] is parallel but level[index] is scalar, where *index* is an index-parallel variable.

The special role of the index-parallel variable, which allows it to select a single scalar value from a parallel variable, is indicated by the fact that it is the only variable that is declared to be parallel where the parallel $ index is required, but does not take the $ notation whenever it is used as an index in the body of the program. See Fig. 3.2.

There is a close relationship between logical parallel variables, responders, and index variables. That is, the set of responders can be and often is saved

```
int scalar a,b,c;
int parallel p[$], q[$], r[$], pp[$,4];
index parallel xx[$], yy[$];
```

Expression	Result
a+b	scalar
a+p[$]	parallel
a+p[xx]	scalar
pp[xx,b]*3+q[$]	parallel
p[xx]+pp[yy,b]	scalar
q[$]+r[$]	parallel
a+pp[xx,b]*3	scalar

Figure 3-2. Expression types.

indirectly by setting a logical parallel variable to TRUE (represented as a one) inside the scope of a statement or directly by being assigned the result of a parallel search in an assignment statement. If the variable is later used in place of the $ parallel index, it is automatically converted to a parallel index variable by selecting the first TRUE (or one) in the field and ignoring the others.

Index variables provide a link between the search phase and the process and retrieve phases. Quantifiers are used during the search phase to restrict processing to the matching associations. The internal identifications of the associations that responded to the search phase are saved. The various ASC control structures retrieve the identification of the responders and assign them to the specified index variable. At any one time, the index variable refers to only one specific association entry and is used to designate that entry during the process and retrieve phases.

Associative items and operators possess two modes. Mode 1 specifies the arithmetic type, i.e., int, real, etc. Mode 2 specifies scalar or parallel. In addition to scalar and parallel, associative operators may be common-left (the left operand is scalar or common to all cells and the right operand is parallel) or common-right (the left operand is parallel and the right operand is scalar or common to all cells). As in conventional languages, mixed-mode expressions are automatically converted to achieve agreement. Table 3-1 indicates that in a mixed-mode expression, the scalar variable is promoted to a parallel variable by broadcasting its value to all active responders in parallel.

Conversely, when a parallel variable has the $ notation replaced with a parallel-index variable, the item is reduced to a scalar type, as shown in Table 3-1a. The scalar–parallel mode of an expression is determined by reducing the statement using operator precedence priority determining the intermediate result type by using the result type in Table 3-1b. Figure 3-2 shows some expressions and their resultant mode-2 types.

There are two types of mixed mode-2 expressions. The scalar variable may be on the left or the right of the operator. For commutative operators such as addition and multiplication, the distinction is trivial and both versions generate an intermediate quadruple of the form

mult common,field1,field2

where the scalar variable is put in the common or first position of the quadruple.

However, when subtraction and division are involved, the result is more complicated. For example, for subtraction, two different operands are required. That is, the expression a[$] − 5 is implemented by providing all PEs in parallel with the common value to be subtracted from their local field a. However, the expression 5 − a[$] requires that 5 be supplied to all PEs and that each PE subtract its local field *a* value from it. Division also requires two separate operators. The two mode-two types, common-left and common-right, are used to designate these two situations. ASC is rich in operator notation; both C and FORTRAN operators are implemented as shown in Table 3-2.

Table 3-1. Scalar Parallel Modes

a. Arithmetic Operation

	operand 2	
operand 1	scalar	parallel
scalar	scalar	parallel
parallel	parallel	parallel

b. Index Operation

variable	result
scalar[sindex, . . .]	scalar
parallel[$]	parallel
parallel[pindex]	scalar
parallel[$,sindex, . . .]	parallel
parallel[pindex,sindex, . . .]	scalar

3.4. Item Declarations

The item declaration statements are shown in Fig. 3-3. The card (cardinal) type is for unsigned integers. Hex, bin, and oct types are all signed integers internally; the designation specifies the type of conversion on input and output. As illustrated with variable *b* in Fig. 3-3, the number of bits in (or the width of) the variable may be specified by the user.

The index parallel type is used in place of the $ notation if a single (scalar)

Table 3-2. Expression Operators

Operation	Operators
add	+
subtract	−
multiply	*
divide	/
less than	.lt. <
less than or equal	.le. <=
equal	.eq. ==
not equal	.ne. !=
greater than or equal	.ge. >=
greater than	.gt. >
compare	.cmp.
NOT	.not. !
OR	.or. ||
AND	.and. &&
exclusive or	.xor. ^^
assignment	=

```
Formats:
 ┌        ┐
 bin
 card
 char
 index      [scalar   variable(:width)([,dimension,...]), .. ];
 int        [parallel variable(:width)[$(,dimension,...)], ..];
 hex
 logical         ( ) indicates optional
 oct
 real
 └        ┘

Examples:
     int parallel a[$], b:16[$], c[$,5,6];
     int parallel e:8[$], f:8[$], g:8[$];
     oct parallel h:24[$];
     hex scalar i, d[3,4];
     index parallel xx[$];
     logical parallel test[$];

     associate a[$], f[$], h[$] with test[$];
```

Figure 3-3. The item declaration statements.

value from the parallel variable is to be used. Note that the $ notation is used in the index parallel declaration because it is a parallel variable. However, when used as an index, the $ is not used to signify that the result is a scalar.

A logical parallel variable may be used to save the responders of a search. The logical parallel variable, with the $ notation, may then be used as an index in place of an index parallel variable. The type of the variable will be converted internally from logical to index just as fixed-point integers are converted to floating-point automatically in a mixed-type algebraic expression. Logical parallel variables can not be used with arithmetic operators, including all comparisons, but they can be used with Boolean operators.

3.5. The Associate Statement

An association between items is established by the **associate** statement, as shown in Fig. 3-4. The tokens following the keyword **associate** are the items in

```
Format:
    associate   item1,item2,... with association_name;

Example:
    int       parallel level[$],sibling[$];
    char      parallel node[$];
    logical   parallel tree[$];

    associate node[$],level[$],sibling[$] with tree[$];
```

Figure 3-4. The **associate** statement.

the association. The token following the keyword **with** is the name of the association. Association names must be logical parallel variables. The association items may be of any parallel type except index.

3.6. The Allocate and Release Statements

When parallel items are declared, their quantity is not specified; memory for items is allocated at run time by the **allocate** and input statements. The **release** statement returns the cell to idle status. Figure 3-5 illustrates **allocate** and **release**.

When a new association entry is needed, memory is allocated for it by the **allocate** statement. An identifier to the newly allocated association entry is returned in the index_variable. The scope of the index_variable is limited to the statement_block. Thus the index_variable should be used only to initialize an association. Once the values for the association are initialized, the index in the index_variable is discarded and not used again. Subsequent association references, retrieval, and modifications are accomplished using associative statements.

When an association entry is no longer needed, its memory allocation is

```
Format:

    allocate index_variable in association_name;
      statement_block
    endallocate index_variable;

    release conditional_expression from association_name;

Examples:

    allocate xx in tree[$]
      node[xx] = a;
    endallocate xx;
         :
    release node[$] .eq. a from tree[$];
         :

Allocate Cycle Structure

    Phase          Statement Part              Example

    search     conditional_expression          tree[$]
  ┌─>retrieve       index_variable              xx
  └─process       statement_block              node[xx] = a;

Release Cycle Structure

    Phase          Statement Part              Example

    search     conditional_expression          node[$] .eq. a
    process       association name             tree[$]
```

Figure 3-5. The **allocate** and **release** statements.

released by the **release** statement. In general, several association entries may be released simultaneously. Thus the **release** statement constitutes a *search, process* cycle where the conditional_expression of the statement is used for the search phase and the process phase consists of releasing all responding association entries.

The **allocate** and **release** statements are very efficient and should be used frequently to conserve memory space.

3.7. The If Statement

The associative **if** statement provides a compound *search, process, complement_search, process* cycle (see Fig. 3-6). The conditional_expression portion is executed in the search phase. All responding associations are active during the **then** statement_block, which constitutes the first process phase. The nonresponding associations are active during the **else** statement_block, which is the second process phase.

If the conditional_expression portion of the **if** statement results in a parallel result (see section 3.3), both statement_blocks of the **if** statement are executed. If the conditional_expression portion of an **if** statement results in a scalar result, the statement behaves like a conventional sequential **if** statement (i.e., only the **then** portion or the **else** portion is executed, not both). The set of active responders is not affected by an **if** statement if the conditional_expression evaluates to a scalar.

```
Format:

        if conditional_expression then

           statement_block1 ( [else    ] statement_block2)
                              [elsenany]

        endif;

Example:

      if a[$] .eq.2  then
         a[$]  =  5;
      else
         a[$]  =  0;
      endif;

Cycle Structure:

      Phase    Statement part             Example

      search   conditional_expression  a[$] .eq. 2
      process  statement_block1        a[$]  =   5
      search   conditional_expression  a[$] .ne. 2
      process  statement_block2        a[$]  =   0
```

Figure 3-6. Associative **if** statement.

The process phases are statement_blocks and may contain any legal associative statement. The nesting of the active responders described earlier applies to parallel **if** statements; i.e., **if** statements with parallel conditional expressions restrict the group of active responders. The effect of cycle nesting depends on whether it occurs in the **then** or **else** portion of the **if**. If it occurs in the **then** statement_block, the effect is that the responders of the nested statement are ANDed with the conditional expression portion of the nesting **if**. If the nesting occurs in the **else** statement block, the responders are ANDed with the complement of the active associations of the nesting **if**.

In the **if–elsenany** statement, the conditional_expression is evaluated. If one or more associations respond, they are set to active and the **then** statement_block is executed (as in an **if** statement). If there are no responders (not any or **nany**), all associations in the nesting statement are set to active and the **elsenany** portion of the statement is executed. The **if–elsenany** statement is parallel only. Figures 3-7 and 3-8 illustrate the **if–elsenany** statement.

3.8. The For and While Statements

Frequently, the same process must be repeated for every entry in a group or subgroup of associations. The **for** statement provides an iterative *search*, *retrieve* cycle for such tasks. As shown in Fig. 3-9, the conditional_expression part of the **for** statement is used during the search phase to find matching association entries. The index-variable field is used to flag all of the responders. The retrieve phase is then executed for each responder in turn, with the index_variable flagging the current entry being processed. The index variable is valid throughout the statement block of the **for** statement and can be used by the programmer to reference items of the current association entry as desired. When the last statement in the statement_block is executed, the index_variable is updated to the next responder

```
Example:

    if b[$] .eq. 11 then
      c[$]  =  1;
    elsenany
      c[$] = 0;
    endif;

Cycle Structure:

    Phase     Statement Part            Example

    search    conditional_expression    b[$] .eq. 11
    process   statement_block1          c[$]   =   1;
    search    conditional_expression    TRUE
    process   statement_block2          c[$]   =   0;
```

Figure 3-7. An example of **if–elsenany**.

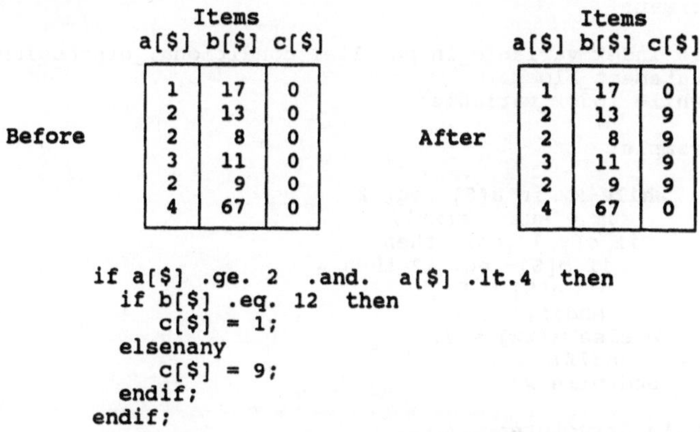

Before

a[$]	b[$]	c[$]
1	17	0
2	13	0
2	8	0
3	11	0
2	9	0
4	67	0

After

a[$]	b[$]	c[$]
1	17	0
2	13	9
2	8	9
3	11	9
2	9	9
4	67	0

```
if a[$] .ge. 2  .and.  a[$] .lt.4  then
  if b[$] .eq. 12  then
    c[$] = 1;
  elsenany
    c[$] = 9;
  endif;
endif;
```

Figure 3-8. The effects of the **if–elsenany** statement.

and the statement block of the **for** statement is re-executed. The **for** statement exits when all responders have been processed.

Note, in Fig. 3-9, that the initial search phase is not repeated; consequently, actions in statement_block1 that might change the results of the expression portion of the **for** statement do not affect the index variable. In addition, a test is used to determine if there were no initial responders. Thus, as in the case of the parallel **if** statement, there is an optional **elsenany** statement block. This block is most useful for handling exceptions.

In many circumstances, it is desirable to redefine the subgroup of associations assigned to the index variable during the execution of the statement. This is

```
Format:

    for index_variable in parallel_conditional_expression
      statement_block1
    (elsenany
      statement_block2)
    endfor index_variable;

Example:

    sum = 0;
    for xx in a[$] .eq. 2
      sum = sum+b[xx];
    endfor xx;

Cycle Structure:

    Phase         Statement Part             Example

    search     conditional_expression        a[$].eq.2
  ┌->retrieve      index_variable            xx
  └-process      statement_block1            sum = sum+b[xx];
```

Figure 3-9. A **for** statement.

```
  Format:

while index_variable in parallel_conditional_expression
  statement_block
endwhile index_variable;

  Example:

     while xx in a[$] .eq. 2
       sum = sum + b[xx];
       if c[xx] .eq.1 then
         if b[$] .eq. 12 then
            a[$] = 5;
         endif;
       else a[xx] = 7;
       endif;
      endwhile xx;

  Cycle Structure:

      Phase     Statement Part            Example

   ┌─>search    conditional_expression    a[$].eq.2
   │  retrieve  index_variable            xx
   └──process   statement_block           sum = sum+b[xx]
                                         if b[$].eq.12 then
                                              :
                                          endif;
```

Figure 3-10. A **while** statement.

achieved by using the **while** statement. As illustrated in Fig. 3-10, the search phase is re-executed at the beginning of each iteration. Execution of the **while** statement stops when there are no responders to the search phase. That is, the body of the **while** statement must contain statements which eventually cause the search phase to return no responders; otherwise, it will loop forever. The **while** statement provides an iterative search, retrieve, process cycle. Figure 3-11 gives an example of the results of a **for** and Fig. 3-12 illustrates the effect of a **while** statement execution.

Since the parallel_conditional_expression of the **while** statement is re-executed, it is not possible to test for an initial no-responders situation and therefore there is no **elsenany** option for the **while** statement. The **for** and **while** statements, in contrast to the **if** statement, do not modify the set of active responders.

3.9. The Loop Statement

The **loop** statement consists of an optional preamble or initialization portion and an iterative portion. The preamble is marked by the keyword **first**. The iterative portion is delineated by **loop** and **endloop**. A **loop** statement may contain any number of conditional terminating **until** statements. These are of two types,

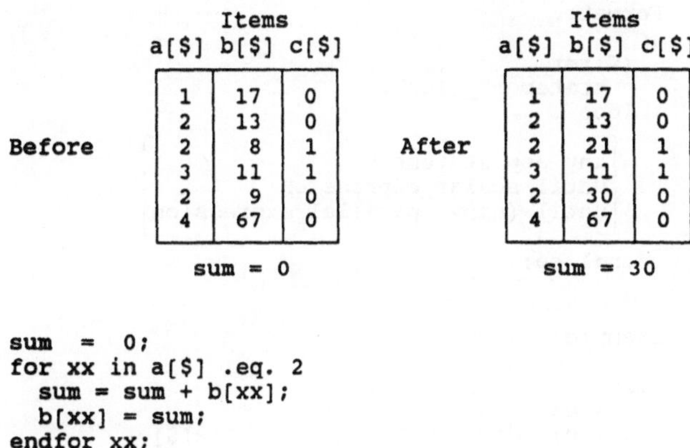

Before

a[$]	b[$]	c[$]
1	17	0
2	13	0
2	8	1
3	11	1
2	9	0
4	67	0

sum = 0

After

a[$]	b[$]	c[$]
1	17	0
2	13	0
2	21	1
3	11	1
2	30	0
4	67	0

sum = 30

```
sum  =  0;
for xx in a[$] .eq. 2
  sum = sum + b[xx];
  b[xx] = sum;
endfor xx;
```

Figure 3-11. The effects of a **for** statement.

format of a **loop** statement and an example. The count() function in the figure returns the number of active responders.

Note that the scalar **until** exits when it is true, but the parallel **until** exits based on responders. Consequently, the loop construct allows both conventional counter-index iteration and responder iteration. Since the **until**s can be placed anywhere, a **loop** statement allows the user to exit a responder iteration at any point in the body, not just at the top of the loop as in the **while** statement. In addition, since both scalar **until**s and parallel **until**s may exist within the same loop, the **loop** statement allows both counter-index and responder iteration to be used in a single construct. The parallel **until** can be used to exit when all

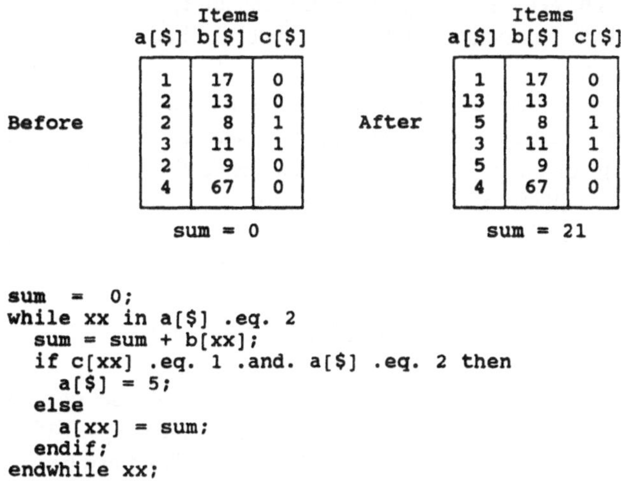

Before

a[$]	b[$]	c[$]
1	17	0
2	13	0
2	8	1
3	11	1
2	9	0
4	67	0

sum = 0

After

a[$]	b[$]	c[$]
1	17	0
13	13	0
5	8	1
3	11	1
5	9	0
4	67	0

sum = 21

```
sum  =  0;
while xx in a[$] .eq. 2
  sum = sum + b[xx];
  if c[xx] .eq. 1 .and. a[$] .eq. 2 then
    a[$] = 5;
  else
    a[xx] = sum;
  endif;
endwhile xx;
```

Figure 3-12. The effects of a **while** statement.

```
Format:

  (first
    statement_block)
  loop
   ┌                                    ┐
   │any asp statement                   │
   │until scalar_expression             │
   │until (nany) parallel_expression    │
   └                                    ┘
  endloop;
```

```
Example:

first
  i = 0;
  j = 0;                                a[$]
loop
  if a[$] .eq. j  then                   3
    i = count();                         2    Result
  endif;                                 1
until i .ge. 4                           1      i = 5
  j = j+1;                               3      j = 3
until j .gt. 10                          4
endloop;                                 3
```

Figure 3-13. The **loop** statement.

responders have been processed (**nany**), or when new responders have been found (without **nany**).

3.10. The Get Statement

Occasionally, it is desirable to select an arbitrary member from a set of responders. The **get** statement provides this capability. The index-parallel variable flags the selected association entry throughout the body of the **get**, but no other action is taken.

Since there is no way to order the entries in an association, the entry flagged by the index-parallel variable is considered "random." However, since no bookkeeping is involved, a second **get** nested inside the first with no intervening modifications will return the same supposedly "random" entry. Figure 3-14 shows a **get** statement. The **get** statement has an optional **elsenany** statement block.

3.11. The Next Statement

Next is similar to **get**, except that **next** updates the set of responders. As a result, only a parallel_variable may be specified (see Fig. 3-15). Unlike **gets**, nested **nexts** will select distinct association entries. **Next** can be used in loops to effect responder iteration, as shown in Fig. 3-16.

Format:

```
get index_variable in parallel_conditional_expression
  statement_block1
(elsenany
  statement_block2)
endget index_variable;
```

Example:

```
get xx in a[$] .eq. 2
  sum = b[xx];
endget xx;
```

Cycle Structure:

Phase	Statement Part	Example
search	conditional_expression	a[$].eq.2
retrieve	index_variable	xx
process	statement_block1	sum = b[xx];

Figure 3-14. The **get** statement.

3.12. The Any Statement

Many times, when a condition exists for only a few elements of a class, all elements must be processed. This is the function of the **any** statement shown in Fig. 3-17. After the conditional_expression is evaluated, a test is made to determine if at least one association entry responded. If so, all of the active associations in the nesting statement are kept active during the process and retrieval phases. If the **any** statement is at the top level, all associations are processed. When no associations respond to the conditional part of an **any**

Format:

```
next index_variable in parallel_variable
  statement_block1
(elsenany
  statement_block2)
endnext index_variable;
```

Example:

```
next xx in result[$]
  sum = sum + B[xx];
endnext xx;
```

Cycle Structure:

Phase	Statement Part	Example
search	parallel_variable	result[$]
retrieve	index_variable	xx
process	statement_block1	sum = sum + b[xx];

Figure 3-15. The **next** statement.

```
loop
until nany result[$]
  :
next xx in result[$]
  sum = sum + B[xx];
endnext xx;
endloop;
```

Figure 3-16. A **next** iteration.

statement, all of the active associations of the nesting statement are kept active and the **elsenany** part of the statement, if present, is executed (see Fig. 3-18).

3.13. The Setscope Statement

As described above in sections 3.2 and 3.7, the results of all parallel searches are ANDed with the responder scope on the top of the scope stack. The **main** statement (section 3.17) initializes the top of the stack to TRUE for all memory cells. The parallel **if** statement automatically ANDs the responder results with the top of the stack and then pushes the result on top of the stack.

The automatic ANDing and stacking of the responders is very effective when one is working with one particular association. However, there are times when it is desirable to temporarily alter the responder scope. This can be done by a parallel expression and the **setscope** statement, as shown in Fig. 3-19. The logical_parallel

```
Format:

     any conditional_expression
       statement_block1
     (elsenany
       statement_block2)
     endany;

Example:

     any  b[$] .eq. 11
       c[$] = 1;
     elsenany
       c[$] = 0;
     endany;

Cycle Structure:

     Phase         Statement Part              Example

     search        conditional_expression      b[$] .eq. 11
     process       statement_block1            c[$] = 1;
     search        conditional_expression      TRUE
     process       statement_block2            c[$] = 0
```

Figure 3-17. The **any** statement format.

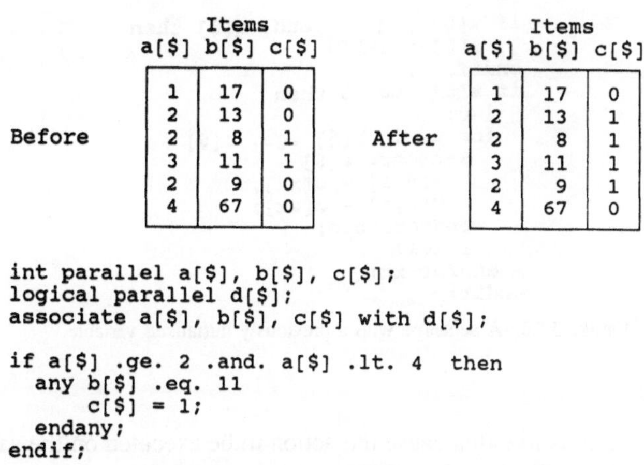

Before

a[$]	b[$]	c[$]
1	17	0
2	13	0
2	8	1
3	11	1
2	9	0
4	67	0

After

a[$]	b[$]	c[$]
1	17	0
2	13	1
2	8	1
3	11	1
2	9	1
4	67	0

```
int parallel a[$], b[$], c[$];
logical parallel d[$];
associate a[$], b[$], c[$] with d[$];

if a[$] .ge. 2 .and. a[$] .lt. 4  then
  any b[$] .eq. 11
      c[$] = 1;
  endany;
endif;
```

Figure 3-18. The effect of the **any** statement.

_expression can be any legal expression but is most often the name of an association or a parallel logical variable previously initialized (see Fig. 3-20).

The **setscope** stacks the current scope and establishes the new one. The new scope may be modified by embedded **if** statements if desired. The **endsetscope** keyword pops the scope stack and re-establishes the scope that was active when the **setscope** statement was executed.

Note that the **setscope** statement's syntax will accept a logical parallel expression. However, since a logical parallel expression is a parallel search, its result will be ANDed with the top of the current stack. Consequently, a **setscope** with a logical parallel expression acts like a parallel **if**.

Setscope is commonly used with an association name as illustrated in Fig. 3-21. Figure 3-21 is a segment of code from a graph-topological sorting algorithm for a directed acyclic graph (dag[$]), shown in Fig. 5-1. Figure 3-22 shows the state of the variables after the first iteration with child equal to one and just before **setscope** on the second pass with child equal to two. If **setscope** is not used, the statement

$$\text{xx[\$]} = \text{FALSE;}$$

does not clear the previous flag since it is outside of the current scope. The incorrect xx[$] field will cause the first one to be selected (the entry just

```
Format:

setscope logical_parallel_expression
  statement_block
endsetscope;
```

Figure 3-19. The **setscope** statement.

```
if x[$] .eq. 2 .and. q[$] then
   z[$] = TRUE;
endif;
if a[$] .eq. 5 then
  i=0;
  for xx in b[$] .ge. c[$]
    setscope z[$]
      x[$,i] = b[xx];
      y[$,i] = c[xx];
    endsetscope;
    i=i+1;
  endfor xx;
endif;
```

Figure 3-20. A **setscope** with a previously initialized variable.

processed). Situations like this cause the action to be executed on the same entry many times. As a result, the selected items are not processed, and in some cases, the looping may not terminate. This is one of the most difficult bugs to detect in ASC. When a programmer is debugging, the contents of index fields should be printed on every iteration of a loop if there is any doubt.

3.14. Maximum, Minimum, *N*th, and Count

The ASC model contains several functions that operate on all active responders in an association. The **maxval** and **minval** functions return the maximum or minimum value of the specified item among the active responders. Similarly, **nthval** returns the *n*th value (the smallest is the first) of an item (see Fig. 3-23). **Them** refers to the most recent responders.

Frequently, it is desirable to use the minimum or maximum of one item to select an association entry and retrieve the value of a second item. The **maxdex**, **mindex**, and **nthdex** functions return an index variable for this purpose. See Fig. 3-24 for an example.

```
loop
 :
if child .eq. node[$] then
   if .not. listed[$] then
      setscope dag[$]
         xx[$] =  FALSE;
      endsetscope;
      xx[$] = mindex(hexsc[$]);
      listed[$] = TRUE;
  endif;
endif;
 :
until nany xx[$]
endloop;
```

Figure 3-21. Setscope needed for index reset.

node[$]	hexsc[$]	current scope	without setscope xx[$]	with setscope xx[$]
1	3000	0	1	0
2	8000	1	0	0
2	2000	1	1	1
1	5000	0	0	0
1	9000	0	0	0

Figure 3-22. Effect of **setscope**.

Prvdex, nxtdex, sibdex, prvval, and **nxtval**, the numeric search functions used for structure-code manipulation, are discussed in section 2.8.1 and Chapter 5.

3.15. Item Equivalences

The **defvar** statement allows the user to fix the location of a variable in memory. The most common use of this statement is to allow the equivalencing of two or more field addresses. For example, the statements in Fig. 3-25 allow the

```
Formats:

    maxval(item)
    minval(item)
    nthval(item,n)
    count()

Examples:
```

a[$]	b[$]	c[$]
1	17	0
2	13	0
2	8	0
3	11	0
2	9	0
4	67	0

(Items)

```
Result:
  i = 8
  j = 13
  k = 4
  l = 9
```

```
int scalar i, j, k, l;
int parallel a[$], b[$], c[$], d[$];
associate a[$], b[$], c[$] with d[$];

if a[$] .ge. 2  .and. a[$] .lt.4  then
  i  =  minval(b[$]);
  j  =  maxval(b[$]);
  k  =  count(them[$]);
  l  =  nthval(b[$],2);
endif;
```

Figure 3-23. The **maxval, minval, nthval,** and **count** functions.

```
Formats:

     maxdex(item)
     mindex(item)
     nthdex(item,n)

Examples:
               Items
        a[$] b[$] c[$]
```

a[$]	b[$]	c[$]
1	17	0
2	13	4
2	8	7
3	11	0
2	9	8
4	67	0

```
Result:
 i = 7
 j = 4
 k = 8

if a[$] .ge. 2  .and. a[$] .lt. 4 then
  i  =  c[mindex(b[$])];
  j  =  c[maxdex(b[$])];
  k  =  c[nthdex(b[$],2)];
endif;
```

Figure 3-24. The **maxdex**, **mindex**, and **nthdex** functions.

three 8 bit integer variables *e*, *f*, and *g* to be treated as a single 24-bit octal variable *h*. Note that the left variable in a **defvar** is defined in terms of the right one, and therefore the right variable must be declared first. Also, the **defvar** must appear before either variable is defined. Variable fields are allocated in reverse order, so *h* must be equivalenced to *g*, not *e*. While an absolute address can be specified as shown for variable *a*, it is highly recommended not to do so.

```
Formats:

deflog "("identifier, Boolean_constant")";

defvar "("identifier, [ integer_constant                        ] ")";
                      [ variable( [ + ] integer_constant)       ]
                                  [ - ]

define "("identifier, constant")";
  constant = 'x'hex_number | 'o'oct_number
           | 'b'bin_number | dec_number

Examples:

   int parallel a[$], b:16[$], c[$,5,6];
   int parallel e:8[$], f:8[$], g:8[$];
   oct parallel h:24[$];

   deflog (TRUE, 1);              defvar (h,g);
   define (eight, 8);             defvar (b,h+8);
   defvar (a,eight);              define (twelve,'x'c);
```

Figure 3-25. The data equivalence statements.

```
lower          higher
addresses   addresses

ggggggggffffffffeeeeeeee
hhhhhhhhhhhhhhhhhhhhhhhh
         bbbbbbbbbbbbbbbb
```

Figure 3-26. Field alignment.

The **defvar** for *b* and *h* illustrate that the alignment of variables may be adjusted using addition and subtraction of constants. Either or both variables in the **defvar** may be modified. Figure 3-26 illustrates how the variables of Fig. 3-25 align.

The **define** and **deflog** statements allow constant integer and logical parameters to be defined. **Deflog** equivalences must be used for assignments to logical parallel variables. As shown, **define** constants may be hexadecimal, octal, binary, or decimal (default).

3.16. ASC Pronouns and Articles

Section 1.7.3 explained how the concept of pronouns in natural language can be used in associative programming. ASC supports the use of **them**, **their**, and **its** as associative pronouns and **a** and **the** as associative articles.

Them refers to the most recent set of responders to a logical parallel expression and eliminates the need to repeat a search. For example, in Fig. 3-27a, a section of code from the **sibdex** algorithm written in ASC, the responders, if any, are to be saved in nxtdex[$]. However, if there are none, nxtdex[$] must not be changed. The responders from the **any** search are automatically saved in **them**. Thus if there are responders, they are moved into nxtdex[$] from **them**. Figure 3-27b gives an example in which the **them** pronoun can be used to count the number of responders.

```
any equal[$] .and. bits[$]
    nxtdex[$] = them;
elsenany
 :
```

a - Update of **nxtdex**

```
if a[$] .gt. 5 .and. b[$] .ne. c[$] then
   cnt = count(them);
 :
```

b - Counting **them**

Figure 3-27. Examples of **them**.

```
if a[$] .gt. 5 then
   if size[$] .ne. 15 then


if a[$] .gt. 5 then
   if their size$ .ne. 15 then
```

Figure 3-28. An example of **their**.

Their is a possessive form of the $ notation. That is, "their size$" is equivalent to size [$], as shown in Fig. 3-28. Note that when the programmer uses **their**, the alternative data-parallel notation size$ is more natural than size[$] and can be read as the plural marker (i.e., read size$ as "sizes").

Its is an automatically declared parallel index variable. **Its** is updated to the most recent index assignment in a **for**, **while**, **next**, or **get** statement—that is, wherever an index_variable is specified in a statement format. The syntax for **its** is similar to that for **their**, as shown in Fig. 3-29. Since **its** refers to a single associative entry, the $ plural/parallel marker is not used. Note that "its size" is equivalent to size[xx]. The figure also demonstrates that an alternative syntax to the **for**, **while**, **next**, and **get** statements can be used when these statements are not nested and no confusion can arise as to what index_variable is being referenced. This syntax eliminates the need to declare index_variables that are to be used only locally (temporarily).

The definite article **the** refers to the last value of a parallel variable that has been reduced to a scalar. Thus if *aaa*[*xx*] and *bbb*[*yy*] were reduced most recently, "the *aaa*" and "the *bbb*" would refer to the reduced values. Note that the definite article marker is maintained for each parallel variable independently. Aaa[the] and bbb[the] may be used as alternate forms.

The indefinite article **a** refers to a random entry of an association. Thus if bi[$] is the busy/idle flag of the association-containing field *bbb*,

value = a bbb;   and   value = bbb[a];

are equivalent to

```
get xx in bi[$]
   value = bbb[xx];
endget xx;
```

```
for xx in a[$] .gt. 5
    if its size .lt. 15 then
       :

for each a[$] .gt. 5
    if its size .lt. 15 then
       :
```

Figure 3-29. Examples of **its**.

The associative pronouns and articles are intended to facilitate the specification, reading, and debugging of ASC programs by having a natural semantic meaning assigned to their familiar natural-language syntax.

3.17. Module Types—Main and Subroutine

ASC supports two module types, main and subroutine. Any program can only have one main module. All others must be specified as subroutines. Every module must be in a separate file and compiled separately.

The subroutine protocol in ASC differs from that in most other modern languages. Most languages, such as C, Pascal, and FORTRAN, use a positional notation in which variables in the calling routine are mapped onto variables in the called routine by position. This is basically a fixed-addressing convention that is contrary to the associative approach supported by ASC; consequently, a more appropriate protocol is used.

In ASC, the actual mappings between fields are specified explicitly, using notation similar to Unix/C file redirection specifications. Thus, if subroutine x is calling subroutine y, with fields *a*[$] and *b*[$] in x being mapped onto *m*[$] and *n*[$] in y as input data and field *o*[$] in y returning data to field *c*[$] in x, the call would be

```
call y n[$]<b[$] m[$]<a[$]     o[$]>c[$];
```

Figure 3-30 gives the formal syntax. Note that any number of fields may be mapped, they may be specified in any order, and the source field may be an expression, as illustrated in the example.

Every module must conclude with an end statement. Subroutine modules may have optional **exit** and **return** statements. The (subroutine) **end** statement automatically generates a return. Figure 3-31 shows the format of a module. The **#include** statement shown in Fig. 3-31 allows any ASC source file to be input and read. Up to ten levels of file indirection are allowed. **#include** is convenient for common (global) data declarations.

```
Grammar:
  sub_call := CALL sub_id args;
  args     := in_arg args | out_arg args | ε
  in_arg   := destination_field < source_field_expression
  out_arg  := source_field_expression > destination_field

Format:
  call subroutine called_field1<calling_field1 ...
                      calling_fieldn>called_fieldn;

Example:
  call bti0 a[$] < b[$] .gt. 5;
```

Figure 3-30. The **call** statement.

```
┌            ┐
│main        │ id
│subroutine  │
└            ┘
#include file_name
 :
..data_declarations..
 :
..body..
(return;)
end;
```

Figure 3-31. A module.

The **exit** statement is intended to provide ASC with a convenient, built-in error-reporting protocol. When one programs in conventional languages, it is common for a routine to report an error by returning a special flag value (e.g., 0 or −1). Unfortunately, these flag values may interfere with legitimate data values, resulting in inconsistent and *ad hoc* error-handling procedures.

In ASC, an error is reported in the routine where it is first detected. Executing the **exit** command causes the next **return** statement to be executed to exit out of all routines back to the operating system. If "exit with trace" is specified, a trace of the routines being exited will be printed. Figure 3-32 shows the difference in

```
main()
{ :
  if((a=sub1()) == ERROR)
    {printf("ERROR detected ...\n"); return(ERROR);}
  else
  :
}

sub1()
{ :
  if( ...) return(ERROR);
  :
}
          a - Conventional Error Handling
```

```
main main
 :
 call sub1 ...
 :
end;

subroutine sub1
 :
 if ... then
   msg "ERROR detected in sub1";
   exit trace;
   return;
 else
 :
              b - ASC Error Convention
```

Figure 3-32. Error conventions.

styles. Note that in the ASC code, there is an absence of error-handling clutter in the calling program, resulting in a smoother program flow. After a **return** statement has been executed, the out_arg (or return) data movements are executed if an **exit** has not been executed.

3.18. The I/O Statements

The **read** and **print** statements shown in Fig. 3-33 embody the association concept of the ASC model. **Read** and **print** both process entire associations. They can also process specific subsets of associations. Memory is automatically allocated in the specified association by a **read** statement to accommodate the number of entries input. **Read** and **print** automatically perform corner turning, so they are compatible with conventional sequential I/O devices such as terminals and printers. For example,

read tail[$], head [$], weight [$] in graph [$];

will produce:

INPUT VALUES FOR graph.
A blank line terminates input.
tail, head, weight,

on the standard output device. Typing

```
1  2  5
1  3  2
3  2  2
⟨new line⟩
```

on the standard input device will cause the following additions to the association *graph*:

tail	head	weight
1	2	5
1	3	2
3	2	2

```
read   (handle) itema[$]  ...  itemn[$] in association[$];
readnl (handle) itema[$]  ...  itemn[$] in association[$];
reread (handle) itema[$]  ...  itemn[$] in association[$];
print  (handle) itema[$]  ...  itemn[$] in
                               logical_parallel_expression;
```

Figure 3-33. The **read** and **print** statements.

If the associative array *result* contains

tail	head	weight	result
1	2	5	1
2	3	9	0
1	3	7	1

the statement

```
print tail[$], head[$], weight[$] in result[$]
```

will produce

```
DUMP OF ASSOCIATION result FOLLOWS:
tail,head,weight,
 1  2   5
 1  3   7
```

One of the advantages of a bit-serial SIMD architecture is that the variables may be of any length. However, one of the problems that arises is that very long decimal numbers are hard to convert to binary numbers on input and output. On the other hand, numbers entered in a base that is a power of 2, such as binary, octal, and hexadecimal numbers, can be converted locally without regard to the remainder of the number. As a result, decimal (*int*) type may be only 32 bits long or shorter, while binary (*bin*), octal *oct*), and hexadecimal (*hex*) variables may be of any length (up to an arbitrary system parameter value).

The **read** and **print** statements automatically read or print the parallel dimension of data. The parallel dimension is always input or output as a column of data. It is denoted by the $ index notation in the first dimension of all parallel variables. Multidimensional arrays of data may also be printed and read one column at a time. For example if an array is declared as

```
int parallel a[$,2,3];
```

then each of the columns may be input by specifying a complete index. However, when the labels for the column are printed prior to input and output, just the array name is given, not the indices. Consequently, the programmer must known in what order to enter the data. Below is an example of a **print** statement and the output header generated.

```
print a[$,0,0] a[$,0,1] a[$,0,2] in test[$];
```

will produce

```
DUMP OF ASSOCIATION test FOLLOWS:
A,A,A,
```

When a large number of array columns are to be input, it is more convenient to specify the **read** statement in a loop. However, since each call to a **read** allocates new cells, the array rows would not be in associative alignment. In order to overcome this problem, the **reread** statement may be used. **Reread** reuses the busy cells specified in the association field. In order to allocate the initial cells, a conventional **read** must be used to input the first column. For example,

```
read input[$,0] in bi[$];
i=1;
loop
   reread input[$,i] in bi[$];
   i = i+1;
   until i > 49
endloop;
```

will input 50 columns into the parallel *input* array. An example of the use of **reread** is given in Chapter 4.

When inputting data for the **read** statement, ASC reads a line (or row) at a time. It counts the items in the row as it performs corner turning. If there are fewer items in the row than specified in the read statement, it outputs an error message. Occasionally, it is desirable to input lines with fewer items than requested. **Readln** should be used for these situations. It will not issue any message if insufficient items are specified. It will supply 0 for the items on the right for which there are no data.

ASC contains an **open** and a **close** statement as illustrated in Fig. 3-34. Also shown in Fig. 3-34 is the optional form of the **read** and **print** statements with a previously opened channel specified. Even if a channel is specified in a **read** statement, the **read** header information is output to the standard output file. The specific workings of the channel operations depends on the host computer and operating system. On most systems, set HOW to 1 for read only, 2 for write only, and 4 for update.

The **msg** statement, shown in Fig. 3-35, provides a means of outputing nonassociative textual comments. The message is always sent to the standard

```
int scalar handle;
handle = open("filename","ext",HOW);
read  (handle) a[$], b[$], c[$] in bi[$];
print (handle) a[$], b[$] in result[$];
close (handle);
```

Figure 3-34. The channel I/O statements.

```
Format:
    msg delimitertextdelimiter variable_list;

Examples:
   msg "The number is:" number;
   msg \He said, "Hello world."\;
```

Figure 3-35. The **msg** statement.

```
int parallel dummy[$];
int scalar parameter1, parameter2;
logical parallel dbi[$];

associate dummy[$] with dbi[$];

allocate xx in dbi[$]
  dummy[xx] = parameter1;
endallocate xx;
allocate xx in dbi[$]
  dummy[xx] = parameter2;
endallocate xx;

print dummy[$] in dbi[$];
release dbi[$] from dbi[$];
```

a - Output of Scalar Parameters

```
read dummy[$] in dbi[$];
next xx in dbi[$]
  parameter1 = dummy[xx];
endnext xx;
next xx in dbi[$]
  parameter2 = dummy[xx];
endnext xx;
```

b - Input of Scalar Parameters

Figure 3-36. I/O for scalar parameters.

output. Any number of variables may be specified after the second delimiter. They will be printed on the line following the message.

Figure 3-36a illustrates that scalars can also be printed by moving them to dummy parallel fields and then output using **print**. Similarly scalars can be input using a **read** as shown in Fig. 3-36b. In this second example, the dbi[$] bit field is updated by the **next** statement so that a **release** statement is not needed. This approach to scalar I/O is somewhat *ad hoc* and awkward. However, if there is a need to input or output a large quantity of scalars, then perhaps the wrong algorithm is being used.

Chapter 8 supplies more details on I/O.

3.19. Interprocessor Communication

In the SITDAC model, there is no direct concept of interprocessor communication. Since the model assumes every association entry has its own dedicated processor, the assumption is that there is minimal need for intercell data movement. The model assumes that what interprocessor communication there is is bimodal. One mode is synchronous and between close neighbors and is most efficiently handled by a grid network. The other mode is random and global and is best handled by flagging the cells which are to receive the data and then broadcasting it to all cells in parallel.

3.19.1 Grid–Network Communication

Many data-parallel algorithms deal with large amounts of data organized into multidimensional arrays. In these situations, intercell communication is often necessary. The current version of ASC supports a one-dimensional CPU, two-dimensional memory configuration as described in section 2.11. Thus a two-dimensional array declaration such as

int parallel image[$,512];

would be mapped onto memory as shown in Fig. 3-37. Intercolumn communication is achieved simply by specifying/modifying the second (column) index. Thus

image[$,i] + image[$,i+1]

will add adjacent columns in an element-by-element data-parallel manner.

Using an analogous notation, interrow communication can be specified by modifying the first dimension index (i.e., [$]). Thus

image[$+1,i] + image[$,j]

will specify that column *i* be added to column *j* with every element of *i* moved (shifted) up one row, as illustrated in Fig. 3-38.

Because of the memory/CPU configuration assumed by ASC, the row–column communication specifications are not symmetrical. For example, adding two rows together in data-parallel fashion would be denoted by

image[i,$] + image [j,$]

if it were supported by a two-dimensional grid in the hardware. In other words, the current assumed hardware configuration limits ASC to the manipulation of columns in parallel.

The selection of the columns may be augmented in two ways. First, the indices of any or all but the first (i.e., [$]) dimension may be modified by scalar algebraic expressions, resulting in the selection of an entire column, in the same way that such a modification would select a word from a multidimensional array in a conventional language.

Second, the $ index of the first dimension may be modified by a positive or negative scalar expression resulting in all items of the selected column being moved or shifted up or down the specified amount. All of the items move the same distance because this movement is achieved by using the one-dimensional

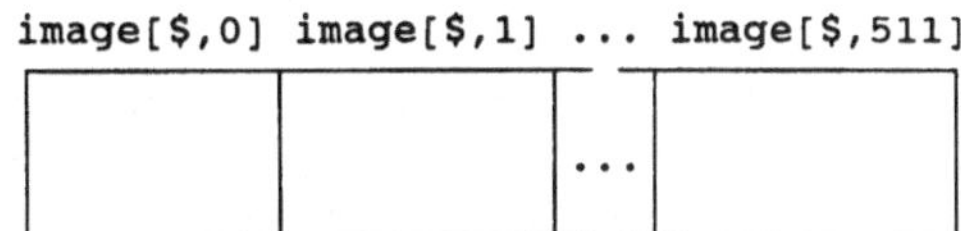

Figure 3-37. A two-dimensional array.

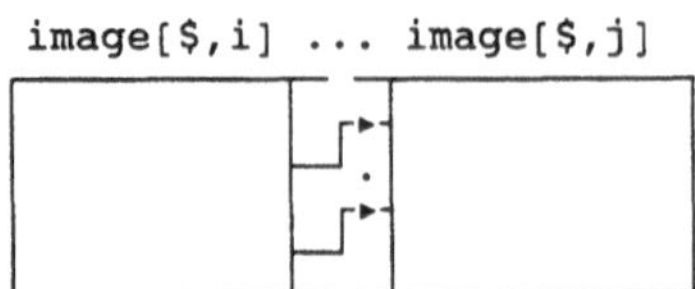

Figure 3-38. The effects of [$+1].

interprocessor communication grid described in bsection 2.10. Section 4.1.2. illustrates the use of this feature.

The actual implementation of this notation may vary from machine to machine. The ASC implementation on the Connection Machine, for example, allows parallel expressions and uses the router to allow random parallel interprocessor communication. Thus general-purpose parallel communication between cells (rows) can be supported in ASC if it is supported by the underlying hardware.

3.19.2. Broadcast Communication

Section 2.13.1 is a good example of the basic technique of broadcast communication. The only difference between the input example and general interprocessor broadcast communication is the source of the data to be broadcast. In interprocessor communication, the data is retrieved from one cell and broadcast to all the others.

3.20. Contiguous Data Allocation

The data-parallel applications that use interprocessor communication described in section 3.19.1 require contiguous data. Because cells may be allocated and released in random order, there is no guarantee that two **allocate** statements executed together will obtain adjacent cells in the interprocessor communication sense.

The contiguous **read** and contiguous **allocate** statements shown in Fig. 3-39 allow the programmer to assure that adjacent cells are allocated. However, contiguous allocation for a few items takes longer and is more wasteful than normal allocation and should be used only when necessary.

The contiguous **read**, like the conventional **read**, allocates as many cells as

```
Format:

  read (handle) item[$] ... contiguously in association[$];
  allocate n index_variable contiguously in association[$];
```

Figure 3-39. Contiguous allocation.

are required by the input data. The contiguous **allocate** requires the programmer to specify the number of cells required. All of the cells allocated are flagged in the parallel-variable index field. The programmer must administer this field if any subdivision of the cell allocation is necessary.

3.21. Indirect Addressing

Associative computation is the antithesis of address-oriented programming, let alone indirect addressing or pointers. However, if ASC is to be used to implement other, higher-level associative or relational languages for such applications as relational data bases, it is essential that the database itself contain the address information that the ASC compiler would normally handle. In order to allow research and development of such applications, ASC has an indirect-address mode of operation. Thus it is possible to have a field of addresses as shown in Fig. 3-40. Note that associative search is still used to select the responders. Because of the SIMD nature of the operation, only scalar-restricted parallel variables (i.e., a[xx]) as shown in Fig. 3-40, can be used for indirect addressing. However, the field addressed is processed in parallel.

3.22. Conclusion

This chapter introduced the ASC language and demonstrated how it is based on the *search*, *process*, *retrieve* cycle of SITDAC associative computing. The next chapter gives several examples of programs written in ASC.

It concluding this chapter, some of the peculiarities of ASC syntax will be reviewed. The parallel-index variables require a [$] suffix when they are declared and when they are used directly in an expression. But the suffix is optional when parallel-index variables are used as indices because of the messy notation, i.e., a[xx[$]] versus a[xx]. Moreover, the ambivalent notation is characteristic of index variables because, when they are used in expressions, they behave as parallel

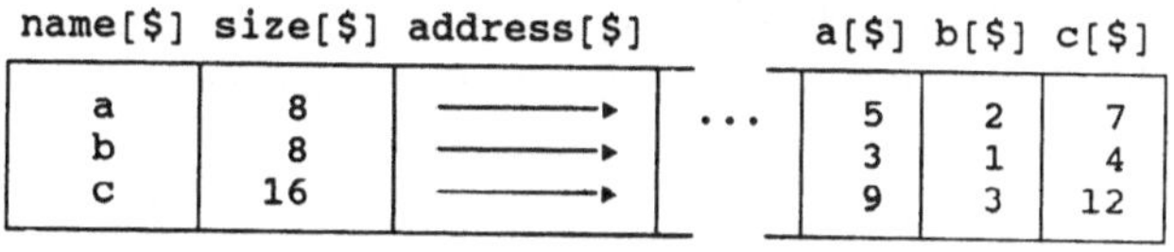

name[$]	size[$]	address[$]		a[$]	b[$]	c[$]
a	8	——→	...	5	2	7
b	8	——→		3	1	4
c	16	——→		9	3	12

```
for xx in name[$] .eq. 'a'
  for yy in name[$] .eq. 'b'
    for zz in name[$] .eq. 'c'
      @c[zz] = @a[xx] + @b[yy];
```

Figure 3-40. Indirect addressing.

variables and process flags for all responders in parallel. However, when used as indices, each selects only one responder.

In most lists, either a blank or a comma delimiter may be used. FORTRAN or C operators may be used, and parentheses are optional in an **if** statement. Some of the syntax style options are shown below:

```
if( ten[$] < twenty[$] ) then ten[$] = twenty[$]; endif;
if( ten[$] .lt. twenty[$] ) then ten[$] = twenty[$]; endif;
if  ten[$] < twenty[$]   then ten[$] = twenty[$]; endif;
if  ten[$] .lt. twenty[$]  then ten[$] = twenty[$]; endif;
until nany ten[$] .gt. 1
until nany ten[$]  >  1
until a .gt. 1
until a  >    1
```

In general, the preferred style is to use FORTRAN logical and comparison operators so that "a = b" is avoided where "a == b" was intended.

The different statement types require a unique explicit **end** keyword, and those statements which incorporate a parallel index variable must terminate the block with a repetition of the variable. This facilities sorting out all of the "end***" statements that tend to bunch together. Furthermore, the scope of the index variable is clearly delineated. Finally, no distinction is made between simple and compound statements, so that

```
if(   )                              (   )
  b;      is not typed where if     {b;
  c;                                  c;}
```

was intended.

This chapter described the associative processing model of computer programming. Associative programming eliminates the need to keep track of the mapping between data structures and memory addresses inherent in conventional programming languages. The associative model expands the concept of a content-addressable memory to a content-addressable array of processors. Associative programming is efficiently supported by SIMD architectures using fine-grain parallelism and is well suited for VLSI fabrication. It supports the sequential-control, parallel-data-manipulation approach encountered in most natural-language "instructional" environments. It is easily written and understood since it does not require recursion or functional composition.

4

Elementary ASC Programs

Chapters 1 and 2 introduced basic SIMD and associative programming concepts. Chapter 3 introduced ASC statements and showed how the search, process, retrieve cycle of SITDAC associative programming can be used to build structured associative high-level statements. This chapter illustrates the use of ASC statements for conventional programming tasks. The initial programs are for simple arithmetic, conditional, and iterative tasks. Examples of a number of input options and north-south grid communication are given. The second program illustrates the use of **count** and **them**. The next section explains how to implement associative stacks and queues. The third section presents an elementary dataflow interpreter that introduces the mask and broadcast-communication technique. The last program is for a minimal-spanning-tree algorithm. It illustrates the use of the **mindex** function, the use of parallel-index variables as indexes into associations, and the use of logical parallel variables as flags for execution control. The ASC version is contrasted with a conventional C version to illustrate the difference in programming style.

4.1. Simple Arithmetic Tasks

4.1.1. Payroll

A typical first program in Pascal or C enables us to input a wage and the number of hours worked and calculate the amount earned. Frequently, such programs deal with I/O and calculate the result for only one set of inputs. In ASC, since I/O is tabular and parallel variables are used, a similar program, as shown in Fig. 4-1, would input a table of wages and hours worked, calculate the earnings in parallel, and output the entire payroll.

```
main payroll

real parallel wage[$], hours[$], total[$];
logical parallel pr[$];

associate wage[$] hours[$] total[$] with pr[$];

read wage[$] hours[$] in pr[$];
total[$] = wage[$]*hours[$];
print wage[$] hours[$] total[$] in pr[$];

end;
```

a - The Payroll Program

```
INPUT VALUES FOR pr
A blank line terminates input.
wage, hours,

3.75  37.5
4.25  14.2
4.25  40.0
4.00  44.0
```

b - Payroll Input

```
DUMP OF ASSOCIATION pr FOLLOWS:
wage, hours, total

3.75  37.5   140.63
4.25  14.2    60.35
4.25  40.0   170.00
4.00  44.0   176.00
```

c - Payroll Output

Figure 4-1. A first ASC program.

4.1.2. Average Age by County

The next program enters a list of student ids, ages, and counties of residence. It computes the average age of the students on a county-by-county basis and prints the result. It illustrates the use of the **associate**, **read**, **for**, and **while** statements.

The **associate** statement on lines *a* in Fig. 4-2 combines two logical associations into one. The first association, for the input data, contains the student id, age, and county information. The second association contains the output information: the counties and their average ages. Since the output counties must be a subset of the input counties, the input association can be augmented with the average-age field and a flag used to specify which entries are to be output, eliminating the need for a separate association. There are two reasons for having a combined association. First, the code is shortened since a second association is not necessary. Second, the code runs faster since data (i.e., the county name) does not have to be moved from one association to another.

Note that this arrangement is in keeping with the associative concept of

```
main avg_age
/* compute the average age of the students on a county
   by county basis. */
int     parallel id[$], age[$], avg[$];
char    parallel county:48[$];
logical parallel bi[$], flag[$];
index   parallel xx[$], yy[$];
int     scalar total, number;

associate  id[$], age[$], county[$],                     a
           avg[$], flag[$]  with bi[$];                  a

read id[$] age[$] county[$] in bi[$];

while xx in bi[$]                                        b
  total=0;
  for yy in county[xx] .eq. county[$]                   c
    total = total+age[yy];
  endfor yy;
  number = count(them[$]);
  release them[$] from bi[$];
  avg[xx] = total/number;
  flag[$] = flag[$] .or. xx[$];                          d
endwhile xx;

print county[$] avg[$] in flag[$];
end;
```

Figure 4-2. Average age by county.

parallel searching. That is, when the desired data is located (i.e., each individual county name is flagged by *xx* of the **while** statement, line *b*), simply flag its location using a logical field (i.e., flag[$], line *d*) for later use (in the **print** statement in this program). This approach is more efficient than moving and reorganizing the data, since the flag is only a one-bit field and is easily manipulated in a bit-serial SIMD computer.

The **for** statement in Fig. 4-2, line *c*, allows the ages of the students to be summed without any need to sort or order the data shown in Fig. 4-3. That is, the logical parallel expression in the **for** statement finds the association entries and the **for** iteration step/find hardware efficiently selects them one by one for processing. Figure 4-3 shows the status of the *xx* and *yy* index variables for the first iteration of the **while** and **for** loops.

The C program in Fig. 4-4 is an interesting comparison. The structures of the programs are basically identical. Each has two loops—one for the counties and one for the students in the counties. Both must calculate or retrieve the number of

id	age	county	xx	yy
1	19	stark	1	1
99	22	summit	0	0
7	17	summit	0	0
41	21	stark	0	1
59	20	summit	0	0

Figure 4-3. Average-age data.

```
main()
{
/*sitr - student roll - list of students in county
  sitc - student count - number of students in county
  cour - county roll - list of counties
  couc - county count - number of counties */

typedef struct student_roll
        {int id, age;
        };
struct county_roll
        {int sitc;
         char *county;
         struct student_roll *sitr;
         } *cour;

int i, j, total, count, couc;

/* input the number of counties to process */
scanf("%d",&couc);
cour = (struct county_roll *)
        malloc(sizeof(struct  county_roll)*couc);
/* input the number of students and county name */
for(i=0; i<couc; i++)                                        a
   {(cour+i)->county = (char *) malloc(sizeof(char)*32);     a
    scanf("%d %s",&(cour+i)->sitc, (cour+i)->county);        a
    (cour+i)->sitr = (struct student_roll *)                 a
       malloc(sizeof(struct student_roll) * (cour+i)->sitc);a
    /* input the students age and id */                      a
    for(j=0; j<(cour+i)->sitc; j++)                          a
      scanf("%d %d",                                         a
         &(((cour+i)->sitr)+j)->age,                         a
         &(((cour+i)->sitr)+j)->id);                         a
printf("The average age for:\n");                            b
for(i=0; i<couc; i++)                                        b
  {count = (cour+i)->sitc;                                   b
   total = 0;                                                b
   for(j=0; j<count; j++)                                    b
     total += ((cour+i)->sitr+j)->age;                       b
   printf("  %s is %d\n",(cour+i)->county,total/count);}     b
  }
```

Figure 4-4. Average-age program in C.

students per county and both use one statement to initialize and an additional statement to calculate the sum. The ASC program must generate a flag field for output control, while the C program can output the values as calculated if a header is preprinted. Each approach takes two statements.

If the two programs are so similar, why bother to use ASC when C will do?! The difference is in the data structure. The ASC data structure is easy and straightforward to understand and use. There is no need to sort the data. If new data is to be added, no change is necessary in the program and no auxiliary programs need to be run. This simple data structure is easily read with one **read** statement.

The C program requires *sorted* data. The program to sort the data by county is as complex as the processing program. (It is not shown. The program in Fig. 4-4 assumes the data has been sorted.) In addition, as shown in Fig. 4-4, the code required to input and dynamically allocate memory in the C program (lines *a*) is more complex than the computational part of the program itself (lines *b*). Taken all together then, the C program requires approximately three times the code, three times the debugging effort, and considerably more computation time.

4.1.3. Convolution

The ASC convolution program illustrates the use of the **contiguous read** and **reread** statements, two types of looping (using a **loop** and a **for** statement), multidimensioned arrays, and grid interprocessor communication.

Convolution, illustrated in Fig. 4-5, is a typical image-processing task in which a two-dimensional weight matrix is overlaid on a two-dimensional section of the image. The individual picture elements (pixels) of the image are multiplied by the weights which align with them. The products are summed and the total is the output value for the pixel at the center of the overlay. This process is repeated for every pixel in the input image. The formula for convolution is

$$\text{pixout}(i,j) = \sum_{m,n=-1,0,1} \text{weight}(m,n) * \text{pixin}(i+m,j+n), \text{ for } i,j = 1 \ldots 512$$

In programming the convolution function, an edge-condition problem must be addressed. When the template is centered on a pixel in the top or bottom row or in the left or right column, a portion of the template "falls off" the image, as illustrated in the lower right-hand corner of the input image in Fig. 4-5. The easiest way to handle the edge condition is to add duplicate rows and columns around the image, making a 512 × 512 image 514 × 514. The convolution function is then calculated for just the original 512 × 512 image, producing a 512 × 512 output.

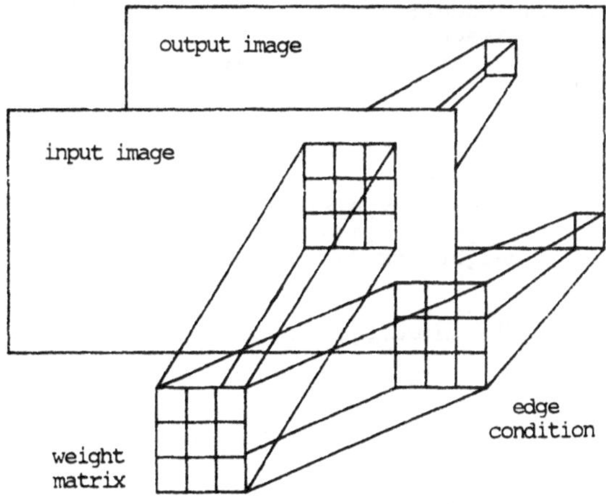

Figure 4-5. Image convolution.

However, boundary rows and columns of zeroes are output to keep the image 514 × 514 so that it may be processed repeatedly with a minimum of data reformatting. During the convolution calculation, special code for edge conditions is not needed since the duplicated boundary pixels provide the necessary values whenever the weight matrix "falls off" the original image.

Figure 4-6 gives the ASC code for convolution. Note that the input image is 514 columns wide and it is assumed that columns 0 and 513 (ASC array indices start at 0 and go to $n-1$) and the top and bottom rows of the image input data are set to supply the proper edge-condition values. Since grid interprocessor communication is required, the individual pixels must be in adjacent cells. Thus the first input into the image association must be made by a **contiguous read** statement.

```
main convolve
define (INPT, 4);

int parallel inn:8[$,514], out:8[$,514], weights:8[$,3],
                 row_id:8[$];
logical parallel image[$], kernel[$];
int scalar i,j,k,l,handle;

associate row_id[$], inn[$], out[$] with image[$];
associate weights[$] with kernel[$];

handle = open("weights",".dat",INPT);
read (handle) weights[$,0] weights[$,1] weights[$,2]
     in kernel[$];
close (handle);

read row_id[$] in image[$] contiguously;
j=0;
loop
out[$,j] = 0;
j=j+1;
until j .ge. 514
endloop;
print out[$,0] in image[$];                                    a
reread inn[$,0] in image[$];
reread inn[$,1] in image[$];
if row_id[$] .ge. 1 .and. row_id[$] .le. 512 then
  j=1;
  loop
    reread inn[$,j+1] in image[$];
    i=1;
    for xx in kernel[$]
       out[$,j] = weights[xx,0]*inn[$+i,j-1]+                  b
                  weights[xx,1]*inn[$+i,j  ]+                  b
                  weights[xx,2]*inn[$+i,j+1];                  b
       i=i-1;
    endfor xx;
    print out[$,j] in image[$];
    j=j+1;
    until j>512
  endloop;
  print out[$,513] in image[$];                                c
endif;
end;
```

Figure 4-6. ASC image-convolution program.

Subsequent inputs to the association use the **reread** command. The **reread** input command allows the columns to be read individually and still line up cell by cell (i.e., rowwise) in the association. That is, **reread** does not allocate new cells as **read** does, but instead reuses the cells in the specified busy/idle flag field.

The kernel is assumed to be 3 × 3 as illustrated in Fig. 4-7 and is input by the first **read** statement. The kernel weights are declared to be in the weights.dat file by the **open** command, which returns a handle for the **read** and **close** commands. Since the rows of the kernel are selected by a **for** loop, they do not have to be contiguous, and therefore a conventional **read** can be used.

The SITDAC model assumes a one-dimensional column of processors, so the convolution formula is written to process a column of the image in parallel. The algorithm processes columns from left to right. Three columns of input ($j-1$, j, and $j+1$) are needed to produce one column of output (j). The algorithm is written using one loop to read-in the next column ($j+1$) of imagery and produce and output the resultant image (column (j)). The entire out image is initialized to zero. The boundary columns of the output image are maintained by outputing the boundary columns (lines *a* and *c*) of zero, and the boundary rows are maintained by inputing a row_id field and using an **if** statement to restrict the generation of the out image to all but the first and last rows.

Note that the ASC code of the assignment statement on lines *b* directly reflects the mathematical formula in the same manner as any conventional FORTRAN or C program with the one exception that columns of pixels are processed in parallel and therefore one fewer nested loop is needed. As the loop statement marches through the columns, the inner **for** statement loops through the rows of the kernel and the assignment statement explicitly specifies the individual columns of the kernel. Figure 4-8 shows a before and after image. The specific convolution kernel shown in Fig. 4-7 is for edge detection and maps uniform intensity regions to zero and transition regions to nonzero.

The algorithm is easily understood if the index values are understood. Note that the indices of the kernel's second dimension go from 0 to 2 instead of -1 to 1. This is due to the fact that negative indices are not allowed in ASC. Therefore the center column of the kernel is column 1, and thus the indices are biased by adding one, giving $-1 + 1$, $0 + 1$, and $1 + 1$ or 0, 1, and 2, respectively. This is standard index biasing and is common in many languages.

The **for** statement is a slightly different approach to kernel-row iteration than is the standard loop. It relies on the fact that the **for** statement will access the rows of the kernel in the same order that they were read. The *i* index is used in the **for**

```
0  1  0
1 -4  1
0  1  0
```

Figure 4-7. A convolution kernel.

```
  0   50 50 ... 50 50   75 75 ... 75 75
  1   50 50 ... 50 50   75 75 ... 75 75
  2   50 50 ... 50 50   75 75 ... 75 75
  :    :  :      :  :    :  :      :
511   50 50 ... 50 50   75 75 ... 75 75
512   50 50 ... 50 50   75 75 ... 75 75
513   50 50 ... 50 50   75 75 ... 75 75
```

a - The Original Image

```
  0   0  0 ...  0  0    0  0 ...  0 0
  1   0  0 ...  0 25  -25  0 ...  0 0
  2   0  0 ...  0 25  -25  0 ...  0 0
  :   :  :      :  :    :  :      : :
511   0  0 ...  0 25  -25  0 ...  0 0
512   0  0 ...  0 25  -25  0 ...  0 0
513   0  0 ...  0  0    0  0 ...  0 0
```

b - The Convolved Image

Figure 4-8. Before and after convolution.

statement in the inn field to specify the amount of the interprocessor communication grid shift. When i is 1, a shift from the lower to higher processors (i.e., a top-to-bottom or north-to-south shift) results. This is the alignment needed when processing the top row of the kernel. Zero or no shift is used for the middle row. Minus one or a shift from higher to lower PEs is used for the bottom row.

Finally, at any one time, only three columns of imagery are required in memory. Thus, by using a triple buffering scheme a considerable amount of memory could be saved. However, in the interest of simplicity and generality, the memory is allocated for both the entire input and output images. Triple buffering would increase the complexity of the dimensioned-array index specifications, and any modern computer has ample memory to hold the data. In addition, this scheme allows a second image-processing function to be performed on the results of the first without having to re-input it.

4.2. Associative Stacks and Queues

Associative programming eliminates the need for encoding order into data structures such as stacks and queues. Associative stacks and queues use the raw data directly to determine order instead. Stacks and queues are implemented simply as dynamically allocated association entries with one of the fields chosen to specify the order of selection (called the *position field*). The stack and queue code segments illustrate the use of the **any**, **allocate**, and **exit** statements.

An associative stack push is accomplished by allocating a new association entry and inserting a larger value in the position field. A pop is simply the selection of the entry with the largest ordinal value in the position field, the return of the associated value(s) of the selected entry, and the release of the entry from the association. Queues are likewise easily implemented. Figure 4-9 shows the state of a stack and a queue association before any action and the state of the associations after either a push or a pop action. Frequently, the position field is a functional data item by itself such as the time of arrival as represented by the time-tag field in Fig. 4-9.

Figure 4-10 shows the ASC code for queue and stack administration. The stack or push operation and the queue operation are identical except for the memory-allocation map variables (astack[$] and aqueue[$]). The first step in pushing a value onto the stack is to determine if there are any idle memory cells by interrogating the global busy/idle flag field with an **any** statement. Unlike conventional busy/idle flags, TRUE indicates that the cell is idle for the global busy/idle flag. If there are no idle cells, an error message is printed using the **msg** command, and the **exit** statement is executed causing the next **return** to abort the program. (The **exit** statement is optional of course, if more sophisticated error handling is desired.) If there are one or more idle cells, the first one is assigned

TIME TAG	VALUE	TIME TAG	VALUE	TIME TAG	VALUE			
0	10	0	10	0	10		17	
not	used	5	17	not	used	20	20	
2	15	2	15	2	15	35	35	35
4	20	4	20	not	used	15	15	15
3	35	3	35	3	35	100	100	100
1	100	1	100	1	100	10	10	10
before		after push 17		after pop->20		before	after push 17	after pop->20

associative stack   conventional stack

TIME TAG	VALUE	TIME TAG	VALUE	TIME TAG	VALUE			
0	10	0	10	not	used		17	
not	used	5	17	not	used	20	20	
2	15	2	15	2	15	35	35	20
4	20	4	20	4	20	15	15	35
3	35	3	35	3	35	100	100	15
1	100	1	100	1	100	10	10	100
before		after queue 17		after next->10		before	after queue 17	after next->10

associative queue   conventional queue

Figure 4-9. Associative stacks and queues.

```
int parallel timetag[$];
int parallel value[$];
logical parallel astack[$];
index parallel xx[$];
int scalar time;

associate
   timetag[$], value[$]
with astack[$];
/* initialize stack */
time = 0;
astack[$] = 0;

/* push val */
any globalbi[$]
  allocate xx in astack[$]
     timetag[xx] = time;
     value[xx] = val;
  endallocate xx;
  time = time + 1;
elsenany
  msg "astack overflow";
  exit;
endany;
```

a - Code to push val

```
int parallel timetag[$];
int parallel value[$];
logical parallel aqueue[$];
index parallel xx[$];
int scalar time;

associate
   timetag[$], value[$]
with aqueue[$];
/* initialize queue */
time = 0;
aqueue[$] = 0;

/* queue val */
any globalbi[$]
  allocate xx in aqueue[$];
     timetag[xx] = time;
     value[xx] = val;
  endallocate xx;
  time = time + 1;
elsenany
  msg "aqueue overflow";
  exit;
endany;
```

b - Code to queue val

```
/* pop val */
any astack[$]
  xx = maxdex(timetag[$]);
  val = value[xx];
  release xx from astack[$];
elsenany
  msg "astack underflow";
  exit;
endany;
```

c - Code to pop val

```
/* dequeue val */
any aqueue[$]
  xx = mindex(timetag[$]);
  val = value[xx];
  release xx from aqueue[$];
elsenany
  msg "aqueue underflow";
  exit;
endany;
```

d - Code to dequeue val

Figure 4-10. Code for stacks and queues.

to the astack busy/idle flag field by the **allocate** statement. **Allocate** causes the index variable *xx* to point to the allocated memory cell so that entries can be made in the timetag and value fields. Finally, the time variable is incremented.

The pop and dequeue procedures are even simpler. After using an **any** statement to assure that there is a stacked value, pop simply looks for the largest (newest) active time tag. It extracts the associated value, releases the memory cell, and returns the extracted value. Dequeue works in exactly the same way, except that it searches for the smallest (oldest) time tag.

The time tag column is shown intentionally out of order in Fig. 4-9 to illustrate that ordering is immaterial. In reality the nature of the stack and queue operations requires them to allocate and release entries in order and, as a result, the time tags would normally be in sequential order. In addition, the time tags are shown to be sequential integers. In reality, they may be any ordered sequence of unique values—numeric, alphabetic, or alphanumeric. (Alphabetic and alphanumeric codes would be retrieved in ASCII numeric order.)

The power of ASC and associative programming is that the data structures are natural and not artificial. In the examples in Fig. 4-9, an artificial time variable and time-tag field were used for illustrative purposes only. In actual application, the time-tag field would be replaced by a more meaningful value such as priority, minutes spent waiting, number of items to process, size of task (memory size needed or CPU time needed) passed as a parameter to the queuing or stacking routine. Moreover, several fields could be used in combination, such as priority and expected execution time. It is obvious that a sophisticated dequeuing routine can be easily programmed when two or more ordering fields are present. In addition, more than one value field can be saved and the value fields can even be used to determine dequeuing order.

It should be emphasized that queues and stacks are ordering data structures and are artifacts of conventional sequential programming. In an associative programming environment the need for these special structures is minimal since frequently the queuing and dequeuing functions are integrated into he algorithm directly using the natural data items with conventional ASC statements to achieve the desired ordering. Section 9.2 gives an example of the use of an associative stack.

4.3. A Dataflow Interpreter

This next program illustrates the necessity for the **setscope** statement. It is a good example of the use of masks and broadcasting as a communication protocol (see section 3.17). It illustrates the use of the **while** and **for** statements. It also introduces some ways parallelism may be enhanced in a more advanced associative computer design.

In dataflow programming, expressions are stated in graph form. The nodes of the graph in Fig. 4-11 can be encoded into templates, as shown in Fig. 4-12. The fields are shown with their symbolic values to make it easy to associate the templates and nodes. The slotno field contains the node label from Fig. 4-11. Note that the edges of the graph are represented as destination addresses in the templates. Thus in the dataflow interpreter, after the node has been evaluated, the value is delivered to the specified template fields.

When a node has links to many other nodes, as node 0 does, broadcasting the value to all nodes and using a mask to select the nodes that are to receive the data is more efficient than using an interconnection network. That is, in a SIMD computer, even with a powerful interconnection network, if the value of a single node is to be sent to more than one node, separate move instructions are required because each transmission requires a separate address.

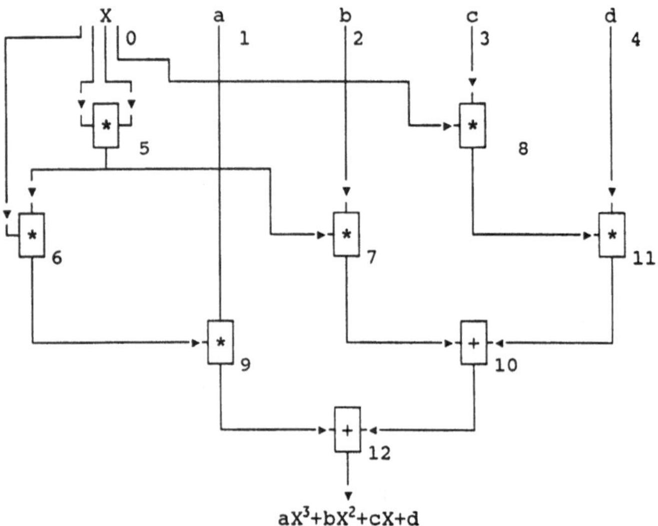

Figure 4-11. A dataflow graph.

Figure 4-13 shows a dataflow template association with masks instead of addresses. If mask 0 from the mask field array in Fig. 4-13 is used to select the PEs to receive the data and the data is broadcast to all PEs in parallel, all destinations are accessed in one step. The distribution is shown graphically in Fig. 4-13 by the arrows and *x*s for node 0 for the *a* field. This approach is very effective for situations where one value is to be sent to many addresses because the only overhead is loading the mask and all destinations are written in parallel.

The dataflow emulator code in Fig. 4-14 shows the basic main program and has comments to mark the location of the two basic steps of the algorithm. The first

slotno	opcode	fielda	fieldb	fieldc	destination
0	INPUT	X			5a,5b,6a,8a
1	INPUT	a			9b
2	INPUT	b			7b
3	INPUT	c			8b
4	INPUT	d			11b
5	MULT	X	X	X^2	6b,7a
6	MULT	X	X^2	X^3	9a
7	MULT	X^2	b	bX^2	10a
8	MULT	X	c	cX	11a
9	MULT	X^3	a	aX^3	12a
10	ADD	bX^2	cX +d	bX^2+cX+d	12b
11	ADD	cX	d	cX +d	10b
12	ADD	aX^3	bX^2+cX +d	aX^3+bX^2+cX+d	13a
13	OUTPUT	aX^3+bX^2+cX+d			

Figure 4-12. Dataflow templates with addresses.

```
slotno opcode flda fldb fldc dest dest   mask[$,i]
                             flda fldb   0123456789

  0     INPUT   X---+          0    1    0000000000
  1     INPUT       |               2    0000000000
  2     INPUT       |               3    0000000000
  3     INPUT       |               4    0000000000
  4     INPUT       |               5    0000000000
  5     MULT    X<--|          6    3    1100000000
  6     MULT    X<--|          2         1000001000
  7     MULT        |          7         0001000000
  8     MULT    X<--+          5         1000100000
  9     MULT                   8         0010000000
 10     ADD                         8    0000000100
 11     ADD                         7    0000010000
 12     ADD                    9         0000000010
 13     OUTPUT                           0000000001
```

Figure 4-13. Dataflow templates with masks.

step performs the execution of the templates that are eligible to be fired and is shown in Fig. 4-15. The second distributes the values and is shown in Fig. 4-16.

One of the advantages of the dataflow parallelism is that it allows nonsymmetrical parallelism. That is, an **add** can be executing at the same time as a **multiply**. For example, nodes 9 and 10 of Fig. 4-11 both are third in the cascade of operations and may be executed in parallel. Unfortunately, the current SITDAC model, since it is based on a conventional bit-serial SIMD computer, does not support this type of parallelism. (However, the extended-model architecture described in section 10.4.5 does.) As a result, the first part of the dataflow template execution engine must test for each opcode type.

The dataflow association has a few more fields than those shown in Fig. 4-12. In particular, as shown in Fig. 4-17 and Fig. 4-14, three ready flags (flag*a*, flag*b*, and flag*c*) and two constant flags (cons*a* and cons*b*) are associated with the argument fields. The ready flags indicate that data values are present in the corresponding operand fields. The constant flag means that an operand value is a constant and must not be overwritten.

The rule for the firing of a dataflow node is that there are data in the input operands but no data in the output operand. The presence of data is denoted by a 1 in the appropriate flag. Thus flag*a* and flag*b* must be TRUE and flag*c* must be FALSE for a node to fire. This is the condition tested for on line *b* in Fig. 4-14. Thus the responders are set to the templates that are eligible to fire in preparation for the template execution code of Fig. 4-15.

Line *a* contains the **while** statement to determine when the process is done. The process is complete when there are no more values in the *a* or *b* operand fields which are not constants.

The execution portion, based on the current SITDAC model hardware, is just a sequence of code to assure that all operations are processed. The code shown in Fig. 4-15 is used because it is simple to read and understand. However, it may be

```
main dataflow

deflog (TRUE, 1);
define (ADD, 1);
define (SUB, 2);
define (MUL, 3);
define (DIV, 4);
define (DIS, 5);    /* distribution node */
define (OUT, 6);
define (NEG, 7);

defvar (mask, masks);

logical parallel flaga[$], flagb[$], flagc[$];
logical parallel consa[$], consb[$];
int parallel fielda[$], fieldb[$], fieldc[$];
int parallel slotno[$], opcode[$], desta[$], destb[$];
hex parallel masks:16[$];
logical parallel dfbi[$], mask[$,16];
index parallel xx[$], yy[$], zz[$];

associate slotno[$] opcode[$]
     flaga[$] consa[$] fielda[$]
     flagb[$] consb[$] fieldb[$]
     flagc[$]          fieldc[$] desta[$] destb[$] masks[$]
with dfbi[$];

read slotno[$] opcode[$]
     flaga[$] consa[$] fielda[$]
     flagb[$] consb[$] fieldb[$] desta[$] destb[$] masks[$]
in dfbi[$];

while zz in flaga[$] .and. .not. consa[$] .or.                  a
            flagb[$] .and. .not. consb[$]                       a
  if flaga[$] .and. flagb[$] .and. .not. flagc[$] then          b
    yy[$] = TRUE;
    /* execute templates  */
   if .not. consa[$] then flaga[$] = 0; endif;
   if .not. consb[$] then flagb[$] = 0; endif;
   flagc[$] = 1;
    /* distribute results */
    yy[$] =0;
  endif;
endwhile zz;
end;
```

Figure 4-14. An ASC dataflow emulator.

somewhat inefficient in that it tests for all opcodes even when they may not be present.

A second approach, given in Fig. 4-18, would use a **switch** statement that branches to the appropriate section of code based on the opcode value selected by a **while** statement. This approach has the advantage of executing code only for opcode values explicitly ready to fire. The extra control overhead is basically a parallel-to-scalar move and a branch, or the equivalent of two compares per iteration versus eight compares. Thus the break-even point is about four distinct opcodes. That is, if fewer than four different opcode types are ready to fire, the version in Fig. 4-18 is faster. When more than four are present, the version in Fig.

```
/* execute templates */
if opcode[$] .eq. ADD then
   fieldc[$] = fielda[$] + fieldb[$];
endif;
if opcode[$] .eq. SUB then
   fieldc[$] = fielda[$] - fieldb[$];
endif;
if opcode[$] .eq. MUL then
   fieldc[$] = fielda[$] * fieldb[$];
endif;
if opcode[$] .eq. DIV then
   fieldc[$] = fielda[$] / fieldb[$];
endif;
if opcode[$] .eq. DIS then
   if .not. consa[$]  then
      fieldc[$] = fielda[$];
   endif;
   if .not. consb[$]  then
      fieldc[$] = fieldb[$];
   endif;
endif;
if opcode[$] .eq. OUT then
   print fielda[$] fieldb[$] in them[$];
endif;
if opcode[$] .eq. NEG then
   fieldc[$] = - fielda[$];
endif;
```

Figure 4-15. The template-execution portion of dataflow.

4-15 is faster. The tradeoff between these approaches is common in ASC programming. And surprisingly, the tradeoff frequently is in the same range of four to ten iterations. The careful programmer must analyze the most likely scenario to make the correct selection. But note that in general, as the amount of data parallelism increases, the more likely it is that many different types of data are present and the first approach (Fig. 4-15) is better.

```
/* distribute results */
for xx in yy[$]                                                    a
   setscope mask[$,desta[xx]]                                      b
      any desta[xx] .and. flaga[$]
      elsenany
         fielda[$] = fieldc[xx];
         flaga[$] = 1;
         flagc[$] = 0;
      endany;
   endsetscope;
   setscope mask[$,destb[xx]]                                      b
      any destb[xx] .and. flagb[$]
      elsenany
         fieldb[$] = fieldc[xx];
         flagb[$] = 1;
         flagc[$] = 0;
   endsetscope;
endfor xx;
```

Figure 4-16. The result-distribution portion of dataflow.

```
        operand a              operand b            operand c
  flaga consa fielda    flagb consb fieldb    flagc fieldc
```

Figure 4-17. The complete argument fields.

Note that the **switch** statement shown in Fig. 4-18 is not implemented in the current verion of ASC. However, the basic equivalent of cascading **if**s, as shown below, is available.

```
if code[xx] .eq. NEG then
    :
else if code[xx] .eq. ADD then
    :
  :
else if . . .
```

The hypothetical **switch** statement was used because it executes more efficiently than the cascading **if**s and thus results in a more favorable comparison. Moreover, section 10.4.5 illustrates that in the enhanced associative computer design, all opcodes can execute in parallel and this section of code is reduced to a single parallel statement.

After the templates have been evaluated, the computed values must be distributed. As mentioned earlier, a mask-and-broadcast approach is used. This approach has several advantages. First, it is faster than other approaches (under certain conditions—see section 10.3). Second, it is more compact and easier to administer. That is, if a list of addresses were to be maintained as opposed to flag

```
/* execute templates */
while xx in yy[$]
  if opcode[xx] .eq. opcode[$] then
    release them[$] from yy[$]
    switch on opcode[xx] to:
      NEG: fieldc[$] =               - fielda[$]; break;
      ADD: fieldc[$] = fielda[$] + fieldb[$]; break;
      SUB: fieldc[$] = fielda[$] - fieldb[$]; break;
     MULT: fieldc[$] = fielda[$] * fieldb[$]; break;
      DIV: fieldc[$] = fielda[$] / fieldb[$]; break;
      DIS: if .not. consa[$] then
              fieldc[$] = fielda[$];
           endif;
           if .not. consb[$] then
              fieldc[$] = fieldb[$];
           endif;
           break;
      OUT: print fielda[$] fieldb[$] in them[$]; break;
    endswitch;
  endif;
 endwhile xx;
yy[$] = TRUE;
```

Figure 4-18. Switched-dataflow execution.

fields, the problem of how large to make the list would arise. Should it be large enough for four links, eight links, or more? Obviously, a compromise size would be selected and special provision for those cases which exceed the size would be required resulting in considerable complications in the program design.

In the mask-and-broadcast approach, the mask has a bit for every cell in the system, and therefore there is no need for code to handle overflow conditions.

The templates contain a separate mask field for values being distributed to fields *a* and *b*. This is necessary because only one destination field address may be broadcast at a time (i.e., field*a* or field*b* but not both). However, as discussed in section 10.4.2, the augmented design would allow local (at the PE) address modification. With such a capability, the two sets of code can be collapsed into one.

Finally, note that the **setscope** statements (lines *b* in Fig. 4-16) are required to set the masks for the broadcast. This is because the broadcast is inside a parallel **if** which has restricted the scope. The **setscope** assures that all template cells are accessible from inside the **if**.

There are two types of iteration in the data-flow program. Both are dynamic, but one, in the distribution phase, is static once the responders are found and is implemented with a **for** statement (line *a* in Fig. 4-16). At the beginning of the distribution phase, the template cells ready for distribution are determined. Note that the ready cells may appear in any order and that a queue or linked list would be required in a sequential dataflow emulation. However, in ASC, the **for** statement via the step/find hardware selects and processes the cells efficiently.

The second is the basic engine iteration. Since the status of the computation can change on every iteration, a **while** statement is required to

1. recognize and process new cells when they become available to fire, and
2. detect that all cells have been processed and exit.

The main loop (line *a* of Fig. 4-14) requires a **while** statement because new template cells are added to the list to be processed during the time of execution. That is, the execution of the **for** distribution loop nested in the **while** loop causes new cells to become eligible to fire; thus the responders to the **while** search change on every iteration.

4.4. Minimal Spanning Tree

The Minimal Spanning Tree (MST) algorithm finds a spanning tree subgraph of a graph with the minimally weighted edges. This algorithm in ASC demonstrates the use of the parallel **if** statement for scoping, the loop **until nany** statement and logical flag fields for flow of control, and the **mindex** function for associative entry selection, as well as the use of a flag field to specify a single associative entry to retrieve or receive a scalar value.

The basic algorithm divides the edges of the graph into four classes or states.

In state 1 are the edges in the MST. State 4 contains the edges eliminated from inclusion in the MST. State 3 contains the edges that have yet to be considered. State 2 contains the edges that connect nodes with edges in state 1 to nodes with edges in state 3.

An iteration of the algorithm consists of simply picking the lowest-weighted edge in state 2, moving it to state 1, and then updating the edges and nodes affected by the selection. This process is repeated until no more edges remain in state 2.

Consider that, as the algorithm advances, whenever an edge is added to state one, all of the other edges connecting the newly selected edge's nodes to other nodes in state 1 are redundant and thus put into state 4. All edges that connect the selected edge's nodes to nodes in state 3 are now candidates for inclusion in the MST and are put into state 2. These updating functions can be applied in parallel.

Figures 4-19 and 4-20 show two different ASC implementations of Prim's

```
main mst
deflog (TRUE, 1);
deflog (FALSE,0);
char parallel nodel[$],noder[$];
int parallel weight[$],state[$];
char scalar nodea, nodeb;
index parallel xx[$];
logical parallel nxtedg[$], graph[$], reachl[$], reachr[$];
associate nodel[$],noder[$],weight[$],state[$],
          reachl[$],reachr[$] with graph[$];
/*   state 1  means edge is in mst
     state 2  means edge bridges between node in mst
              and node not in mst.  A candidate edge.
     state 3  means neither node of edge has been processed yet.
     state 4  means edge is not in mst.        */
read nodel[$], noder[$], weight[$] in graph[$];
/* select first edge, set to state 2, remainder to state 3 */
state[$] = 3;
if graph[$] then state[mindex(weight[$])] = 2; endif;
reachl[$] = FALSE;  reachr[$] = FALSE;
while xx in state[$] .eq. 2  /* while candidate edges remain */
/* Select candidate edge with minimum weight. */
 if state[$] .eq. 2 then nxtedg[$]= mindex(weight[$]); endif; a
 state[nxtedg[$]] = 1;
 nodea = nodel[nxtedg[$]];  nodeb = noder[nxtedg[$]];
 /* update edge status */
 reachl[$] =
   nodea .eq. nodel[$] .or. nodeb .eq. nodel[$] .or. reachl[$];
 reachr[$] =
   nodea .eq. noder[$] .or. nodeb .eq. noder[$] .or. reachr[$];
 if (state[$].eq.2 .or. state[$].eq.3) .and.
     reachl[$] .and. reachr[$] then state[$] = 4;
 endif;
 if state[$] .eq. 3 .and. (reachl[$] .or. reachr[$]) then
  state[$] = 2;
 endif;
 nxtedg[$] = FALSE;  /*clear for next iteration */
endwhile xx;
print nodel[$] noder[$] weight[$] in state[$] .eq. 1;
end;
```

Figure 4-19. A MST program using a parallel-state variable (ASC).

```
main mst
deflog (TRUE, 1);
deflog (FALSE, 0);
char parallel nodel[$],noder[$];
int parallel weight[$];
char scalar node1, node2;
index parallel xx[$];
logical parallel nxtedg[$], graph[$], reachl[$], reachr[$];
logical parallel state1[$], state2[$], state3[$], state4[$];
associate nodel[$],noder[$], weight[$], state1[$], state2[$],
     state3[$], state4[$], reachl[$], reachr[$] with graph[$];

read nodel[$], noder[$], weight[$] in graph[$];
/* select first edge, set to state 2, remainder to state 3 */
if graph[$] then
  state2[mindex(weight[$])]=TRUE;
  state3[$] = .not. state2[$];
endif;
reachl[$] = FALSE;  reachr[$] = FALSE;
while xx in state2[$]; /* while candidate edges*/
/* Select candidate edge with minimum weight. */
  if state2[$] then
     nxtedg[$]  =  mindex(weight[$]);
  endif;
  state1[nxtedg[$]] = TRUE;
  state2[nxtedg[$]] = FALSE;
  node1 = nodel[nxtedg[$]];
  node2 = noder[nxtedg[$]];
/* update edge status */
  reachl[$] =
    node1 .eq. nodel[$] .or. node2 .eq. nodel[$] .or. reachl[$];
  reachr[$] =
    node1 .eq. noder[$] .or. node2 .eq. noder[$] .or. reachr[$];
  if (state2[$].or.state3[$]) .and. reachl[$].and.reachr[$] then
     state2[$] = FALSE; state3[$] =FALSE; state4[$] = TRUE;
  endif;
  if state3[$] .and. (reachl[$] .or. reachr[$]) then
     state2[$] = TRUE; state3[$] = FALSE;
  endif;
  nxtedg[$] = FALSE;  /*clear for next iteration */
endwhile xx;
print nodel[$] noder[$] weight[$] in state1[$];
end;
```

Figure 4-20. A MST program using logical-state flag fields (ASC).

algorithm given in Baase [1978] (pp. 127–132). Note that the program in Fig. 4-19 is a direct reflection of the verbal description of the algorithm. The power of associative computing lies in the ease with which the language can capture natural parallelism in conventional algorithms. For example, the first **if** statement (line a) inside the **while** in Fig. 4-19 sets the scope to all edges in state 2 so that the edge with the minimum weight can be found in parallel. Confusing, complex linked-list data structures and serializing loop-control statements are not needed to convert inherently parallel search statements into sequential code for an efficient implementation of Prim's algorithm, as is required in the C version shown in Figs. 4-21, 4-22, and 4-23.

Two ASC implementations of the MST algorithm are presented. In both,

```
#include <stdio.h>
#include <stdlib.h>
#include <alloc.h>
#include <stdarg.h>
#include <conio.h>

 struct linknode
   {  int vtx;
      int wgt;
      struct linknode *link;
   };

 struct v2link
   {  struct v2link *v2l;
      int    weight;
      struct v2link *parent;
      int    vset;
      struct linknode *adjlist;
   };
```

Figure 4-21. Data-structure definitions (MST program in C).

two flag fields (reach*l* and reach*r*) are used to record which nodes have been reached. If both nodes of an edge have been reached and the edge is not in state 1, then it is not needed and is set to state 4. The use of logical flag fields is an efficient way of saving information from one iteration to the next.

The program in Fig. 4-20 uses not only flag fields reach*l* and reach*r* but four other flag fields as well, to represent the four edge states instead of a single-state field. Both versions of the program are correct and both work. However, the second version executes more efficiently because searching for state numbers is replaced by setting the mask register to a flag field. The first version is included because it is more readable, especially for programmers new to associative computing who are not quite accustomed to using logical parallel flag fields to control the flow of a program.

Contrasting Figs. 4-19 and 4-20 with Figs. 4-21, 4-22, and 4-23 reinforces the conclusion of section 4.1.2. The main reason ASC is easier is that the linked lists required for efficient sequential execution are replaced by a simple tabular data structure which can be searched in parallel in one step for the minimum weighted edge.

Again, a large portion of the C program is dedicated to I/O and the generation of the internal data structure, as shown in Fig. 4-22. More code is required to search and maintain the linked list for the minimal edge. Thus the C code on line *a* in Fig. 4-23 is equivalent to the ASC operation **mindex**(weight[$]). The C code closely follows the algorithm given in Baase using the same variable names and step designations. The reader interested in more details of the C code is encouraged to consult Basse [1978], p. 130.

```
main(int argc, char *argv[], char *env[])
{
  char path[30];
  FILE *handle;
  int cnt,i,ecnt,x,y,ecount;
  int tail,head,wt,minwgt;
  struct v2link *header,*vlink,*v2lo, *v2pnt, *ypnt, *xpnt,
         *oldpnt, *savv2l;
  struct linknode *pnt, *savpnt;

  strcpy(path,argv[1]);
  handle = fopen(path,"r+");
  printf("Enter count for nodes and edges.\n");
  fscanf(handle,"%d %d",&cnt,&ecnt);
  printf("echo cnt = %d\n",cnt);

  header = calloc(cnt+1,sizeof(struct v2link));
  for(i=0; i<cnt; i++) (*(header+i)).adjlist= NULL;
   for(i=0; i<ecnt; i++)
     {printf("Enter tail, head weight\n");
      fscanf(handle,"%d %d %d",&tail,&head,&wt);
      if(tail >= cnt)
        printf("ERROR - OOR tail\n");
      else
        {vlink = header + tail;
         pnt = calloc(1,sizeof(struct linknode));
         pnt->vtx = head;
         pnt->wgt = wt;
         pnt->link = (*vlink).adjlist;
         (*vlink).adjlist = pnt;
         (*vlink).weight = 99;
        }

     if(head >= cnt)
       printf("ERROR - OOR head\n");
     else
       {vlink = header + head;
        pnt = calloc(1,sizeof(struct linknode));
        pnt->vtx = tail;
        pnt->wgt = wt;
        pnt->link = (*vlink).adjlist;
        (*vlink).adjlist = pnt;
        (*vlink).weight = 99;
       }
   }
```

Figure 4-22. Data-input and data-structure generation (MST program in C).

```
/*Step 1 - Initialize edges to state 1 and 3 */
 ecount = 0;
 v2lo=header+cnt;
 v2lo->v2l=NULL;
 xpnt=header;
 xpnt->vset = 1;
 for(i=1; i<cnt; i++) (*(header+i)).vset=3;
/*Steps 2, 3 and 4 */
   while(ecount < cnt-1)
     {pnt = (*xpnt).adjlist;
      while(pnt != NULL) /* traverse the adjacency lists */
        {y = pnt->vtx;
         ypnt = header+y;
         if(ypnt->vset == 2 && pnt->wgt < ypnt->weight)
           {ypnt->parent = xpnt; ypnt->weight = pnt->wgt;}
         if(ypnt->vset == 3)
           {ypnt->vset = 2;    ypnt->v2l = v2lo->v2l;
            v2lo->v2l = ypnt; ypnt->parent = xpnt;
            ypnt->weight = pnt->wgt;}
         pnt = pnt->link;}
  /*Step 5 */
    if(v2lo->v2l == NULL) {printf("No MST\n"); return;}
  /*Step 6 - traverse v2links to find minimal weight */
    minwgt = 99;                                                   a
    v2pnt = v2lo->v2l;                                             a
    xpnt  = v2lo->v2l;                                             a
    oldpnt = v2lo;                                                 a
    while(v2pnt != NULL)                                           a
      {if((*v2pnt).weight < minwgt)                                a
         {minwgt = (*v2pnt).weight;                                a
          savv2l = oldpnt;                                         a
          xpnt = v2pnt;}                                           a
          oldpnt = v2pnt;                                          a
          v2pnt = (*v2pnt).v2l;}                                   a
     if(minwgt == 99)                                              a
      {printf("ERROR - minimum weight not found\n"); return;}
     else                                                          a
      {savv2l->v2l = xpnt->v2l;                                    a
       xpnt->vset = 1;                                             a
       ecount++;}}                                                 a
  /* Step 7 - output results */
   printf(" head tail weight\n");
   for(i=0; i<cnt; i++)
      printf("%d %d %d\n",i,
         (*(header+i)).parent-header,(*(header+i)).weight);}
```

Figure 4-23. Link list searching (MST program in C).

4.5. Conclusion

This chapter demonstrated the use of the most important ASC statements. Several ASC examples using **for**, **while**, **if**, **read**, **print**, **allocate**, and **release** were presented. In addition, arithmetic calculations, associative queues and stacks, grid and mask and broadcast interprocessor communications, flag fields to control flow, and the **mindex** operation were illustrated.

5

Associative Data Structures

Massively parallel bit-serial SIMD computers such as the MMP* with 16K processors and the Connection Machine† with 64K processors eliminate the need for time-sharing a single central processing unit with a multitude of data elements, thus avoiding the classic memory–CPU bottleneck. And although these machines were designed with the traditional data-addressing mechanisms, they can be programmed as associative computers, using massive parallel searching in place of address calculation, reducing data structure and programming complexity.

Chapter 3 introduced the ASC language and Chapter 4 gave simple examples of its use. Section 4.1.3 gave an example of conventional data-parallel computation for a simple two-dimensional-array data structure. This chapter describes a method for implementing in ASC a completely general hierarchy of data structures, which can be processed in parallel. The programs in Chapter 9 make heavy use of structure codes.

The first sections of this chapter

- review associative programming,
- introduce the concept of structure codes,
- explain how data structures and associations are related and that a structure code can be viewed simply as an additional element of a data structure, and
- illustrate the dynamic nature of associative data-structure references.

Section 5.7 describes how structure codes can be modified to produce new data organizations. The subsequent sections describe how linked lists can be implemented using structure codes and how structure-code functions can be used to manipulate them. Section 5.13 discusses input and output functions for lists and describes how structure codes are generated on input and used to format the output lists. Section 5.14 describes how structure codes can be used for graphs.

*The Massively Parallel Processor was built for NASA by the Goodyear Aerospace Corporation.
†The Connection Machine is made by Thinking Machines, Inc., of Cambridge, Mass.

5.1. An Associative Program

The impact of associative programming can be best explained by analyzing the fundamental components of a program. A program contains two major types of information, the procedural component and the identification component. The procedural part specifies the operations to be performed and the order in which they are to be executed. The identification component selects the data to be operated on by the procedural component. The identification component uses a field's address within a memory (i.e., its position in the program's data structure) to select it.

As described in section 1.9, the positional information content of a program's data structure is established by two mappings. The first mapping connects the problem data and the logical data structure used by the algorithm. The second connects the logical data structure and the physical organization of the computer's memory. A third mapping is required to map the physical organization into a time-sliced sequence of scalar data elements. These three mappings are combined into an addressing function, which in conventional programs is embedded into the sequential flow of control. In associative processors, an address function is stored explicitly with the data elements. Associative programming identifies the data to be processed by preceding each block of code to be executed by an associative search.

5.2. Structure Codes

The data structures, arrays, and data types of conventional languages can all be mapped onto the general concept of associations. For conventional data structures, the address function is a constant consisting of a path name. For example, the data structure specification shown in Fig. 5-1 is used by the compiler to establish the fixed path names shown. The path name is constant because of the requirement in conventional computers that the addresses be determined at compile time.

The array address function is more complex. In addition to the constant portion, consisting of the array's name, variables can be used because the regular structure allows run-time address calculation. Run-time calculation requires that indices be numerical. However, certain languages such as Pascal use data typing to map non-numerical address values into numerical ones at compile time. The association data structure in associative programming encompasses all of the above types of data organizations.

When the implicit address functions of conventional languages are stated explicitly in a content-addressable computer, the explicit address function values state specifically the positions of the objects in the data structure space generated by the address function. For this reason, the individual explicit address function

```
struct blood_pressure { int low;
                        int high;
                      };

struct medical_record { char patient;
                        int  age;
                        blood_pressure pressure;
                      };

medical_record record[many];
```

```
Constant Path Names:

     record.patient
     record.age
     record.pressure.high
     record.pressure.low
```

Figure 5-1. Data-structure path names.

values are referred to as *structure codes*. Thus, in Fig. 5-2, age and size are the structure codes for 50 and large, respectively.

Structure codes can be thought of as if they were a unique type of data item. In reality they are not. They are just like the other data items in an associative object in that they can be searched for and manipulated by all ASC associative programming statements. Structure codes are unique only in that they contain structural information on how one data element of the problem relates logically to other data elements. Any field or subset of fields in an association may be thought of as structure codes.

5.3. Data Structures as Extended Associations

The associative concept is most commonly introduced in terms of attribute–value pairs. All conventional data-organization techniques can be viewed as extensions of the attribute–value pair concept. Specifically, an array can be thought of as an attribute–value pair with a compound attribute consisting of a constant portion, the array name, with variable modifiers, the indices, as shown in Fig. 5-3. The dimension of the array determines the number of variables.

structure code	data element
age	50
size	large
color	blue
patient	jones

Figure 5-2. A simple scalar structure.

attribute			value
constant	variable	variable	
A	I	J	3

A [I , J]= 3

Figure 5-3. Compound attributes.

On the other hand, a data structure as shown in Fig. 5-4 is an attribute–value pair with a compound value. The fields of the data structure constitute the components of the compound value. Thus arrays and data structures can both be viewed as generalizations of attribute–value pairs. In fact, all multiattribute, multivalued data objects can be viewed as extended associations.

5.4. Simultaneous Multiple Data Organizations

In an associative memory there is no hard distinction between the attribute portion and the value portion of an attribute–value pair. That is, the same datum can be retrieved by searching for the matching attribute or the matching value. For example (color $) and ($ blue) would both select (color blue).

Thus, in effect, either the attribute portion or the value portion can be defined as the constant portion of an address function. It is only by convention that the attribute portion is considered the address function.

By extension to associative triples, any one component of the triple can be considered to be the address function, with the other two components being the compound value, as shown in Fig. 5-5. Moreover, any combination of two components can be considered to be a compound address function with the third component a simple value. In general, if there are *n* components in an object there are

```
struct emp {
                int emp#;
                int birth_yr;
                int birth_day;
               };
```

attribute	value		
	field1	field2	field3
emp	emp#	birth_yr	birth_day

Figure 5-4. Compound values.

address function	compound	value
sofa	color	red
table	size	big
chair	weight	heavy

a - Object
Address Function

compound	address function	value
sofa	color	red
table	size	big
chair	weight	heavy

b - Attribute
Address Function

compound	value	address function
sofa	color	red
table	size	big
chair	weight	heavy

c - Value
Address Function

Figure 5-5. Multiple data organization.

$$\sum_{k=1}^{n-1} C_k^n = 2^n - 2$$

sets of address functions, where $C_k^n = n!/(k!(n - k)!)$.

In an associative computer, all of these address functions are available to the programmer simultaneously. There is no *a priori* reason to select one set of address functions and its inherent data organization over any other. Therefore, all can be used at the programmer's discretion, intermingled in any way without any need for reordering. Multiple simultaneous data organizations are impossible in conventional and parallel-sequential computers, since the data structures must be sorted to be efficiently accessed and they can be ordered in only one way at a time. Frequently, auxiliary data structures such as inverted lists are employed to overcome this limitation of conventional computers.

5.5. Generalized Array Data Structure Codes

Arrays are the canonical forms of data structures. As shown in Fig. 5-6, their address functions form a natural hierarchy of complexity. Scalars are zero-

ADDRESS FUNC TYPE	EXAMPLE	ARRAY TYPE
constant	a	0-dimensional
constant+x_1	a(x_1)	1-dimensional
constant+x_1+x_2	a(x_1,x_2)	2-dimensional
constant+x_1+..+x_n	a(x_1,..+x_n)	n-dimensional

Figure 5-6. A hierarchy of address functions.

dimensional arrays. They are represented by the class of address functions consisting only of constants. The address functions for one-dimensional arrays each consists of constants plus one variable. Two-dimensional arrays have two-variable address functions, and so on. The most common example of address functions for arrays are the row-major and column-major ordering functions generated automatically for indexed arrays by most high-order languages such as FORTRAN, Pascal, and C.

One-dimensional arrays can be stored using a straightforward extension of scalar structure codes. The structure code consists of the object name (the constant portion of the address function) and the position of the value in the construct (the variable portion of the address function). The variable component for one-dimensional arrays is simply the ordinal position of the data element in the array. Thus, for example, the one-dimensional object $A = (1\ 5\ 4\ 3\ 2)$ would have the structure code shown in Fig. 5-7.

The structure code for two-dimensional arrays is a natural extension of one-dimensional arrays as shown in Fig. 5-8. The extension of structure codes to higher-dimensional arrays is obvious. Canonical-array structure codes can be composed to make structure codes for arbitrarily complex compound data structures.

One-dimensional arrays are logical data structures that are natural for use with several common problem data structures such as vectors, lists, and strings. Two-dimensional arrays are logical data structures which are natural for dealing

structure code		data element
constant part	variable part	
object name	element position	value
A	1	1
A	2	5
A	3	4
A	4	3
A	5	2

Figure 5-7. A one-dimensional array.

structure code			data element	
constant part	variable part			
object name	row position	col	value	
B	1	1	5	
B	1	2	3	B=(5 3)
B	2	1	7	(7 6)
B	2	2	6	

Figure 5-8. A two-dimensional array.

with matrices and imagery. The mapping from these problem data structures to the logical data structure is the identity mapping. Consequently, for ease of reading, where no confusion can arise, the terms *vector* and *matrix* will be used interchangeably for one-dimensional and two-dimensional arrays, respectively.

5.6. Associative Data Structure References

It is not uncommon to consider matrices as collections of vectors. Thus if the constant portion of the structure code shown in Fig. 5-8 is modified to include row position, the constant address B 1 is shared by two values representing the vector (5 3) and B 2 represents (7 6). Similarly, if the constant portion is modified to include column position instead of row position, B 1 represents $(5\ 7)^{-1}$ and B 2 represents $(3\ 6)^{-1}$.

An important property of structure codes is the ability to reorganize them as illustrated above. The . operator will be used to indicate the basic code grouping and can be thought of as a concatenation operator. The symbol $ is used as a placeholder. Thus the code B.1.$ represents the vector (5 3), B.$.2 represents $(3\ 6)^{-1}$, and so on. (The . operator is not currently implemented.)

5.7. Data Structure Code Manipulation

The concept of combining data structures to form new data structures at run time is common in some languages, such as Lisp. For example, lists can be grouped together to form lists of lists, and so on. This can be done because of the generalized method of data storage for lists. However, in conventional languages, this capability is not easily extended to other types of data structures such as arrays. In associative computing, it is possible to create new data structures from existing data structures at run time for all types of data organizations. That is, structures such as arrays of arrays of lists of arrays can be generated, decomposed, and manipulated with ease.

In order to describe how the structure codes for two arbitrary data structures can be combined to generate the structure codes for a combined data structure, several definitions are necessary. Let DS_j be a data structure of dimension r with address function A_j. Then $A_j = a_j0.a_j1..a_jr$ are the $r+1$ components of the structure code. By convention, the 0th component is the constant portion which is the name of the data structure. Let $A_j(m)$ stand for the structure code of A_j for the mth element of DS_j. Let 0^1 denote the constant value 0, 0^2 denote 0.0, 0^3 denote 0.0.0, and so on. Then 0^n denotes the constant zero-structure code for a function with n components. Similarly, let $A^n(x)$ denote the first (leftmost) n components of a structure code. The depth of a component is equivalent to the number of components to its left.

Then if DS_l is the complex data structure obtained by inserting data structure DS_k, with dimension s, as the mth element of the DS_j, with dimension r, at depth d, the address function A_l for DS_l has dimension $d + s$ and is given by

$$\begin{aligned} A_l(x) &= A_j(x).0^{d+s-r} && \text{for } x \neq m \\ A_l(x) &= A_j^d(x).A_k(y) && \text{for } x = m, \\ & && \text{for all } y \text{ in } DS_k \end{aligned}$$

The data structure insertion operation is denoted by

receiving_data_structure$\|$
[element,depth]inserted_data_structure.

If a complex structure is to be built by a number of insertions, they may occur in any order; i.e., if $m_1 \neq m_2$, then

$$(A_l \,\|[m_1,d_1]\, A_k) \,\|[m_2,d_2]\, A_j = (A_l \,\|[m_2,d_2]\, A_j) \,\|[m_1,d_1]\, A_k.$$

Figure 5-9 gives an example. DS_a is an "empty" vector with address function $A_a = (1\ 2)$. DS_b and DS_c are both matrices with the same address function $A_b = A_c = (1.1, 1.2, 2.1, 2.2)$. The composition $A = (A_a \,\|[1,1]\, A_c) \,\|[2,1]\, A_b$ is shown. Clearly, arbitrarily complex hierarchical data structures can be composed from the basic canonical forms.

Figure 5-10 shows the conventional nested-loop statements required by a conventional language (such as C, FORTRAN, or Pascal) to perform the same operation. Note that the data must be physically moved (resorted) so that the physical memory layout maps correctly onto the logical layout. This requires that the number of items in all arrays be known at run time. In associative programming languages that use structure codes, the address function is modified as specified by the address-composition function above. The number of data items is immaterial, and the intent of the data reorganization is clear. The new address function is not hidden inside a number of loops that need to be untangled.

	Aa	Value
DSa	1	nil
DSa	2	nil

DSa=
(nil nil)

	Ab	Value
DSb	1.1	7
DSb	1.2	14
DSb	2.1	3
DSb	2.2	8

DSb=(7 14)
(3 8)

	Ac	Value
DSc	1.1	9
DSc	1.2	15
DSc	2.1	6
DSc	2.2	2

DSc=(9 15)
(6 2)

OBJ NAME	VEC POS	MAT R	MAT C	VAL
A	2	1	1	7
A	2	1	2	14
A	2	2	1	3
A	2	2	2	8
A	1	1	1	9
A	1	1	2	15
A	1	2	1	6
A	1	2	2	2

A =
((9 15) (7 14))
((6 2) (3 8))

Figure 5-9. A vector of matrices.

The structure-code mechanism is completely general. Lists, for example, are simply a special case of data structures. They are vectors whose elements are atoms or other lists. Address-function composition can be applied to list-structure codes to generate the structure codes for any complex nested list. Figure 5-11 illustrates the structure codes for a list. Section 5.9 describes lists in more detail. Since, as described above, arrays and data structures are both just generalizations of associations, the application of this technique to data structures is straightforward, although not as intuitive.

```
for (i=1, i<2, i++)
  for (j=1, j<2, j++)
    { a[2,i,j] = b[i,j];
      a[1,i,j] = c[i,j];
    }
```

Figure 5-10. Conventional data reorganization.

OBJECT NAME	VECTOR POSITION	VECTOR POSITION	VECTOR POSITION	VALUE
LIST	1	0	0	THIS
LIST	2	1	0	IS
LIST	2	2	1	A
LIST	2	2	2	LIST

LIST = (THIS (IS (A LIST)))

Figure 5-11. A list.

5.8. Synonymous Data Structures

In some applications, it is desirable to view data structures in two or more ways. For example, a string can be thought of as a single variable containing a list of characters or as an array of characters. As can be seen in Fig. 5-12, this dual approach to referencing strings is a natural artifact of using associative addressing techniques. The string as a whole can be accessed by the structure code S.$, while the *n*th character in the string can be accessed by S.n. Note that this capability is due to the parallel-associative implementation of structure codes and does not require multiple variable declarations or equivalences.

5.9. Lists and Linked Lists

Lisp list representation is a good example of the use of linked lists. In conventional sequential computers, the linked-list mechanism allows lists to be searched, divided, and concatenated easily. New list segments can be inserted into the middle of existing lists. Lists can be searched for specific items or patterns, and

S = "A STRING"

OBJECT NAME	POSITION	VALUE
S	1	A
S	2	
S	3	S
S	4	T
S	5	R
S	6	I
S	7	N
S	8	G
S	9	null

Figure 5-12. A string.

sections can be deleted from anywhere in the list. The only problem with the linked-list data structure is that link following is inherently sequential.

Fortunately for associative processors, the data structure code mechanism described in section 5.7 can be used to represent Lisp lists in particular and any type of linked list in general. Moreover, structure codes allow lists to be manipulated as easily in array processors as they are in sequential computers, and in addition, all of the elements of a list can be searched and processed in parallel.

Normally, Lisp lists are stored as binary trees, as illustrated in Fig. 5-13. But Lisp lists can be represented as conventional tree structures also. A node in the tree may be either an atom or a sublist. Atoms are at the leaves of the tree. Sublists are at internal nodes. The root of the tree is associated with the entire list.

In a tree, the level of the root node is 0. The level of any other node is 1 plus the level of its parent. The component position of a node is obtained by counting the number of siblings to its left, including itself. For example, in Fig. 5-14, if node A is at level n, then children X, Y, and Z are at level $n+1$, and the component position of X is one, Y is two, and of Z is three.

Figure 5-15 shows how lists can be stored using structure codes that are composed of the component position numbers ordered by level. Note that only leaf (atom[$]) nodes are listed. The structure code (sc[$]) of a leaf node is given by the position number of each node on the path from the root to that leaf node. The path is specified from left to right, with the level-0 position being the most significant digit. If there are fewer nodes than digits in the code, the code is zero-filled on the right. The position of the root node is not specified, since it is the same for all atoms in the list. Instead, the name of the list is specified in a separate field (dsid[$]).

For example, the first level of the tree structure shown in Fig. 5-13 consists of three components, the atom THIS and two sublists, (IS A) and (NESTED (LISP LIST)). The number of the component position for THIS is one, and it is stored in the leftmost digit of the code with 0 fill on the right. The second component sublist has two sub-subcomponents, IS and A. Their structure codes consist of the

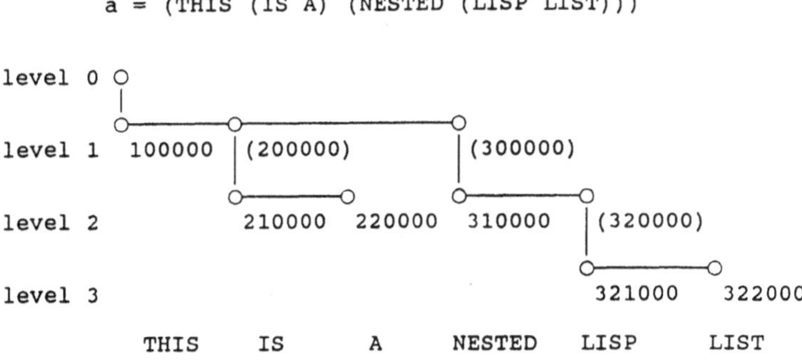

Figure 5-13. A list in binary tree form.

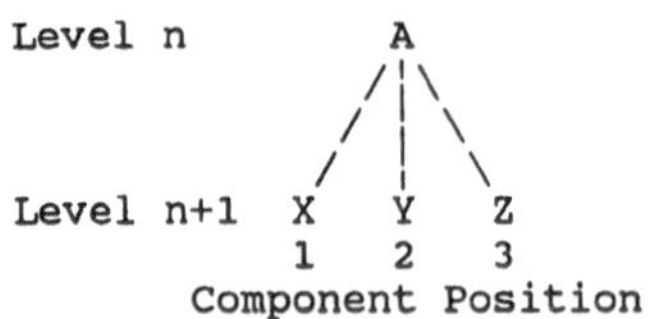

Figure 5-14. Level and position defined on a tree.

component position of their parent node, 2, and their own component position, 1 or 2 followed by 0 fill, giving 210000 as the code for IS and 220000 as the code for A. The third component sublist has an atom and another sublist as sub-subcomponents. The structure code for the atom is the code of the parent node, 3, plus its position code, 1, with 0 fill; thus NESTED has the code 310000. Finally, the codes for the sub-sublist consisting of (LISP LIST), is obtained by the digit for the position code of the grandparent, 3, followed by the position code for the parent, 2, and then the code for each of the component atoms, 1 and 2. This gives 321000 and 322000 for LISP and LIST, respectively.

The entire list and sublists of the interior nodes can be found in one parallel step by searching. For example, the sublist, (NESTED (LISP LIST)), which is in the third component position, is represented by the interior node whose code is 300000. All of the components of the list including the nested sublist can be identified by searching for all nodes with values greater than or equal to its component position and less than its next-right sibling's structure code, 400000.

5.10. Structure-Code Functions

Six functions are provided in ASC to facilitate list structure-code manipulation. They are **fstcd, prvcd, nxtcd, trncd, trnacd**, and **prefix**. Table 5-1 details the workings of these functions. Figure 5-16 shows the effect of the structure-code functions on an abstract list tree. The **fstcd** (first structure code) function returns the structure code of the first child of the input node. The **prvcd** (previous structure code) function returns the structure code of the sibling node to the left of

dsid[$]	sc[$]	atom[$]
a	100000	THIS
a	210000	IS
a	220000	A
a	310000	NESTED
a	321000	LISP
a	322000	LIST

a=(THIS (IS A) (NESTED (LISP LIST)))

Figure 5-15. Structure codes for a list.

Table 5-1. Effects of Structure-Code Functions

Function	Input code	Output code
fstcd	122000	122100
prvcd	122000	121000
ntxcd	122000	123000
trncd	122000	120000
trnacd	122000	100000
prefix	122000	122

the current node. If the current node is the leftmost sibling, an error indication is returned. The **nxtcd** (next structure code) function returns the structure code of the sibling node to the right of the current node. If the current node has the maximum value of 15 (F in hexadecimal) in its rightmost nonzero digit, the function returns an error indication. Also, in general, it may return a code for a node which is not present in the tree. The **trncd** (truncate structure code) function returns the code of the parent of the current node by zeroing the rightmost nonzero digit of the input code. The **trnacd** (truncate all structure code) function returns the code of the ancestor node which is the first descendant of the root node of the tree. It is obtained by truncating all but the leftmost digit of the input code. The **prefix** function returns the left nonzero digits of a structure code. This function is used to obtain structure-code fragments that can be used to generate new structure codes by concatenation.

5.11. List Manipulation

As an example of list manipulation, consider inserting the list *b* in place of atom *A* in list *a* of Fig. 5-17a. The ASC code is shown in Fig. 5-18. Figure 5-17

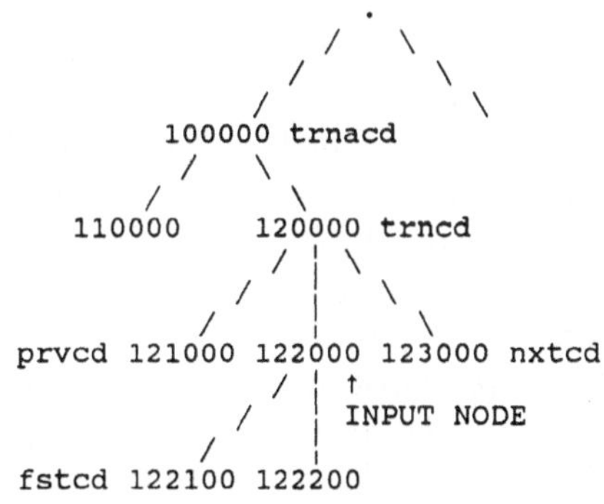

Figure 5-16. The list functions illustrated on a tree.

dsid[$]	sc[$]	atom[$]
a	100000	THIS
a	210000	IS
a	220000	A
a	310000	NESTED
a	321000	LISP
a	322000	LIST
b	100000	AN
b	200000	ASC

a=(THIS (IS A) (NESTED (LISP LIST)))
b=(AN ASC)

a - Lists Before Insertion

dsid[$]	sc[$]	atom[$]
a	100000	THIS
a	210000	IS
a	310000	NESTED
a	321000	LISP
a	322000	LIST
a	221000	AN
a	222000	ASC

a=(THIS (IS (AN ASC)) (NESTED (LISP LIST)))

b - List After Insertion Operation of a ¦¦[2,2] b

Figure 5-17. List manipulation.

shows the list data structures before and after insertion. Note that the data is not moved; the insertion is achieved by changing the structure name and structure codes. The row with atom *A* is blank in Fig. 5-17b to indicate that the associated memory cell has been released and therefore is not logically present, but actually is still there.

The first step in Fig. 5-18 is to find the atom *A* in list *a*. This task requires only one step since the atoms of the list can be searched in parallel. *A* is deleted from the list. Only one step is needed, since the **release** statement simply resets the local associative and global cell busy/idle flags.

Then the elements of list *b* are inserted into list *a* in parallel by concatenating the prefix of the structure code for *A* onto the structure codes for *b*. The concatenation is achieved in one pass by moving the digits of the *b* structure codes to the right and inserting the *A* structure code digits on the left. The scd (structure code digits) and sc (structure code) fields are aligned by the **defvar** and **hex** parallel statements in Fig. 5-18 so that an index value of 0 for scd is the leftmost digit of sc and an index of 5 is the rightmost digit (see Fig. 5-19).

If the prefix of variable *A*'s code were modified with the **prvcd** or **nxtcd**

```
define(CODESIZE, 6);
defvar (scd, sc);

int scalar delta,i,j;
hex parallel sc:24[$], scd:4[$,6], scsize:4[$];
index parallel xx[$];
logical parallel dsbi[$], list[$];
char parallel dsid[$], atom[$];

    :
/* Find atom A in list a */
get xx in dsid[$] .eq. "a" .and. atom[$] .eq. "A"
    release xx[$] from list[$];
/* Insert b at A's location */
    delta = CODESIZE - scsize[xx];
    if dsid[$] .eq. "b" then
      j=0;
      loop
          i=j+delta;
          loop
            scd[$,i] = scd[$,i-1];
            i = i-1;
            until i .le. j
          endloop;
          scd[$,j] = scd[xx,j];
          j = j+1;
          until j .ge. delta
      endloop;
      dsid[$] = "a";
      scsize[$] = scsize[$]+delta;
    endif;
endget xx;
    :
```

Figure 5-18. ASC code for list insertion.

function before inserting it into list *b*'s codes, list *b* would be inserted before or after atom *A*. However, when inserting in front of or behind an atom, caution must be exercised to avoid generating a structure code that already exists. In section 5.13, a paragraph describes how the list input function **scin** can leave holes in a list's data structure that can be filled in later.

Sublists are deleted from a list by the **release** statement in the same way the single atom *A* was deleted in Fig. 5-18. When one or more atoms are deleted, a hole may appear in the tree structure. The **nxtcd** and **prvcd** functions, which simply modify an input structure code, do not check for holes. In addition they may generate codes which are not present in the tree even though the input node may have siblings. There are three search functions which search the structure-code field to find the next and previous siblings in these cases.

```
 sc:   ssssssssssssssssssssssss
scd:   000011112222333344445555
```

Figure 5-19. Structure code alignment.

5.12. Structure-Code Searching Functions

The three functions are **nxtdex**, **prvdex**, and **sibdex**. **Nxtdex** and **prvdex** have second forms, **nxtval** and **prvval**, analogous to **mindex/minval** and **maxdex/maxval**. The **nxtdex** function is equivalent to a greater-than search followed by a **mindex** search, as illustrated in Fig. 5-20. The **nxtdex** function itself, however, is an assembly-language routine that combines the search and **mindex** operation into one function that takes no more time to perform than either a search or the **mindex** function alone (see section 2.8 for more details on implementation). The **nxtval** function performs the same searches as **nxtdex**, but extracts and returns the value at the node found. Both functions return 0 if the input code is the largest code in the structure.

The **nxtdex** function skips holes of any size. Figure 5-20 shows that **nxtdex** finds the next-largest node in the structure, whether it is an interior node or a leaf node, and that it finds interior nodes before their descendants. Recall, however, that in a list structure, interior nodes are not listed.

Prvdex is similar to **nxtdex**. **Prvdex** is composed of a search for the structure codes less than the input code and then a search for the maximum code among the responders. The above comments about **nxtdex** and **nxtval**, modified in the obvious ways, apply to **prvdex** and **prvval**.

Sibdex is a combination of **nxtdex** and **prvdex**. That is, given an input

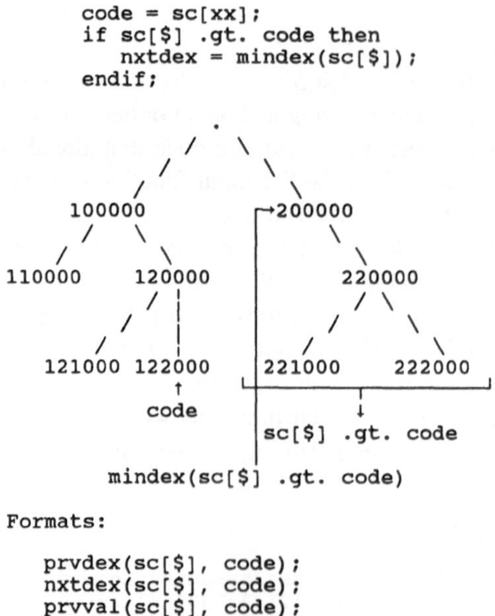

Figure 5-20. The effect of the **nxtdex** function.

structure code, **sibdex** returns two parallel-index variables that flag the **nxtdex** and **prvdex** nodes. This function is very useful for expression parsing. Consider the example in Fig. 5-21. Once an operator has been selected, its operands can be identified in one step by the **sibdex** function. In Fig. 5-21, **nxtcd** and **prvcd** can be used to find the operands, but once the operation has been reduced to the (temporary) result *temp*, as shown in Fig. 5-22, there are holes in the data structure which **nxtcd** and **prvcd** can not handle. However, the **sibdex** function can handle both the initial case before any reduction and subsequent cases after any number of reductions.

The **nxtdex, prvdex,** and **sibdex** functions are extensions of the **mindex** and **maxdex** functions. The original **mindex, maxdex, prvdex,** and **nxtdex** algorithms are described in Falkoff [1962]. These routines illustrate the power of the one-dimensional parallelism of an associative array of processors. They enable the associative array to find in one step data items with a specific relationship to another item. On a conventional parallel (multiple-instruction, multiple-data) computer, the searches require at least log *n* steps, and on a sequential computer they take *n* log *n* steps. See Chapter 2 for more detail.

5.13. Structure-Code I/O (SCIO)

There are several special I/O functions for inputing and outputing lists. The two basic functions are **scin** (structure-code input) and **scot** (structure-code output). **Scin** expects a parenthesized list as input. It generates the internal structure-code representation and returns a flag field marking the newly generated

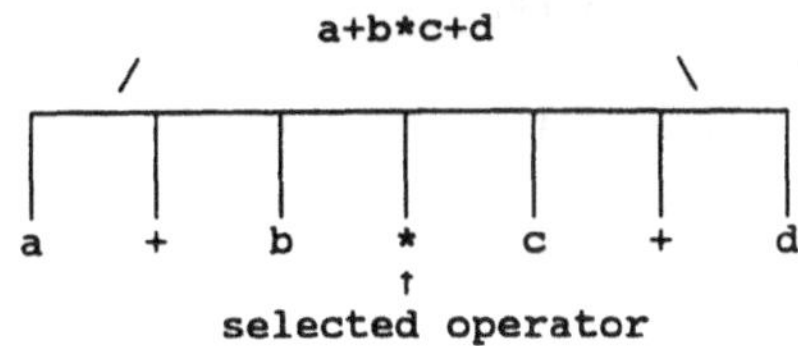


```
define (MULT,42);
operator[$] = atom[$] .eq. MULT;
operands[$] = sc[$] .eq. prvcd(sc[operator[$]]) .or.
              sc[$] .eq. nxtcd(sc[operator[$]]) ;
```

sc[$]	atom[$]	operator[$]	operands[$]
..10	a	0	0
..20	+	0	0
..30	b	0	1
..40	*	1	0
..50	c	0	1
..60	+	0	0
..70	d	0	0

Figure 5-21. Reduction.

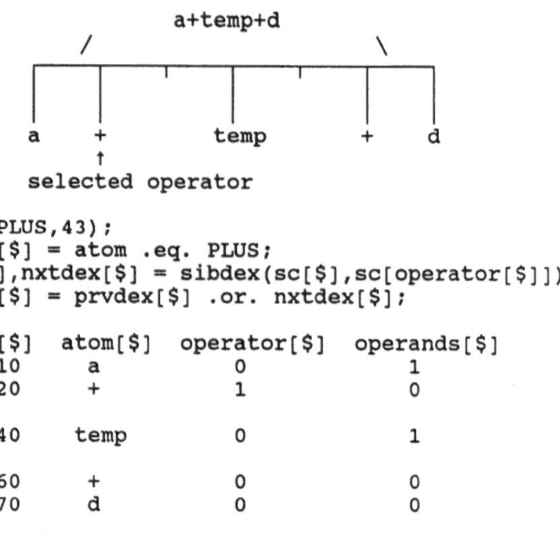

a+temp+d
a
+
temp
+
d
selected operator
define (PLUS,43);
operator[$] = atom .eq. PLUS;
prvdex[$],nxtdex[$] = sibdex(sc[$],sc[operator[$]]);
operands[$] = prvdex[$] .or. nxtdex[$];
sc[$] atom[$] operator[$] operands[$]
..10 a 0 1
..20 + 1 0
..40 temp 0 1
..60 + 0 0
..70 d 0 0
Format
sibdex(sc[$], code)

Figure 5-22. Reduction using **sibdex**.

entries. **Scot** takes an internal structure-code field, atom field, and busy/idle flag and outputs a parenthesized list. For example, **scin** would input the list

(THIS (IS A) (NESTED (LISP LIST)))

and produce

sc[$]	atom[$]	bi[$]
100000	THIS	1
210000	IS	1
220000	A	1
310000	NESTED	1
321000	LISP	1
322000	LIST	1

while **scot** inputs the latter and outputs the former.

There are four different versions of **scin** and **scot**. Figure 5-23 gives their format. The standard **scin** function operates as described above. It assumes that the structure-code field is six digits long with four bits per digit. **Scin8** is similar to **scin** except that it assumes a six-digit structure-code field with eight bits per digit. **Scin** is sufficient for most general-purpose applications, allowing six levels of nesting and 16 branches per node. **Scin8** also allows six levels of nesting but accommodates 256 branches per node. Since most structure-code manipulation is bit-serial, **scin** executes approximately twice as fast as **scin8**. (Section 5.13.2 and

```
┌      ┐
│scin  │
│scin8 │ (atom_field, sc_field, busy/idle_flag);
│scinl │
└      ┘
scinp (atom_field, sc_field, busy/idle_flag,
       pred_id, head_flag, term_id, pred_flag);

┌      ┐
│scot  │
│scot8 │ (atom_field, sc_field, busy/idle_flag);
│scotl │
│scotp │
└      ┘

┌      ┐
│scst  │
│scst8 │ (atom_field, sc_field, busy/idle_flag, list);
│scstl │
│scstp │
└      ┘
scstp (atom_field, sc_field, busy/idle_flag,
       pred_id, head_flag, term_id, pred_flag);
```

Figure 5-23. Scin/scot/scst formats.

Fig. 5-28 give an example of structure-code association declaration and manipulation.)

Scinl is the same as **scin** except that it terminates sublists explicitly with a nil, as shown in Fig. 5-24. **Scinp** produces a structure code suitable for Prolog, where the predicate is the parent node of its arguments and lists are terminated by nils (see Fig. 5-25). These last two functions are provided to establish a common format with existing systems. If format consistency is not of concern, the standard structure code and **scin** and **scot** can be used just as effectively as **scinl**, **scinp**, **scotl**, and **scotp**.* More details on **scinp** are given in section 9.8.

The **scin** algorithm increments the position counter when a comma is encountered, allowing holes to be inserted into the structure code. For example, the list (THIS, IS) would have the structure code shown in Fig. 5-26. Thus, if list *a* in Fig. 5-17 had been specified as a=(THIS (IS ,) (NESTED (LISP LIST))), we could have inserted list *b* into the hole directly instead of having to search for atom *A*, provided the structure code of the hole was known.

The last set of functions in Fig. 5-23, the **scst** functions, allow the programmer to specify list constants at compile time and save the location of the hole. For example,

type[$] = scst(atom[$], sc[$], bi[$], (, type , , ,));
value[$] = scst (atom[$], sc[$], bi[$], (, , , , value));
result[$] = scst(atom[$], sc[$], bi[$], (the, answer is,)) .or. type [$] .or. value[$];

*In standard LISP list notation, there are often many right parentheses at the right end of the list. **Scin** allows the use of "]" to indicate the correct number of closing right parentheses, for example, (THIS (IS A) (NESTED (LISP LIST].

```
sc[$]     atom[$]
100000     THIS
210000     IS
220000     A
230000     nil
310000     NESTED
321000     LISP
322000     LIST
323000     nil
330000     nil
400000     nil

(THIS (IS A) (NESTED (LISP LIST)))
```

Figure 5-24. A terminated list.

will cause the following data structure to be generated:

sc[$]	atom[$]
200000	TYPE
500000	VALUE
100000	THE
300000	ANSWER
400000	IS

These functions are used primarily for generating templates which can be filled with atoms during processing and then output as messages. The commas in the above example provide holes for variables to be inserted later. For example,

```
atom[type[$]] = BEST;
atom[value[$]] = YES;
scot(atom[$], sc[$], result[$]);
```

where BEST and YES are equivalenced to the appropriate ASCII constant, will result in

```
sc[$]     atom[$]
100000     THIS
110000     IS
111000     A
112000     nil
120000     NESTED
121000     PROLOG
121100     LIST
121200     nil
130000     nil
200000     nil

THIS(IS(A) NESTED(PROLOG(LIST)))
```

Figure 5-25. A Prolog list.

```
sc[$]   atom[$]
100000   THIS
300000   IS
```

Figure 5-26. Holes in structure codes.

(THE BEST ANSWER IS YES)

A more detailed example of the use of **scin**, **scot**, and **scst** is given in section 5.13.4.

5.13.1. Associative Scanning

All of the **scin** routines assume that the input character stream has been scanned and broken into tokens. This section describes a short algorithm for scanning a string and breaking it into tokens in an associative computer. The algorithm as shown in Fig. 5-27 assumes that the characters in the input stream are initially stored one character per PE in a contiguously allocated block.

The algorithm begins by spreading the character field into neighboring PEs so as to produce all possible initial permutations of the tokens in the input stream. In Fig. 5-28, it is assumed for simplicity that the maximum token length is six characters. Note that the spreading operation is very efficient, being nothing more than a move field with a one-PE shift.

After the tokens have been spread, the algorithm proceeds as a conventional sequential scanning algorithm using a finite-state automaton to recognize the tokens in parallel. The automaton has three states: in_token, token_found, and no_token. Note that all tokens (except the first and last) in the string must begin and end with a delimiter. Thus the first step is to flag each PE with a delimiter in the first (leftmost) character position as in_token. All others are marked as no_token.

The algorithm processes the characters from left to right. If a PE is in the in_token state and a second delimiter is detected, the PE's state is changed to token_found. No other action is needed. When all characters have been processed, the tokens can be processed by using **for** iteration on the PEs in the token_found state.

The algorithm given in Fig. 5-27 is the basic one. It assumes that delimiters are not tokens, and thus that 3*5 must be written as 3 * 5 (with spaces). Also, as written, there is a maximum-length token. The reader should realize that by adding a few additional states to the automaton, both of these restrictions are easily overcome.

5.13.2. The Structure-Code-Generation Algorithm

The input structure-code-generation algorithm is shown in Fig. 5-29. The algorithm basically checks for parentheses to determine the nesting level. The level of nesting determines the structure-code digit position being processed. The top level is the leftmost digit position. The bottom level (level 6) is the rightmost

```
main scanner

define(blank, 'x'20);
define(in_token, 1);
define(no_token, 2);
define(token_found, 3);
defvar(rittok, tokchr+8);
defvar(leftok, tokchr);
char parallel tokchr[$,6], leftok:40[$], rittok:40[$];
/* map of tokchr(t), rittok(r) and leftok(l)
     lllll
     tttttt
      rrrrr                              */
int parallel state[$];
logical parallel tbi[$];
index parallel xx[$];

associate tokchr[$], state[$] with tbi[$];

read tokchr[$,0] contiguously in tbi[$];
/* terminate last token with a blank */
allocate xx in tbi[$]
  tokchr[$,0] = blank;
endallocate xx;
/* spread characters */
rittok[$] = leftok[$+1];
/* scan tokens */
state[$] = no_token;
if tokchr[$,0] .eq. blank then
  /* flag the token preceeding the blank */
  state[$-1] = in_token;
endif;
/* flag first token */
state[tbi] = in_token;

i=1;
loop
  if state[$] .eq. in_token .and.
     tokchr[$,i] .eq. blank
  then
     state[$] = token_found;
  endif;
  i = i+1;
  until i .ge. 6
endloop;
end;
```

Figure 5-27. The scanner routine.

digit position. The number of atoms and sublists since the last left parenthesis on the current level is the value written into the digit. In the simple overview given here, only four token types are distinguished: left and right parenthesis, comma, and atom.

The algorithm generates a maximum-level field (mlevel[$]) which saves the maximum level of the associated structure code. That is, mlevel contains the number of nonzero digits in the code. The mlevel value is used frequently in low-level structure-code processing.

When a left parenthesis is detected, a new level is entered, signalling a move

```
Original       Spread
character      character
field          field

  a            abc^de          - first token
  b            bc^de^
  c            c^de^f
  ^            ^de^f^          - second token
  d            de^f^.
  e            e^f^..
  ^            ^f^...          - third token
  f            f^....
  ^            ^.....
  :
```

Figure 5-28. Spreading the character string.

```
subroutine gencode
/* NOTE: - Some declarations have been eliminated to
         simplify the figure  */
defvar(sc, scd);
hex parallel sc:24[$], scd:[$,6];
logical parallel list[$];
char parallel tokens[$];
int parallel mlevel[$];

associate sc[$], tokens[$], mlevel[$] with list[$];

position = 1;
level = -1;
for xx in state[$] .eq. token_found
 if token_type[$] .eq. left_paren then
   setscope .not. list[$]
     if level .ge. 0 then
        scd[$,level] = position;
     endif;
     level = level + 1;
     mlevel[$] = level+1;
   endsetscope;
   call push stack<position;
   position = 1;
 else if token_type[$] .eq. comma then
   position = position + 1;
 else if token_type[$] .eq. right_paren then
   setscope .not. list[$]
      scd[$,level] = 0;
      level = level - 1;
      mlevel[$] = level+1;
   endsetscope;
   if level .ge. 0 then call pop stack>position; endif;
   position = position + 1;
 else
   setscope .not. list[$]
     scd[$,level] = position;
   endsetscope;
   allocate xx in list[$]
      atom[xx] = token;
   endallocate xx;
   position = position + 1;
 endif;
endfor xx;
end;
```

Figure 5-29. Structure-code generation.

to the next-right digit in the structure code. Since all entries from now until the matching right parenthesis have a common left prefix representing the current position in the structure code, the structure code digit for *all unallocated* entries is set to the current position value. (This is an application of data replication during computation, section 2.13.2.) The level index is incremented and the mlevel value updated. The position value of the current level is saved on a stack, and the position value of the new level is initialized to 1 (see Fig. 5-30a). The mlevel value is shown as the rightmost (seventh) digit of the structure-code field.

When a right parenthesis is detected, it signals a return to the previous level. The effect on the structure-code association is shown in Fig. 5-30b. The unallo-

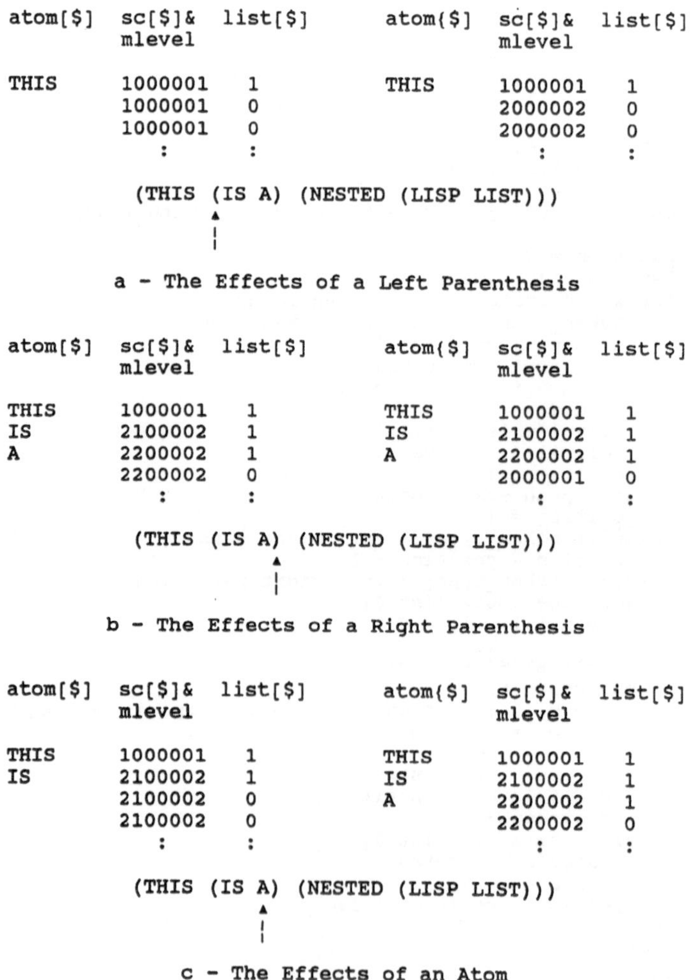

atom[$] sc[$]& mlevel list[$] atom($] sc[$]& mlevel list[$]
THIS 1000001 1 THIS 1000001 1
1000001 0 2000002 0
1000001 0 2000002 0
: : : :
(THIS (IS A) (NESTED (LISP LIST)))
a - The Effects of a Left Parenthesis
atom[$] sc[$]& mlevel list[$] atom($] sc[$]& mlevel list[$]
THIS 1000001 1 THIS 1000001 1
IS 2100002 1 IS 2100002 1
A 2200002 1 A 2200002 1
2200002 0 2000001 0
: : : :
(THIS (IS A) (NESTED (LISP LIST)))
b - The Effects of a Right Parenthesis
atom[$] sc[$]& mlevel list[$] atom($] sc[$]& mlevel list[$]
THIS 1000001 1 THIS 1000001 1
IS 2100002 1 IS 2100002 1
2100002 0 A 2200002 1
2100002 0 2200002 0
: : : :
(THIS (IS A) (NESTED (LISP LIST)))
c - The Effects of an Atom

Figure 5-30. The effects of the different token types.

cated entries must be updated, and the position value of the previous level must be restored. Before returning to the previous level, the structure-code digit of each unallocated entry corresponding to the current level is reset to 0. The level index is decremented to update it to the value of the previous level, and the mlevel field of the unallocated entries is updated to reflect the decreases in structure-code length.

The atom token type provides for the processing of atoms on the given level. The position value for the current level for all unallocated entries must be updated. One of the unallocated entries with the correct structure code is allocated, and the token is stored in the atom field. The position value is then incremented. The effect of this action is shown in Fig. 5-30c.

The fourth case is that of commas. Since commas leave holes in the data structure, the only action that needs to be taken is to increment the position counter.

Figure 5-31 shows the structure-code fields at the intermediate point of just having processed token *A* and illustrates how they change for the next three tokens. The sc and token fields are not in the same association and are not physically aligned as indicated in the figure. In particular, there are never any parentheses or commas in the **scin** or **scot** atom field. The alignment is used to illustrate the action taken in the structure-code association in response to processing the tokens in the input association.

When token *A* is processed, two left parentheses have been scanned, causing the left two digits of all the then unallocated entries to be preloaded and the mlevel value to be set to 2. Token *A* is an atom case and updates the unallocated scd[$,1] to 2 before the next cell is allocated and *A* is moved into the atom field. This is the state shown in the left sc[$] column of Fig. 5-31. Again, the mlevel value is shown as the rightmost digit of the structure-code field. The arrowhead to the left of the column points to the token just processed.

The next token is a right parenthesis, which causes the second digit of the

```
tokens[$]   sc[$]& list  sc[$]& list  sc[$]& list  sc[$]& list
& atom[$]   mlevel [$]   mlevel [$]   mlevel [$]   mlevel [$]
  (
  THIS      1000001 1    1000001 1    1000001 1    1000001 1
  (
  IS        2100002 1    2100002 1    2100002 1    2100002 1
  A        ◂2200002 1    2200002 1    2200002 1    2200002 1
  )                     ◂
  (                                  ◂
  NESTED    2200002 0    2000001 0    3000002 0   ◂3100002 1
  (
  LISP      2200002 0    2000001 0    3000002 0    3100002 0
  LIST      2200002 0    2000001 0    3000002 0    3100002 0
  )          ▴            ▴            ▴            ▴
  )          |            |            |            |
  )         level 2      level 1      level 2      level 2
            position 2   position 3   position 1   position 2
```

Figure 5-31. The effects of the structure-code-generation algorithm.

unallocated entries to be cleared. Level is decremented, mlevel is updated, and position is restored from the top of the stack and then incremented (to 3). This last procedure allows the algorithm to count a parenthesized sublist with any number of elements as just one element on the current level. This result is shown in the second-from-left sc[$] column.

The left parenthesis that is scanned next causes the left digit of the unassigned entries to be updated to the current position (3), and then the level incremented to 2, the mlevel updated, and the position count reset to 1 as shown in the third sc[$] column from the left.

The rightmost column shows the result of processing token NESTED. Similar to A, the atom case causes the current position value to be written in the current-level digit of the unallocated entries, so that, when the next cell is allocated and the token is moved into the atom field, the structure code will have been set to the correct value. The position count is incremented in anticipation of the next atom.

5.13.3. The List-Generation Algorithm

Just as pronouncing words backwards is more complex than simply reading them from right to left, the **scot** algorithm is considerably different from **scin**. In particular, **scin** threw away the explicit structure information (i.e., parentheses and commas) and encoded it in the structure-code notation. For example, the length of the nonzero portion of the structure code represents the level of the associated atom in the nested list.

Scot is the inverse of **scin** in that **scin** assigned to the input atoms structured codes in increasing order. **Scot** searches for the lowest structure codes first and outputs them in order. The complication is determining the number and type of parenthesis (if any) to print between adjacent atoms. As control flows from one atom to the next, there are three cases to consider:

1. the structure codes of the two atoms are of the same length,
2. the structure code of the first atom is shorter than that of the second, and
3. the structure code of the first is longer than that of the second.

Each of these cases has two subcases. In the easiest subcase, there are either no, all left, or all right parentheses between atoms. In the more difficult case, there may be both left and right parentheses between atoms.

Figure 5-32 illustrates the easy subcase for all three cases. In Fig. 5-32a, case 1, the structure codes are of the same length and are identical except for the last digit, which differs by only one. This case means that the two atoms should be printed as consecutive atoms in a list. If the last digit differs by more than one, say n, then there are holes in the list, and if holes are to be printed,* $n-1$ commas must be printed between the two atoms.

*In many applications where only the relative ordering is important, it is desirable to ignore holes when printing the output list.

```
sc[$] atom[$]     sc[$] atom[$]     sc[$] atom[$]

112000   a        112000   a        112400   a
113000   b        113100   b        113000   b

 ...a b...         ...a (b...        ...a) b...


112430   a        112000   a        112430   a
112450   b        114110   b        114000   b

 ...a,b...         ...a,((b...       ...a)),b...

 a - Case 1        b - Case 2        c - Case 3
```

Figure 5-32. Relationship between structure codes and parentheses.

Figure 5-32b shows case 2. Here the code for the first atom is shorter than the code for the second. The initial portions of the codes are identical up to the last digit of the shorter code. This leftmost-differing digit is called the *branch digit*. In this case, the difference in code length signals a difference in list levels to be indicated in list form by left parentheses between the two atoms. The number of parentheses is determined by the difference in length of the code—one parenthesis per digit, as illustrated. Again, if the branch digits differ by more than one, holes may be printed if desired.

Case 3, shown in Fig. 5-32c, is the mirror image of case 2. Thus the first code is longer than the second, and right parentheses instead of left are printed.

Now consider case 1 in Fig. 5-33a. It shows the difficult subcase in which both the left and right parentheses must be printed between the atoms. Since the codes are of the same length, the atoms must be on the same level. However, since the branch digit is not in the last position of the structure code, the atoms must be in different sublists. Accordingly, if the branch digit is at level *l*, *l* sets of right and left parentheses must be printed. Note that all right, then all left parenthesis must be printed to achieve ". . a)) ((b . .", not ". . a) () (b . ." or ". . a() ()b . .".

The difficult subcase of case 2 shown in Fig. 5-33b can be interpreted directly

```
sc[$] atom[$]     sc[$] atom[$]     sc[$] atom[$]

123000   a        123000   a        112400   a
131000   b        131100   b        121000   b

...a)(b...        ...a)((b...       ...a))(b...


123200   a        123000   a        112430   a
131100   b        131110   b        121000   b

...a))((b...      ...a)(((b...      ...a)))(b...

 a - Case 1        b - Case 2        c - Case 3
```

Figure 5-33. The effect of both left and right parentheses.

from the preceding cases. In particular, it is a combination of the difficult subcase of case 1 and the easy subcase of case 2. Therefore, the number of right- and left-parenthesis sets is determined by the distance of the branch digit from the end of the shortest code. The number of additional right parentheses is determined by the difference in the lengths of the codes as in the easy subcase of case 2.

The processing of the difficult subcase of case 3, shown in Fig. 5-33c, can be determined by a straightforward analogy of the previous cases.

By reviewing the above analysis, it can be seen that the procedure for generating lists from structure-code associations is to print atoms in the order of their structure codes from smallest to largest. By saving the structure code of the previously printed atom, the number of right and left parentheses to be printed before printing the current atom can be determined. First, one right parenthesis is printed for every digit by which the previous code is longer than the current code. Second, a right parenthesis is printed for every nonzero digit to the right of the branch digit. Third, a left parenthesis is printed for every nonzero digit to the right of the branch digit. Then a left parenthesis is printed for every digit by which the previous code is shorter than the current one. Finally, the atom is printed. The algorithm works correctly even for the first atom in a list, if the previous structure code is initialized to all 0s. It is shown in Fig. 5-34. The algorithm can be augmented in the obvious ways to print commas for holes, as discussed previously.

5.13.4. An Example of Structure-Code I/O

The association in Fig. 5-35 represents a semantic network. The **while** loop in the code shown in Fig. 5-36 will search the data base following the IS_A link. The nested **for** loop will print all foods that the current animal will eat. The combined program will print all the foods the initial animal and its superclasses will eat.

The *a* lines in Fig. 5-36 will generate the structure-code association shown below:

psc[$]	pel[$]
100000	ANIMAL
500000	FOOD
200000	LIKES
300000	TO
400000	EAT

The outer **while** loop changes the an_slot element as it searches up the network. The inner **for** loop changes the fd_slot element as the various foods are found. Starting with SYLVIA assigned to animal will result in the output

(CAT LIKES TO EAT FISH)
(CARNIVORE LIKES TO EAT MEAT)

```
prvcod = 0;
prvlen = 0;
active[$] = scbi[$];
loop
  until nany scli[$]
  nextok[$] = mindex(sc[$]);
  stcode = sc[nextok];
  length = mlevel[nextok];
  call findbranch code1<stcode code2<prvcod result>branch;
  /* calculate differences */
  i = prvlen-length;
  j = 0;
  if i .lt. 0 then j = -i; i = 0; endif;
  k = length-branch;
  if k .lt. 0 then k = 0; endif;
  /* print )s */
  l = i+k;
  loop
    until l .le. 0
    msg ")";
    l = l-1;
  endloop;
  /* print (s */
  l = j+k;
  loop
    until l .le. 0
    msg "(";
    l = l-1;
  endloop;
  /* print token */
  msg token[nextok];
  release nextok[$] from scbi[$];
endloop;
end;
```

Figure 5-34. The generate-list algorithm.

5.14. Structure Codes for Graphs

Many structure code formulations can be developed. In this chapter, a code designed for trees based on the concepts of tree level and node position was developed and discussed. Potter [1983] describes an approach based directly on the binary tree representation of Lisp lists. Structure codes can be designed for any type of data structure, but *n*-dimensional arrays typically do not need them, since the regular data structure allows indices to be calculated and data files do not

```
object     attribute  value

sylvia     is_a       cheetah
cheetah    is_a       cat
cat        eats       fish
cat        is_a       carnivore
carnivore  eats       meat
```

Figure 5-35. A semantic network.

```
main zoo

define (EATS, 'x'65617473);
define (IS_A, 'x'69735f61);

char scalar animal;
index parallel xx[$], an_slot[$], fd_slot[$];
char parallel pname[$], object[$], attribute[$], value[$],
              pel[$];
int parallel psc[$];
logical parallel pbi[$];

associate pname[$] psc[$] pel[$] with pbi[$];
associate object[$] attribute[$] value[$] with zoo[$];

an_slot[$]  = scst(pel[$],psc[$],pbi[$],(ANIMAL , , , ,));      a
fd_slot[$]  = scst(pel[$],psc[$],pbi[$],( , , , , FOOD));       a
result[$]   = scst(pel[$],psc[$],pbi[$],(, LIKES TO EAT ,))     a
              .or. an_slot[$] .or. fd_slot[$];                  a

read object[$] attribute[$] value[$] in zoo[$];

unproc[$] = zoo[$];
animal = object[zoo];

while xx in object[$]    .eq. animal .and.
            attribute[$] .eq. EATS   .and.
            unproc[$]
  unproc[$] = FALSE;
  animal = value[xx];
  pel[an_slot] = animal;
  for yy in object[$]    .eq. animal .and.
            attribute[$] .eq. EATS
      pel[fd_slot] = value[yy];
      scot(pel[$], psc[$], result[$]);
  endfor yy;
endwhile xx;
end;
```

Figure 5-36. An example of SCIO for messages.

normally need them because there is typically no structure between records in a file.

The structure code described here, however, in addition to being used on trees, can be used on any general graph. Consider the problem of performing a topological sort on a directed acyclic graph (dag). In the dag shown in Fig. 5-37, the two paths from the root node to the common subexpression ($a + i$) give the + node two structure codes, as shown in Fig. 5-38. This and subsequent ambiguous structures can be handled in two ways.

The first approach, which expands the dag into a tree, allows faster algorithms but is limited to smaller data structures. It is to simply replicate the entries for each unique structure code, giving the data structure codes shown in Fig. 5-39. Note that the atoms must have an id field so the different structure code entries can be identified as belonging to the same atom. If there are many back edges, this approach can lead to many replicated entries using considerable memory, but since

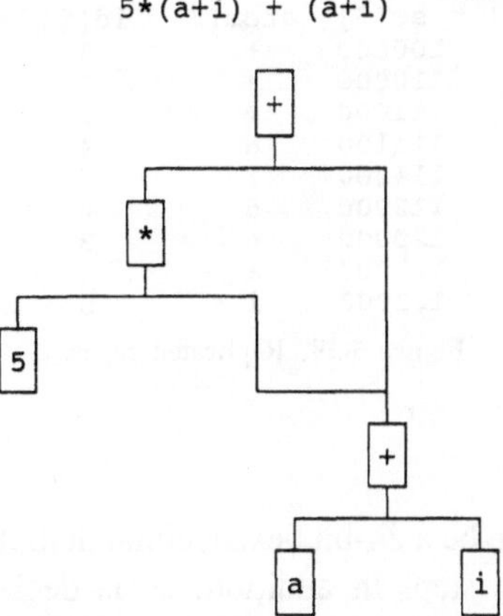

Figure 5-37. A directed acyclic graph.

a complete copy of all the data is presented at every entry, all of the data can be processed in parallel at every level.

The second approach trades tree searching time for memory. In this approach, when multiple paths to a node exist, the node is entered in the data structure once for each path. However, the node's descendants are limited to one structure-code prefix—the prefix from the minimum structure code for the node (see Fig. 5-40). As a result, the data structure is smaller, but if the algorithm requires traversing the graph's edges, the need to do a minimum search on each node may slow execution time. An id field is needed here as well to set the scope for the minimum search. This approach can be viewed as composing trees.

Figures 5-41, 5-42, and 5-43 show the code for the sorting routine. The basic algorithm (Aho and Ullman [1986], p. 560) consists of not listing a node until all of its parents have been listed. When a node is listed, its children are marked as having their parent listed (plisted), and then its left child is selected as the next node to process if possible. The result is that the evaluation dependencies represented by the interior node structure are preserved when the order of listing is reversed.

Note that in Fig. 5-41 the structure code is six hexadecimal digits or 24 bits

sc[$]	sc[$]	atom[$]
	100000	+
	110000	*
120000	111000	+
121000	111100	a
122000	111200	i
	112000	5

Figure 5-38. Structure codes for a DAG.

sc[$]	atom[$]	id[$]
100000	+	1
110000	*	2
111000	+	3
111100	a	4
111200	i	5
112000	5	6
120000	+	3
121000	a	4
122000	i	5

Figure 5-39. Replicated codes.

long. By defining hexsc to be a 24-bit hexadecimal field, the entire structure code can be compared in one step. In addition, sc is declared as an array of six hexadecimal digits, each 4 bits long. Since hexsc and sc are equivalenced by a **defvar**, they provide two different forms of access to the same structure code. The sc field allows the program in Fig. 5-43 to modify the structure codes to calculate the left-child and right-child codes given the parent's code. (See the plistr and plistl routines in Fig. 5-42).

The algorithm implementation consists of selecting an interior, unlisted node whose parents are listed (plisted[$]). The order and listed fields are set for all entries with the same node id (see Fig. 5-43 line *a*). In order to visit the children of the node, the leftmost 0 in the code must be found and set to 2 for the right child and to 1 for the left child. All entries that match these codes have their plisted[$] flag set by routines plistr and plistl.

The left child is visited last because we must traverse to the left descendant if possible. Thus in the plistl subroutine, shown in Fig. 5-42, the entry for the left child with the smallest structure code is selected. Back in the main program (Fig. 5-43), after returning from plistl, the parent's structure code is restored and the *xx* variable is reset. The **if** and **any** statement combination in subroutine unlchild (Fig. 5-42, lines *a*) checks the conditions for advancing to the left child. It must be an interior node, and all entries with the same node name must have their plisted flag set. If the conditions are true and the node has not yet been visited (that is, listed[$] is FALSE), it is marked TRUE (visited) and its order field is assigned a value. The loop variable *xx* which flags the next node to be processed is updated to the selected left child before returning to the top of the loop.

sc[$]	atom[$]	id[$]
100000	+	1
110000	*	2
111000	+	3
111100	a	4
111200	i	5
112000	5	6
120000	+	3

Figure 5-40. Minimal structure codes for a DAG.

```
main dag

deflog (TRUE, 10);
deflog (FALSE, 0);

defvar (sc, hexsc);

int scalar i,cnt;
char scalar lchild;

int parallel order[$];
hex parallel hexsc:24[$], sc:4[$,6];
char parallel node:16[$];
logical parallel interior[$], listed[$], dag[$], plisted[$],
                 cand[$];
index parallel xx[$], yy[$];

associate hexsc[$], node[$], interior[$] with dag[$];
```

Figure 5-41. DAG sort: data declarations.

```
subroutine seti
/* find left most zero in hexsc[xx]
   set i to digit position          */
i=0;
loop
until sc[xx,i] .eq. 0
  i=i+1;
endloop;
end;

subroutine plistr
/* i indexes left most zero digit */
sc[xx,i] = 2; /* generate right child code */
if hexsc[xx] .eq. hexsc[$] then
   plisted[$] = TRUE;  /* set plisted */
endif;
end;

subroutine plistl
/* i indexes left most zero digit */
sc[xx,i] = 1; /* generate left child code */
if hexsc[xx] .eq. hexsc[$] then
   plisted[$] = TRUE;
   if .not. listed[$] .and. interior[$] then
   /* select unique sc for next left child */
     lchild = node[mindex(hexsc[$])];
   endif;
endif;
end;


subroutine unlchild
/* search for unprocessed left child */
if lchild .eq. node[$] .and. interior[$] then                  a
  any .not. plisted[$]                                         a
  elseany
     if .not. listed[$] then
        order[$] = cnt; cnt=cnt+1; listed[$]=TRUE;
        xx[$] = mindex(hexsc[$]);
     endif;
  endany;
endif;
end;
```

Figure 5-42. DAG sort: subroutines.

```
cnt=1; listed[$]=FALSE; plisted[$]=FALSE;

read hexsc[$], node[$], interior[$] in dag[$];

get xx in dag[$]   plisted[xx] = TRUE; endget xx;
/* find next node with all parents listed and process it */
while xx in .not. listed[$] .and. plisted[$] .and. interior[$]
 if node[xx] .eq. node[$] then /* establish node ordering */
    order[$] = cnt; cnt=cnt+1; listed[$]=TRUE;                    a
 endif;
 loop
   call seti;
   call plistr;
   call plistl;
   sc[xx,i]=0; /* restore sc of parent node */
   setscope dag[$] /* clear xx */
     xx[$] = FALSE;
   endsetscope;
   /* search for unprocessed left child */
   call unlchild;
 until nany xx
 endloop;
endwhile xx;

print node[$] order[$] in dag[$];

end;
```

Figure 5-43. DAG sort: body of the main program.

CAUTION: Inclusion of this algorithm is for pedagogic reasons only. It does not imply that this is the proper approach for minimum register usage optimization on an associative computer. Note that this is a sorting algorithm hidden in dag's clothing. As with all problems that use sorting algorithms on a sequential computer, it is much more efficient to search the raw data directly than to sort. In Asthagiri and Potter [1991], it is shown that register usage can be optimized by searching the source code directly.

5.15. Conclusion

Conventional programs contain a control component and an address-generation component. The address-generation component implements an address function which maps the logical organization of the variables, data structures, and arrays onto the computer's memory. The generation of the address function is a significant portion of a sequential program. Associative programming and associative data structures substantially reduce the programming effort by replacing address generation with parallel searching.

In particular, associative processing and parallel searching are the antithesis of pointers. Pointers are the **goto**s of data structures. The proper use of pointers remains one of the most difficult concepts to teach. Associative data structures do away with the need for pointers. For example, as described above, a simple, natural association of data eliminates the need for linked lists. The "search, don't point" approach of associative programming is more natural, easier to implement, and more easily understood.

This chapter has presented a unified approach for representing arbitrarily complex data structures in content-addressable memories and associative computers. This approach to data structures in associative computers has the advantages of

1. automatically extracting fine-grain parallelism,
2. eliminating much of the complexity of the nonalgorithmic address computation in program development,
3. allowing multiple data structures to be associated with each datum, and
4. allowing the data structures themselves to be modified.

6

ASC Recursion

The previous chapters have concentrated on the basic concepts of associative computing and the basic ASC statements and data structures which support them. This chapter describes the **recursewhile-stack** construct. The basic ASC language does not support general recursion. However, it has a structured construct which supports the stacking of variables and recursive execution.

First, the basic construct and its flow of control is described, including how the flow maps onto a depth-first tree search. Then a brief example is given. The third section gives a few rules on when and how to use the recursive statements. The penultimate section gives a detailed example of using recursion to search for a consistent pattern match in a data base.

The following two chapters will describe how patterns can be compiled into special ASC statements and their associative data structures to achieve a nonrecursive procedural program.

When programming a problem in ASC, it may be apparent after several layers of nesting that the logical parallel expression portions of the nested **for** or **while** statements are essentially identical. In such situations there are two definite advantages to using the recursive constructs. First, if explicit nesting is used, the nesting is limited to a predetermined level. The **recursewhile** construct allows nesting to a level as deep as the data requires and the internal stacks will allow. Second, the compactness of the recursive form greatly reduces the amount of repetitious programming effort.

6.1. The Recursewhile Construct

The **recursewhile-stack** construct actually consists of two statements: **recursewhile** and **stack**. Their general form and interrelationships are diagrammed in Fig. 6-1. The basic flow of control for the **recursewhile-stack** construct is diagrammed in Fig. 6-2. The statement keywords (**recursewhile**, **stack**, and

```
recursewhile parallel_index in logical_parallel_expression
  body1
stack stack_list then bodya endstack;
  body2
endrecursewhile parallel_index;
```

Figure 6-1. The **recursewhile-stack** construct.

endrecursewhile) and their corresponding logic are enclosed in boxes of asterisks (*). First, the **recursewhile** statement is executed. It initializes an internal counter to zero; then if there are responders to the logical parallel expression, the body1 code is executed. The **stack** statement between body1 and body2 is composed of two parts. The first part is executed at the end of executing body1. The second part is executed at the beginning of body2. When the first part is executed, the stack-list variables are stacked. (Any number of scalar and parallel variables may be saved. There are two stacks one for scalars and one for parallel variables.) Then the internal counter is incremented, bodya is executed, and control passes back to the beginning of the **recursewhile** statement via path *a*. The **recursewhile** is executed as if it were a new separate statement. This process repeats recursively until the evaluation of the **recursewhile**'s logical parallel expression results in no responders.

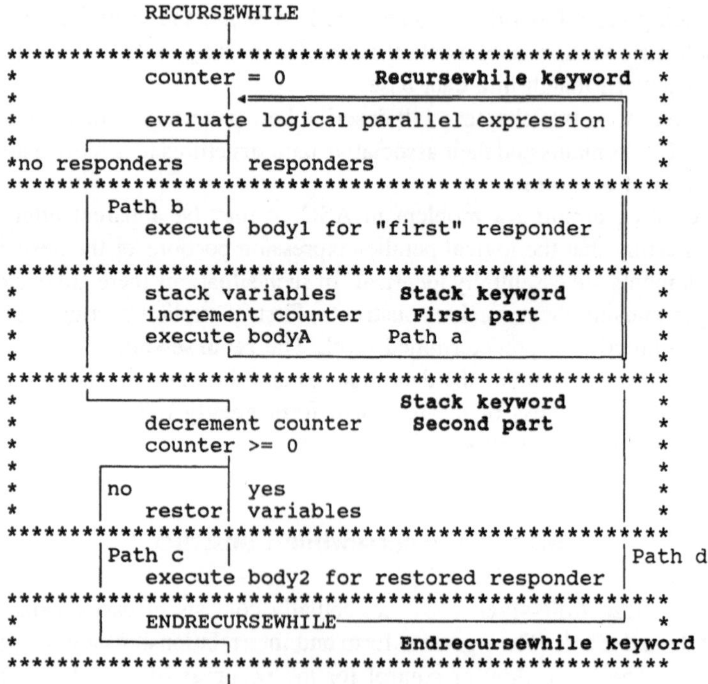

Figure 6-2. Recursewhile flow of control.

When there are no responders, control passes down to the second part of the **stack** statement via path *b*. The second part of the **stack** statement decrements the internal counter. If the count is negative, control passes out of the control structure to the statement following the **endrecursewhile** (path *c*). If the count is non-negative, the stacked variables are restored to the values on the top of the stacks, the stacks are updated, and the second body of code (body2) is executed. When **endrecursewhile** is reached, control passes back to the top of the **recursewhile** statement via path *d*. The logical parallel expression is recalculated and the parallel index is updated according to the rules for a **while** statement.

Any number of conventional ASC statements may be in the bodies of the **recursewhile** statement. The statements may be entirely in body1 or body2 or in both. If more than one statement is in both bodies, the begins and ends must be nested, as in any other piece of structured code. However, a **recursewhile** statement may have only one **stack** statement and may not contain any nested **recursewhile** statements.

The bodya part of the **stack** statement may also contain any legal ASC statement. The stack portion of the **stack** statement allows the programmer to specify what variables need to be saved to establish a recursive environment. The bodya portion allows these variables to be re-initialized. In particular, the variables which the **recursewhile** uses in the logical parallel expression normally need to be saved (i.e., stacked) and then reinitialized to the descendant values before re-executing the **recursewhile** statement.

One of the most appropriate applications of the **recursewhile** construct is as the control structure for a depth-first tree search. The diagram in Fig. 6-3 illustrates how the **recursewhile** construct flows for a depth-first search. The logical parallel expression of the **recursewhile** statement generates the descendants (if any) of the start node [statement (1) in Fig. 6-3]. The descendants are flagged by the parallel index of the **recursewhile** statement. The **recursewhile** control logic selects one of the descendants and stores it in the parallel index variable [statement (2) of Fig. 6-3]. The body1 portion of the **recursewhile** statement is executed for the selected descendant specified by the parallel index

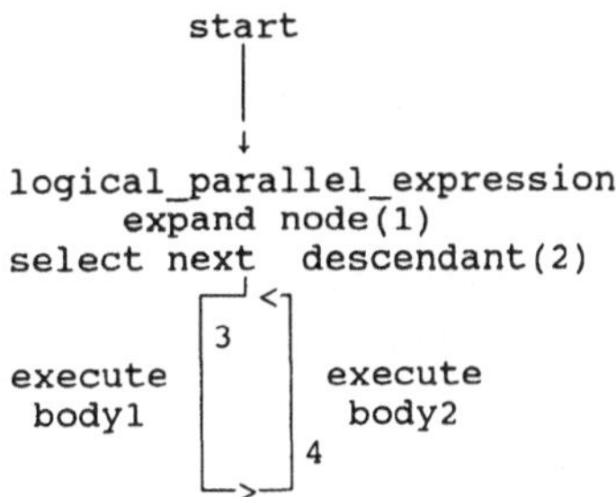

Figure 6-3. A **recursewhile** tree search.

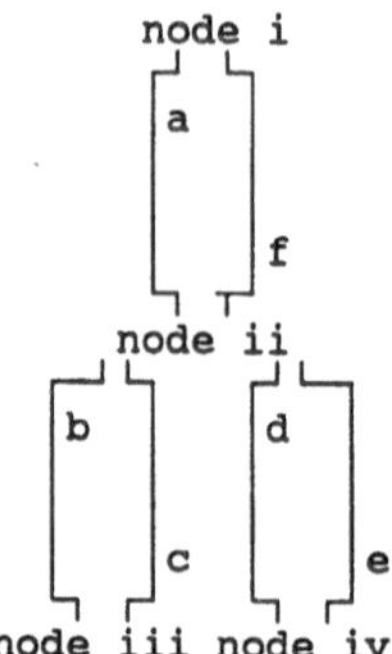

Figure 6-4. Order of expansion of a tree search.

(edge 3 of Fig. 6-3). When the **stack** statement is reached at the bottom of edge 3, the state of the specified scalar and parallel variables are stacked. This sequence represents one traversal of path *a* in Fig. 6-2.

Figure 6-3 shows a trace of the execution of the **recursewhile-stack** construct over the search space for one complete iteration—down and up one branch of the tree. Body1 of the **recursewhile** (edge 3 of Fig. 6-3) is executed on the traversal down the branch. Body2 (edge 4) is executed on the way back up the tree. Figure 6-4 shows the flow of execution over three branches of a tree search. Edge *a* of Fig. 6-4, which corresponds to edge 3 of Fig. 6-3 and represents the execution of body1 for the first responder of node *i*, is traversed first. Edge *b* of Fig. 6-4, which also corresponds to edge 3 of Fig. 6-3 but represents execution of body1 for the first responder of node *ii*, is traversed second. Control then passes to node *iii*. When control returns from node *iii*, edge *c* of Fig. 6-4, which corresponds to edge 4 of Fig. 6-3 and represents the execution of body2 for the first responder of node *ii*, is traversed. The **recursewhile** statement is re-evaluated for node **ii**, and the second responder is selected.* Then body1 is executed for the second responder of node *ii*. This is represented in Fig. 6-4 by edge *d*. Edges *d* and *e* in Fig. 6-4 correspond to edges 3 and 4 in Fig. 6-3 and represent the execution of body1 and body2 for the second responder of node *ii* in a manner identical to edges *b* and *c* for the first responder.

Every time node *ii* is entered from the bottom (i.e., via path *d* in Fig. 6-2), a new evaluation of the logical parallel expression is made. If one or more responders is present, body1 (edge 3 of Fig. 6-3) and eventually, after possible recursion, body 2 (edge 4 of Fig. 6-3) are executed for the next responder. If there are no responders, the counter is decremented, the environment variables are restored from the stack, and body2 is executed for the stacked iteration of the parent node.

*The **recursewhile** is a **while** statement. That is, the body of the statement must update the variables in the logical_parallel_expression to advance to the next responder. Actually of course, the statement always selects the first responder, the updated variables having eliminated the previously selected responder.

When there are no more responders and the internal counter goes negative, the root node of the search tree has been reached and the **recursewhile** construct exits.

6.2. A Simple Recursewhile Example

Figure 6-5 is a brief example of a **recursewhile** statement which will perform a depth-first search on the simple data base in Fig. 6-6. The unprocessed (unproc) flag is used to ensure that each node is visited once and only once. The **recursewhile** begins by finding the is_a descendants of the node called sylvia. Body1 clears sylvia's unproc flag so that she will not be processed again. The **stack** statement saves the node name (in variable animal) on the stack and then updates it to the sibling's node name (animal = value[xx]).

Note that when **recursewhile** is reentered at a leaf node of the is_a link—i.e., animal = carnivore (see Figs. 6-6 and 6-7)—there will be no responders, and therefore body1 and body2 will not be executed with animal set to the leaf-node value (carnivore or mammal in this case). Consequently the leaf nodes must be searched for an eats link in the bodya portion of the stack statement. Since interior as well as leaf nodes are processed by bodya, the one search statement suffices, and both fish and meat are found as foods for sylvia, corresponding to nodes cat and carnivore. The code shown in Fig. 6-5 would have to be modified slightly to find an eats link for the initial animal (i.e., sylvia).

6.3. How to Use Recursewhile

Before discussing the next **recursewhile** example, some rules of thumb for using **recursewhile** recursion will be discussed. First, if the parallel index variable (i.e., variable *xx* in Fig. 6-5) that flags the node being expanded is to be used in

```
read object[$], attribute[$], value[$] in zoo[$];
unproc[$] = TRUE;
animal = "sylvia";
recursewhile xx in animal        .eq. object[$] .and.
                   attribute[$] .eq. "is_a"    .and.
                   unproc[$]
  unproc[xx] = FALSE;
  stack animal then
    animal = value[xx];
    if animal .eq. object[$] .and. attribute[$] .eq. "eats"
    then
       food[$] = YES;
    endif;
  endstack;
endrecursewhile xx;
```

Figure 6-5. A depth-first search.

object	attribute	value
sylvia	is_a	cheetah
cheetah	is_a	cat
tiger	is_a	cat
tiger	eats	people
cat	eats	fish
cat	is_a	carnivore
cat	is_a	mammal
carnivore	eats	meat

Figure 6-6. Mealtime data base.

body2, it can not be changed (i.e., re-initialized for the next recursion) until after it is stacked in the **stack** statement. Similarly, the parallel indices of all of the straddling control statements must be stacked to preserve their value for the body2 portion. Variable reinitialization is the primary reason for the bodya portion of the **stack** statement.

The traversal through the search space can be controlled by a global parallel-variable flag. The corresponding bit in the flag is turned off as each node in the space is visited or eliminated by pruning. Frequently this flag is called *unprocessed* (unproc).

If the success or failure of a search is recorded by a global scalar status flag, then the flag can be included as a part of the **recursewhile** search expression. If the flag is initialized to SUCCESS before the search and is then set to FAIL whenever the search fails, an AND tree is modeled. In an AND tree every node of the entire tree must be TRUE. If any node is FALSE, the search stops and the construct is exited. Figure 6-8 shows the assignment of status to FAIL in bodya, but it could be in body1 or body2.

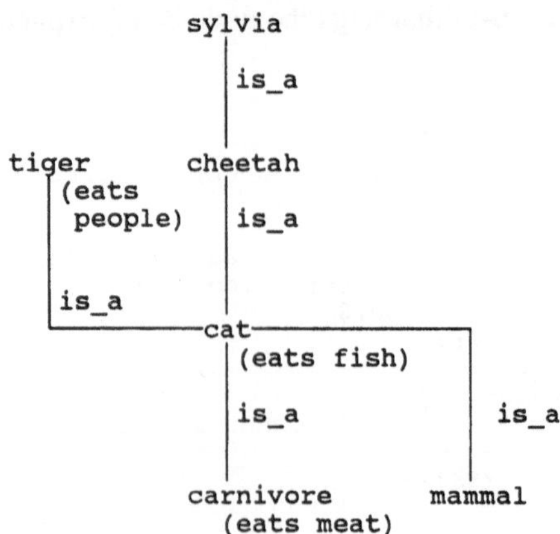

Figure 6-7. Mealtime in tree form.

```
read object[$], attribute[$], value[$] in zoo[$];
unproc[$] = TRUE;
animal = "sylvia";
status = SUCCESS;
recursewhile xx in animal       .eq. object[$] .and.
                   attribute[$] .eq. "is_a"    .and.
                   status       .eq. SUCCESS   .and.
                   unproc[$]
  unproc[xx] = FALSE;
  stack animal then
    animal = value[xx];
    if animal .eq. object[$] .and. attribute[$] .eq. "eats"
    then
       food[$] = YES;
    else /* exit if any node does not have an eats link */
       status = FAIL;
    endif;
  endstack;
endrecursewhile xx;
```

Figure 6-8. An AND-tree search.

An OR tree (exit on first solution) can be modeled in two ways. First, we can use the complement of the AND tree case above; a global flag can be set to FAIL and tested for FAIL in the logical parallel expression of the **recursewhile** statement. As soon as the search is successful, setting status to SUCCESS will cause the construct to exit (see Fig. 6-9). Again, the assignment of SUCCESS to status may be done in any of the three statement bodies.

Another way to model an OR tree or to implement a pruning algorithm is to use the unproc flag. Whenever the search is successful and exiting is desired, setting unproc to FALSE for all remaining entries will cause the **recursewhile** statement to find no responders, causing the recursion to unwind and exit (see Fig. 6-10). Unproc is set to FALSE inside a **setscope** statement to assure that every unproc is cleared regardless of the scope of the nesting **if** statement.

A local backtrack flag used in the **recursewhile** search can be used for backtracking. Normally, the flag is set to FALSE before entering the construct and also, perhaps conditionally, at the bottom of body2 of the recursewhile statement.

```
read object[$], attribute[$], value[$] in zoo[$];
unproc[$] = TRUE;
animal = "sylvia";
status = FAIL;
recursewhile xx in animal       .eq. object[$] .and.
                   attribute[$] .eq. IS_A      .and.
                   unproc[$]    .and.   .not. status
  unproc[xx] = FALSE;
  if "success" then status = SUCCESS; endif;
  stack animal then
    animal = value[xx];
  endstack;
endrecursewhile xx;
```

Figure 6-9. An OR-tree search.

```
read object[$], attribute[$], value[$] in zoo[$];
unproc[$] = TRUE;
animal = "sylvia";
recursewhile xx in animal       .eq. object[$] .and.
                   attribute[$] .eq. "is_a"    .and.
                   unproc[$]
  unproc[xx] = FALSE;
  stack animal then
    animal = value[xx];
    if animal .eq. object[$] .and. attribute[$] .eq. "eats"
    then
      food[$] = YES;
      setscope zoo[$]          /* exit on first solution */
        unproc[$] = FALSE;
      endsetscope;
    endif;
  endstack;
endrecursewhile xx;
```

Figure 6-10. An OR search with **unproc**.

The flag can be set to TRUE at any place in body1 or bodya. If it is set in bodya, as shown on lines *a* in Fig. 6-11a, it behaves as a conventional backtrack. That is, it exits the current level and backtracks to the previous level. If the flag is set in body1 as shown on line *b* in Fig. 6-11b, it causes backtracking to occur at all levels below the current level, since the current values will be stacked before the backtrack flag is detected by the **recursewhile**. The value of the flag can be used for testing anywhere in body1, body2, or bodya. The backtracking process can be stopped by setting the flag to FALSE. The

backtrack = FALSE;

statement at the end of body2 in Fig. 6-11a will stop the backtrack process after one level. Of course, the flag can be set as the result of any logical expression. For example, a counter could be used to cause backtracking to any desired level.

A brief analysis of Fig. 6-11 will show that if the flag is set to FALSE in body1, the current node will not be expanded. As a result, bodya and body2 will be entered with all variables set to their current values. The local flag can be tested for FALSE in these sections of code if they are not to be executed with the current values.

Before considering a more difficult example of **recursewhile**, it should be noted the **recursewhile** constructs which contain nested **for** and **while** statements which may or may not straddle the stack statement are best understood by reading both body1 and body2 as a contiguous sequence, ignoring the **stack** statement.

6.4. A Complex Recursewhile Example

Looking for a set of consistent bindings in a pattern-matching language like OPS5 (Brownston *et al.* [1985]) is an example of a complex recursive tree search.

```
read object[$], attribute[$], value[$] in zoo[$];
unproc[$] = TRUE;
backtrack = FALSE;
animal = "sylvia";
recursewhile xx in animal       .eq. object[$] .and.
                   attribute[$] .eq. "is_a"    .and.
                   unproc[$]                   .and.
                   .not. backtrack
  unproc[xx] = FALSE;
  stack animal then
    animal = value[xx];
    if animal .eq. "feline" then                         a
       backtrack = TRUE;                                 a
    else
       if animal .eq. object[$] .and. attribute[$] .eq. "eats"
       then food[$] = YES; endif;
    endif;
  endstack;
  backtrack = FALSE;

endrecursewhile xx;
```

a - Backtrack at feline

```
read object[$], attribute[$], value[$] in zoo[$];
unproc[$] = TRUE;
backtrack = FALSE;
animal = "sylvia";
recursewhile xx in animal       .eq. object[$] .and.
                   attribute[$] .eq. "is_a"    .and.
                   unproc[$]                   .and.
                   .not. backtrack
  unproc[xx] = FALSE;
  if animal .eq. "feline" then backtrack = TRUE; endif;     b
  stack animal then
    animal = value[xx];
       if animal .eq. object[$] .and. attribute[$] .eq. "eats"

       then food[$] = YES; endif;
  endstack;
  backtrack = FALSE;

endrecursewhile xx;
```

b - Backtrack below feline

Figure 6-11. Backtracking.

At any one instance, the depth of the tree search varies, depending on the number of instantiated facts in the system. The process is illustrated in Figs. 6-12 through 6-16. Figure 6-12 shows the left-hand side or pattern portion of a rule. Symbols enclosed in angle brackets (⟨⟩) are variables. This simple rule form is sufficient for the current discussion. A more detailed description of an OPS5 rule format is given in Chapter 7. Figure 6-13 shows three facts that match the patterns in the rule in Fig. 6-12. Figure 6-14 shows the actual entries in the binding association which would be made given the patterns in Fig. 6-12 and the facts in Fig. 6-13. Each entry in the binding association represents one variable binding. When a pattern with

```
(R5  (P1  <X>  <Y>   5  )
     (P2  <X>   4   <Z> )
     (P3   9   <Y>  <Z> )
  -->
```

Figure 6-12. A rule with three patterns.

more than one variable is bound to a fact, multiple entries are made. The multiple entries are related logically by having the same time-tag id.

In Fig. 6-15, the multiple entries of the binding association corresponding to a single time tag are put into a single row corresponding to the multiple bindings created by matching a pattern to a fact. Figure 6-15 is not an ASC data structure; it is simply a more intuitive style of presenting the binding-association data for the current discussion.

Given the binding-association entries for individually matched patterns as shown in Fig. 6-14, the task of searching it for a set of consistently bound pattern variables for the entire rule is as follows: First, an entry from the binding association is selected at random. This entry is labeled (*i*) in Figs. 6-14 and 6-15. Next a pattern-variable search is performed to identify all entries in the binding association which have the same pattern id and time tag. This search will find bindings for all of the variables in the pattern. All the responders to this search are related in that they were made as the result of a single, locally consistent fact. These entries are labeled (*ii*) in Figs. 6-14 and 6-15. Each of the responders will be processed in turn (by a **for** statement) searching for globally consistent bindings. The third marker, (**iii**) in Figs. 6-14 and 6-15, illustrates such a search. That is, the entries marked with (*iii*) are responders to a search for variable id ⟨*x*⟩ and value 17 which are the parameters of the first responder to the (*ii*) step. These two steps, (*ii*) and (*iii*), represent one iteration of a consistent binding search. Figure 6-16 shows how three iterations of the search algorithm can find a set of globally consistent bindings for three variables. Boxes (*ii*) and (*iii*) (solid lines) are the first level. Boxes (*iv*) and (*v*) (double solid lines) are the second level, and boxes (*vi*) and (*vii*) (lines of asterisks) are the third level.

Once the global variables of the consistent binding have been identified, the individual variable binding entries can be verified in exactly the same way as the original new entry was processed. As a result, a rule which is being searched for a consistent set of bindings is processed recursively. Figure 6-17 gives the recursive **recursewhile-stack** construct needed to perform the search.

```
( P1  17   3   5 )
( P2  17   4   8 )
( P3   9   3   8 )
```

Figure 6-13. Facts that match the patterns.

```
associate time_tag[$], rule_id[$], pattern_id[$],
          variable_id[$], variable_va[$] with ba[$];
```

time _tag	rule _id	pattern _id	variable _id	variable _va	markers i	ii	iii
1	R5	P1	<X>	17		1	1
1	R5	P1	<Y>	3	1	1	
2	R5	P2	<X>	17			1
2	R5	P2	<Z>	8			
3	R5	P3	<Y>	3			
3	R5	P3	<Z>	8			

Figure 6-14. Entries in the binding association.

The code of Fig. 6-17 is somewhat complex due to the special requirements of the problem. For example, a method must be found that assures that a given variable is bound to the same value for every pattern in which it occurs (called a comprehensive match). That is, if the variable ⟨*x*⟩ appears in three patterns, but has only two entries in the binding association, one for pattern1 and one for pattern2, and both entries have value 17, a straightforward search for consistent bindings would succeed even though pattern3 had no entries in the table because it had not been matched. This problem can be overcome if the binding association is initialized with nil bindings for every pattern-variable combination in the rule. These entries assure that every variable is bound to something for every pattern in which it appears.

A comprehensive match can be assured if all entries in the table which match the variable id are flagged initially. (The first **if** statement in Fig. 6-17 sets pats[$]. The lines in the statement are marked by an *a* on the right side of the figure.) Then

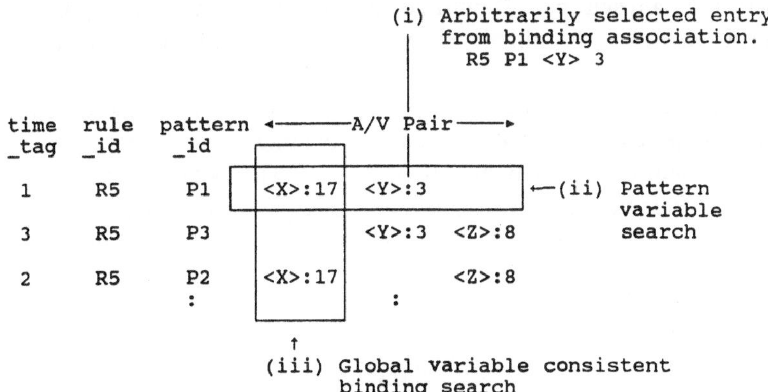

Figure 6-15. Relationship between the pattern-variable search and the global-variable consistent-binding search.

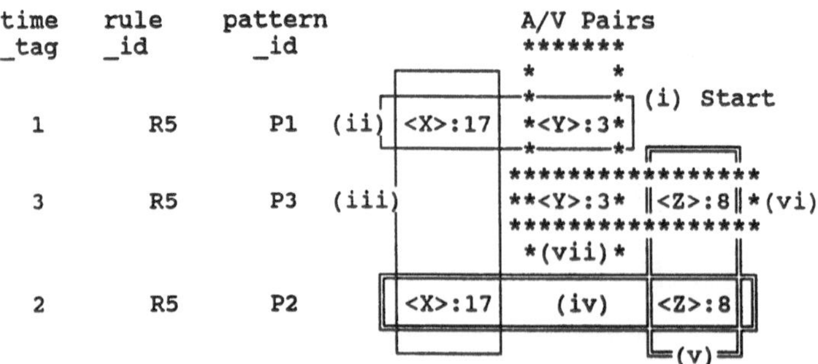

Figure 6-16. Path of a consistent binding search.

the iterative search for a binding consistent with entry *xx* from among the pats[$] is executed by the "for yy in pats[$]" statement (line *b*). First, the candidates are tested to filter out those with nil bindings (**while zz**–block *c*.). The remainders are passed down recursively to complete the search. When a successful candidate has been found, control returns to statement block *d*, which eliminates all competing binding entries for the variable, including the nil entries. Therefore, after all variables have been processed, pats[$] will flag nil bindings only if no consistent binding was found for a given variable. The test for this situation is the **any** statement after the **endwhile zz** (block *e*). Status is set to FAIL if any nil unproc entries are found.

A second complexity involves the pats[$] flag field. It is saved by stacking, as are the parallel index variables *xx*, *yy*, and *zz* before reentering the **recursewhile**. Note that when an index variable is used in a **recursewhile**, it is re-initialized automatically as a part of the statement's execution. However, pats[$] is set in the then body of a parallel **if** (block *a*), which does not execute if there are no responders. As a result, pats[$] must be set to FALSE in the **elsenany** part of the parallel **if** (line *f*) or be initialized to FALSE in the bodya part of the **stack** statement.

A third complexity is the "tree trimming" factor. The **while zz** statement identifies all possible alternative consistent bindings. Thus when a consistent binding is found, the alternatives may be deleted. This is done in the parallel **if**, immediately following the **stack** statement (block *d*). This statement eliminates alternatives by setting the unproc[$] flag to false. This in effect prunes the search tree.

6.5. Conclusion

This chapter has presented the **recursewhile-stack** construct. It is a very powerful statement construct but is limited to certain situations. In particular, it

```
while qq in unproc[$] .eq. NEW
  status = SUCCESS;
  recursewhile xx in pattern_id[qq] .eq. pattern_id[$] .and.
                     timetag[qq]    .eq. timetag[$]    .and.
                     unproc[$]      .eq. NEW
    unproc[xx] = FALSE;
    if variable_id[xx] .eq. variable_id[$] .and.              a
      (att_value[xx]   .eq. att_value[$]   .or.               a
             nil       .eq. att_value[$])  .and.              a
       pattern_id[xx]  .eq. pattern_id[$]  .and               a
         unproc[$]     .eq. NEW                               a
    then pats[$] = TRUE; elsenany pats[$] = FALSE;  endif; af
    any pats[$]
      for yy in pats[$]                                       b
        while zz in pattern_id[yy] .eq. pattern_id[$] .and. c
                    att_value[$]   .ne. nil           .and. c
                    pats[$]                           .and. c
                    unproc[$]      .eq. NEW                 c
          status = SUCCESS;
          unproc[zz] = FALSE;
stack zz[$] yy[$] zz[$] pats[$] then qq[$] = zz[$]; endstack;
          if status then                                      d
             result[$] = result[$] .or. zz[$];                d
             unproc[zz] = FALSE;                              d
               if variable_id[zz] .eq. variable_id[$] .and. d
                  pattern_id[zz]  .eq. pattern_id[$]  .and. d
                  unproc[$]       .eq. NEW                  d
               then  unproc[$] = FALSE; endif;              d
          else
            status = FAIL;
          endif;
        endwhile zz;
        any att_value[$] .eq. nil .and.                       e
            pats[$]               .and.                       e
            unproc[$]    .eq. NEW                             e
          result[$] = FALSE;                                  e
          status = FAIL;                                      e
        endany;                                               e
      endfor yy;
    elsenany
      status = FAIL;
    endany;
    if status then
      result[$] = xx[$] .or. result[$];
      fa_status[xx] = FALSE;
    endif;
  endrecursewhile xx;
endwhile qq;
```

Figure 6-17. Recursewhile inference engine.

requires that the descendants of a node can be obtained by a parallel search in a **recursewhile** statement. It requires that the same code be able to expand all of the descendant nodes. The programmer must decide what to save (stack) prior to recursion, and the programmer must control the construct's execution by use of global (i.e., nonstacked) variables. However, the **recursewhile-stack** construct can efficiently execute a tree-search strategy to variable depths with backtracking capability.

7

Complex Searching

Chapter 6 described the **recursewhile** construct and showed how it could be used to search for a consistent binding to any level. However, as noted, there are some restrictions on the use of **recursewhile**. In particular, it can perform a depth-first tree search with AND or OR nodes, but not both. This chapter describes an approach for implementing general-purpose complex searching. First, an associative data structure which supports several levels of ANDing and ORing is introduced. Then the ASC statements which use the data structure are described. The flow of control for these statements is given in detail. These statements can be used to hand-code simple patterns. Chapter 8 describes how general, arbitrarily complex patterns can be compiled into the AND constructs.

Complex searching addresses searching techniques needed to accommodate and/or pattern matching typical in rule-based systems. In associative computing, searching is done in the cells in parallel. Thus the parallel **if** statement

```
if color[$] .eq. red .and. size[$] .eq. big then . . .
```

requires that the color and size fields be in the same association so that the responders from the two searches can be ANDed to yield the responders for the complete search. However, it is often desirable to store data in more-complex data structures, which may be spread across several associative cells. In these cases, a new statement, **andif**, can be used to connect searches logically.

Figure 7-1a illustrates a fact data base which can be searched by an **andif** statement. Note that the fact association entries implement a semantic network. If the network were implemented by having a specific field for the object and each attribute as shown in Fig. 7-2a, a conventional parallel **if** could be used to search it using associative (entry by entry) ANDing as shown in Fig. 7-3. However, the data structure would be quite rigid. For example, if a new attribute type such as "material" is to be added to the database, a new field must be defined, as illustrated in Fig. 7-2b, and the programs modified and recompiled. On the other hand, in the organization of Fig. 7-1, universal attribute and value fields are used.

attribute[$]	value[$]	object[$]
color	red	table1
size	big	table1
size	big	table3
color	red	table2
size	small	table2
color	green	table3

a - Original Database

attribute[$]	value[$]	object[$]
color	red	table1
size	big	table1
size	big	table3
color	red	table2
size	small	table2
color	green	table3
material	wood	table1
material	plastic	table3
material	metal	table2

b - Modified Database

Figure 7-1. Fact association.

Thus new attributes and values such as (material, wood), (material, plastic), and (material, metal) can easily be added at run time for each object, as shown in Fig. 7-1b.

7.1. A Brief OPS5 Background

A LHS (left-hand side) pattern of the OPS5 production rule represents a pattern which is to be matched against a database of facts called Working Memory

color[$]	size[$]	object[$]
red	big	table1
red	small	table2
green	big	table3

a - Original Database

color[$]	size[$]	material[$]	object[$]
red	big	wood	table1
red	small	plastic	table2
green	big	metal	table3

b - Modified Database

Figure 7-2. Specific attribute fields.

```
     red        1              big     1                1
     red        1             small    0                0
    green       0              big     1                0

color[$] .eq. "red"   size[$] .eq. "big"    color .eq. "red"
                                                   .and.
                                              size .eq. "big"
```

Figure 7-3. Entry-by-entry ANDing.

Elements (WME). The LHS pattern is organized into subpatterns* of sets of attribute–value pairs. The LHS pattern is enclosed by a set of parentheses. The first entry in the subpattern is the set name (called a *class* in OPS5) and must be a constant (e.g., name1 in Fig. 7-4). The remaining entries are paired off with the first item, starting with the ^ character, being a constant attribute name (^A1, for example). The second element (e.g., ⟨X⟩ or 31) is the value and may be a constant (31) or a variable (⟨X⟩). All variables begin with ⟨ and end with ⟩.

In general, a condition may be present between the attribute and the value which must be satisfied for the match to be successful. Thus, ^A4 < ⟨X⟩ is interpreted as meaning that the value bound to ⟨X⟩ by matching ^A1 must be greater than the value associated with ^A4. If no condition is specified and the value is a constant, the WME being matched must match exactly. If the value is a variable and the variable is bound, the binding must match the WME. If the variable has not been previously bound, it is bound to the value of the WME. Double angle brackets (⟨⟨ ⟩⟩) indicate OR. Curly brackets({ }) mean AND. Thus, ^A16 ⟨⟨18 21 65⟩⟩ indicates that ^A16 may match a WME with the value 18, 21, or 65, and ^A10 {>5 <15} indicates that any value matching A10 must be greater than 5 and less than 15.

If the pattern is successfully matched, the right-hand side (RHS) of the pattern is executed. A rule is successfully matched only when first, all of the patterns are matched by WMEs in the database and in addition, the variable bindings due to the matching are consistent. That is, if the variable ⟨*Y*⟩ is bound to 5 by the successful match of a rule, it must be bound to 5 wherever it appears in all patterns.

The RHS of the rule consists of actions to be taken, such as deleting the matching fact or inserting a new fact composed of pieces of matched facts. In Fig. 7-4, (delete 2) means that the WME that matches subpattern 2 should be deleted from the database. Similarly, (modify 1 ^A1 100) states that the WME matching the first subpattern should be modified by changing the value associated with ^A1 to 100. WMEs may also be inserted as shown in Fig. 7-4. See Brownston *et al.* [1985] for a more-detailed discussion of the OPS5 programming language.

*Frequently, the term *pattern* is used for both the entire LHS and the subpatterns of the LHS. The meaning is usually clear from the context.

```
(P R1
    ( name1 ^A1 <X>   ^A2 31 ^A3 <Y>   ^A4 < <X>)         <-LHS
    ( name2 ^A10   {>5 <15}   ^A16 <<18 21 56>> <Y>
            ^A5 <Y>)                                       <-LHS
-->
    ( delete 2)                                            <-RHS
    ( modify 1 ^A1 100 )                                   <-RHS
    ( insert name3 ^B1 <X> ^B2 <Y>)                        <-RHS
)
```

a - A Prototype OPS5 Rule

```
(name1 ^A1 5 ^A3 2 ^A2 15 ^A4 2 ^A16 99 ^A21 yes)
```

b - A Prototype Working Memory Element

Figure 7-4. An OPS5 rule and memory.

In most OPS5 implementations, the context sensitivity of the pattern is handled by the RETE algorithm (Forgy [1982]). The rule subpatterns are compiled into a single network, and then the WMEs are passed through the network. A token stored at a terminal node of the network represents a unique set of objects which completely matches all the patterns of a single rule. Each object to be added to or deleted from the production system database is passed through the network, causing changes to intermediate and terminal nodes. By saving state information in the nodes, the algorithm computes the matches for an object only once. The algorithm, designed for sequential computers, essentially trades a larger data space and an increased amount of data fetching/storing (which are still relatively cheap for this algorithm on sequential machines) for a reduced number of match operations (which are expensive for this algorithm).

7.2. Pattern Data Structures

7.2.1. ORed Association Entries

In the standard tabular format of ASC associations, the fields in an entry are ANDed while the individual association entries are ORed. For example, in Fig. 7-5, the first entry can be uniquely identified by ANDing the tests:

a[$] .eq. d .and. b[$] .eq. e

The AND sequence could also include

c[$] .eq. f

but this third test is not needed in this example. On the other hand, the single parallel search

```
a[$]  b[$]  c[$]

 d     e     f
 d     h     i
 g     h     f
```

Figure 7-5. ASC association ANDing.

a[$] .eq. d

will find the same two responders as would first searching for

a[$] .eq. d .and. b[$] .eq. e

and then searching for

a[$] .eq. d .and. b[$] .eq. h.

This sequence implies that the responders to both queries are sought. Combining these two searches into one by the distributive law gives

a[$] .eq. d .and. (b[$] .eq. e .or. b[$] .eq. h)

which produces the same result as just

a[$] .eq. d

in this example. In other words, independent association entries are automatically ORed during searching.

Associative data structures can be designed to take advantage of the entry-by-entry ANDing and entry ORing to represent Boolean search patterns. For example, assume that patterns of the form

a[$] .eq. 3 .and. (b[$] .eq. 5 .or. b[$] .eq. 7)

are to be processed. If many of these patterns exist, but there are relatively few facts, then the patterns (see Fig. 7-6a) may be stored in an associative-memory data structure as shown in Fig. 7-6b (dc stands for don't care—i.e., match everything). The facts can be converted into sequential code and tested in parallel against all of the patterns. Thus if a fact has *a* equal to 4, *b* unspecified, and *c* equal to 6, then the code in Fig. 7-6c would test all patterns of the form shown in Fig. 7-6b for a match. This process is called "passing the facts past the rules."

One problem with this approach is that it allows only one test, i.e., .eq.. This is true because in a SIMD computer only one instruction can be broadcast at a time. However, a compare (.cmp.) operator for associative computers has been developed (Haston [1987]) which executes in approximately the same amount of time as .eq. but checks for all three conditions and sets individual status flags in each PE memory to TRUE depending on whether the result was less than, greater than, or equal to.

```
  a[$] .eq. 3 .and. (b[$] .eq. 5  .or.  b[$] .eq. 7)
 (a[$] .eq. 4 .or.   a[$] .eq. 5) .and. c[$] .eq. 6

                     a - Test Patterns


               tsta[$]  tstb[$]  tstc[$]

                  3        5        dc
                  3        7        dc
                  4       dc         6
                  5       dc         6

                b - Associative Memory


                 a = 4; b = dc; c = 6;
               if
                 tsta[$] .eq. a  .and.
                 tstb[$] .eq. b  .and.
                 tstc[$] .eq. c
               then

                 c - Parallel Search
```

Figure 7-6. Associative memory layout for a pattern.

7.2.2. The .cmp. Operation

The test patterns of Fig. 7-6a now must be modified to specify which test is desired. This is accomplished with a 3-bit field which has the same format as the status flags (i.e., .lt., .eq., .gt.). Thus the test code for .eq. is 010, for .lt. it is 100, and for .gt., .le., .ne., .ge., .nil. and .dc. it is 001, 110, 101, 011, 000, and 111, respectively. The multiple-result codes such as .ge. and .ne. are obtained by ORing the acceptable conditions. Thus the code for .dc. is 111 which will match everything, and the code for nil or false is 000 which will match nothing. See Fig. 7-7a and b for the modified test patterns and associative memory representation. Note that the example has been changed to include tests other than .eq. In addition, Fig. 7-7c has been changed to the .cmp. operator, which has an argument that specifies the field that contains the correct test codes.

The .cmp. operator first generates the proper status-register code for all tests in parallel. It then bitwise ANDs the status register with the specified test-code field and then ORs the results of the three bits into one. If a bit is TRUE (i.e., one), the test passes for the association entry; if it is zero, it fails. Figure 7-8 illustrates the results for all possible combinations. Note that the code for .dc. will always produce a TRUE and the code for nil will always produce a FALSE.

7.2.3. The AND Extension Field

The last pattern in Fig. 7-7a contains two tests on the *a*[$] variable. Since both tests must be TRUE for the pattern to be TRUE, the tests must be ANDed.

```
 a[$] .lt. 3 .and. (b[$] .eq. 5  .or.  b[$] .ge. 7)
(a[$] .ne. 4 .or.   a[$] .eq. 5) .and. c[$] .le. 6
(a[$] .gt. 5 .and.  a[$] .lt. 9) .and. c[$] .ne. 5
```

a - Test Patterns

andext[$]	tsta[$]	cmpa[$]	tstb[$]	cmpb[$]	tstc[$]	cmpc[$]
0	3	100	5	010	nil	000
0	3	100	7	011	nil	000
0	4	101	nil	000	6	110
0	5	010	nil	000	6	110
1	5	001	nil	000	5	101
1	9	100	nil	000	5	101

b - Associative Memory

```
a = 4; b = dc; c = 6;
if
   tsta[$] .cmp(tst[$]). a .and.
   tstb[$] .cmp(tst[$]). b .and.
   tstc[$] .cmp(tst[$]). c
then
```

c - Parallel Search

Figure 7-7. Test pattern storage.

fact	tst	value	status code	result
5	100(lt)	2	001	0
5	100(lt)	5	010	0
5	100(lt)	7	100	1
5	010(eq)	2	001	0
5	010(eq)	5	010	1
5	010(eq)	7	100	0
5	001(gt)	2	001	1
5	001(gt)	5	010	0
5	001(gt)	7	100	0
5	110(le)	2	001	0
5	110(le)	5	010	1
5	110(le)	7	100	1
5	101(ne)	2	001	1
5	101(ne)	5	010	0
5	101(ne)	7	100	1
5	011(ge)	2	001	1
5	011(ge)	5	010	1
5	011(ge)	7	100	0
5	000(nil)	2	001	0
5	000(nil)	5	010	0
5	000(nil)	7	100	0
5	111(dc)	2	001	1
5	111(dc)	5	010	1
5	111(dc)	7	100	1

Figure 7-8. Results of the .cmp. operation.

Yet, in order to perform the two tests in parallel, they are entered into two separate association entries, which (as discussed in section 7.1.1) are automatically ORed. In order to signify that these two tests are related, not disjoint, an AND extension field (andext) is added to the association. The AND extension field contains the ID code of all of the association entries which form a logical AND condition. In Fig. 7-7b, there is only one logical AND consisting of two entries both with andext code one. Additional logical ANDs would have different codes. The ZERO code is reserved for ORed entries. To test for the condition that all of the ANDed entries are true, the AND extension field must be processed in software.

Figure 7-9a gives an example of a lengthy test specification for an OPS5-type rule. The LHS of the rule is a complex pattern consisting of two simpler patterns. The first pattern reads, roughly, "Search for a boy with the name Joe or Tom and an age of 18, 21, or 65." The second pattern reads, "Search for a girl with the name Jane, Amy, or Mary with an age between 10 and 18." Figure 7-9b shows that the ANDing of the ORed tests in the first pattern requires a separate entry for every possible combination. The second pattern is more complex in that the ANDed age tests must be accomplished by using an AND extension mechanism. The ORed name test requires that the ANDed tests be repeated three times, each with a different AND extension id. See Haston [1987] for more details.

7.3. Local and Global Variables

There are two basic configurations of variables in rule-based patterns. If a variable is bound in a pattern but not used in any other pattern or if it is bound and used (i.e., tested) only in the same pattern, then it is a local variable. If a variable is bound in one pattern and used in one or more other patterns or also bound in another pattern, it is a global variable.

The local–global classification is clear when the structure of the test pattern association is modified to include variables as shown in Fig. 7-10a. Figure 7-10b shows that a local variable binding can be stored in the test pattern association as it is bound during WME matching. If the pattern calls for a subsequent test of the variable's binding, it is available for such from the cell's own memory and as a result does not require any intercell communication. It is therefore a local variable. Figure 7-10b illustrates the contents of the test pattern association after WME

(^a 2 ^b 9 ^c 3) (read as attribute *a*, value 2, etc.)

has been processed.

Variables that appear in multiple tests will have bindings stored in multiple cells. In general, the variable may be bound in one cell and tested in any other. This requires intercell or global communication.

The data structure described here is adequate when using conventional ASC statements for matching patterns that have only constants and local variables.

```
(P R1
   (boy  ^name <<joe tom>>         ^age <<18 21 65>>)
   (girl ^name <<jane amy mary>> ^age {>10 <18}    )
      -->
```

a - A Complex LHS

rule id	ce	class	attribute 1 ext	prd	val	var	attribute 2 prd	val	var
R1	1	boy	0	=	joe		=	18	
R1	1	boy	0	=	joe		=	21	
R1	1	boy	0	=	joe		=	65	
R1	1	boy	0	=	tom		=	18	
R1	1	boy	0	=	tom		=	21	
R1	1	boy	0	=	tom		=	65	
R1	2	girl	1	=	jane		>	10	
R1	2	girl	1	=	jane		<	18	
R1	2	girl	2	=	amy		>	10	
R1	2	girl	2	=	amy		<	18	
R1	2	girl	3	=	mary		>	10	
R1	2	girl	3	=	mary		<	18	

b - The Association for the LHS.

Figure 7-9. An association for a complex pattern.

Under these circumstances, the rules may be stored in associative memory and the facts passed by them as they are entered or modified.

If it is desirable to store the facts and pass the rules by them, the facts can be represented as conventional association entries and the rules can be compiled into sequential code using the ASC **andif** and **andfor** constructs described in the following sections. The preferred method depends on the relative size of the fact base versus the rule base and the speeds at which they change. The larger component is usually stored in memory, and the elements of the smaller one are passed by the memory as they are input or changed.

When global variables are present, however, more complicated situations can arise. In these situations, the rules must be passed by the facts. The next sections

```
 a[$] .lt. 3 .and. (b[$] .eq. 5       .or.  b[$] .ge. 7):<x>
(a[$] .le. 4  .or.  a[$] .eq. 6):<y> .and. c[$] .le. 6 :<z>
```

a - Test Patterns

a	tsta	vara	b	tstb	varb	c	tstc	varc	bindx	bindy	bindz ...
3	100	nil	5	010	<X>	nil	nil	nil	nil	nil	nil
3	100	nil	7	110	<X>	nil	nil	nil	9	nil	nil
4	110	<y>	nil	nil	nil	6	011	<z>	nil	2	3
6	010	<y>	nil	nil	nil	6	011	<z>	nil	nil	nil

b - Associative Memory

Figure 7-10. Modified test pattern association.

describes the ASC statements that allow patterns to be efficiently implemented for both local and global variables. See Haston [1987] for a lengthier discussion of doing rule-based pattern matching using ASC.

7.4. The Andif Statement

Consider the **if** statement in Fig. 7-11. It represents the form of a generic pattern. Note in particular that if the three patterns (*a*, *b*, and *c*) are true simultaneously, the three actions (*d*, *e*, and *f*) will be performed. One of the problems with this notation is that, often, the subactions are directly related to the corresponding subpatterns and are meant to be effected on the corresponding responders. Thus action *d* depends on matches performed in part *a*, action *e* depends on pattern *b*, and *f* depends on *c*. Expressing these dependencies with conventional structured statements results in awkward cumbersome syntax.

The statement in Fig. 7-12 expresses relationships between patterns and actions in a much more intuitive manner. Still the requirement that *a*, *b*, and *c* must all have true responders is not clear. The **andif** statement in ASC allows both relationships to be expressed in structured form, as shown in Fig. 7-13.

The conditions and actions of the **andifs** are treated in exactly the same manner as standard parallel ASC **ifs**. However, when **andifs** are used, none of the actions will be executed if any of the conditions fail (i.e., no responders). Moreover, after each condition is tested, the responders are stacked prior to the next condition test and restored prior to the execution of the corresponding **andthen** body. This results in a direct relationship between the condition (**andif**) portion of a compound **andif** and the action (**andthen**) portion.

The requirement for the successful execution of a compound **andif** statement is that every **andif** condition must have one or more responders, but the responders of the individual **andif** tests are not ANDed as they are with conventional nested **if** statements. Thus, the major distinction between the **andif** and the parallel **if** statements is that the responders of tests in a parallel **if** are ANDed together on an entry-by-entry basis (see Fig. 7-3), while the **andif** requires that two or more related entries from one or more association must be matched.

When using nested **andifs** as in

andif attribute[$] .eq. color .and. value[$] .eq. red
andif attribute[$] .eq. size .and. value[$] .eq. big

```
if  a .and. b .and. c
then d .and. e .and. f endif;
```

Figure 7-11. A generic pattern.

```
if  a then d .andif.
      b then e .andif.
        c then f endif;
```

Figure 7-12. A structured pattern.

each **andif** condition will have its own set of responders. It is desirable to specify the **then** action for each corresponding set separately. Thus the **andif** statement requires a parallel_index flag which saves the state of the current responders. The corresponding **andthen** keyword is followed by the corresponding index flag. The compiler produces code to restore the scope to the value of the index flag at this time. The effect of this approach is shown in Fig. 7-14. The value field of the "color, red, table1" entry is modified to blue but the "size big table1" entry is untouched because the modification comes after the second **andthen** and therefore applies only to the responders of the first **andif**, as is appropriate for conventional structured programming techniques. The syntax for **andif** is given in Fig. 7-15.

7.5. The Andfor Statement

More general constructs can be built if an **andfor** statement is introduced. The **andif** statement described above can be thought of as an AND node in a search tree. The **andfor** is an iterative OR node. That is, if an **andfor** statement is included in a nested AND construct, the entire construct will succeed iteratively for every successful binding of the **andfor** index variable. If there are no *initial* responders to the **andfor** statement, the entire **and** construct fails and no **andthen** portions are executed.

On the other hand, if the **andfor** is in the middle of an **and** construct, the **andthen** portions belonging to **andif** statements placed after the **andfor** that use the **andfor** index variable will be executed exactly for those situations where the entire and construct is true for the specific index variable bindings. The **andthen** portions corresponding to the **andif** above the **andfor** will be executed if and only if the **andfor** has at least one successful execution.

```
andif a
   andif b
      andif c
      andthen f endandif;
   andthen e endandif;
andthen d endandif;
```

Figure 7-13. An **andif** pattern.

```
andif xx in attribute[$] .eq. color .and.
           value[$] .eq. red   .and.
         object[$] .eq. table1
    andif yy in attribute[$] .eq. size  .and.
              value[$] .eq. big   .and.
             object[$] .eq. table1
    andthen yy
    endandif yy;
 andthen xx
     value[$] = 'blue';
 endandif xx;
```

a - An **andif** Pattern and **then** Action

attribute[$]	value[$]	object[$]
color	red	table1
size	big	table1
size	big	table3
color	red	table2
size	small	table2
color	green	table3

b - Fact Association Before the **andif** Pattern

attribute[$]	value[$]	object[$]
color	blue	table1
size	big	table1
size	big	table3
color	red	table2
size	small	table2
color	green	table3

c - Fact Association After the **andif** Action

Figure 7-14. Pattern matching.

As an example of a combined **andif** and **andfor** construct, consider the rule prototype shown in Fig. 7-16. It is similar in form to an OPS5 (Brownston *et al.* [1985]) rule except that the action is specified immediately after each pattern instead of in a separate action side. This allows easy reference to the patterns. For example, (fact_id ^d ⟨x⟩ ^e ⟨z⟩) is a new fact generated by combining variable

```
andcons and_block endandcons;

andif index_variable in parallel_conditional_expression
    (and_block)
andthen index_variable
   statement_block
endandif index_variable;

andfor index_variable in parallel_conditional_expression
    (and_block)
andthen index_variable
   statement_block
endandfor index_variable;
```

Figure 7-15. And constructs syntax.

```
(rule_id_a                                   +(fact_id)^-1
  (pat_id_1 ^a <x> ^b <y> ^c <x>) --> +(^d  <x>)^-1  -(^b <y>)^-2
  (pat_id_2 ^a <y> ^b  3        ) --> +(        )^-1
  (pat_id_3         ^b <z> ^c <z>) --> +(^e  <z>)^-1
)
```

Figure 7-16. A prototype associative rule.

bindings from pat_id_1 and pat_id_3. The -1 exponents in Fig. 7-16 signify that the components (fact-id), (^d ⟨x⟩), and (^e ⟨z⟩) all belong to the same action, which is specified as a vertical column. This notation is considerably more compact than the equivalent OPS5 rule as shown in Fig. 7-17.

Figure 7-18 shows the ASC code corresponding to the rule in Fig. 7-16. Since the bottommost **andif** may have more than one responder and a new fact_id must be generated for each one, a **for qq** in the statement is required to process each responder at the bottommost **andif**. For each iteration of the **for** statement, a new cell is allocated and its *e* field is set to the value bound to variable ⟨*z*⟩, which is in the *c* field flagged by *qq*. The *pp* flags are accumulated in *rr* so that the *d* field can be initialized in parallel in the **andthen** portion of the **andfor** to the value of $a[xx]$.

The $-$(^b ⟨y⟩)$^{-2}$ action specified for pat_id_1 in Fig. 7-16 means that for every successful match, a new fact similar to the one matched by pat_id_1 is to be generated without the *b* attribute. This is accomplished by the allocate block at the end of the **andthen** block of the **andfor** statement of Fig. 7-18. A new fact cell flagged by *pp* is obtained by calling **allocate**. Since this code is in the **andthen** block of a **for** statement, *yy* points to only one entry, and only one new cell is allocated at a time. The -2 superscript signifies that this action is separate from the superscript -1 action.

Figure 7-19 shows the result of an example. Given the facts listed in Fig. 7-19a and assuming that pat_id_1 is equal to 1, pat_id_2 is equal to 2, and pat_id_3 is equal to 3, the **andfor** of Fig. 7-18 will produce two *xx* responders. In the first iteration, *xx* is bound to the entry with fact_id equal to 1 and *tt* equal to 1. The first **andif** fails with this binding (i.e., there is no $a[\$]$ equal to $b[yy] = 5$) and no action is taken.

During the second **andfor** iteration, *xx* is bound to the entry with fact_id equal to 1 and *tt* equal to 4. The first **andif** matches fact_id 2 with *tt* 3, so control passes to the second **andif**. It successfully matches both fact_id 3s (*tt* equal to 2

```
( rule_id_a
    (pat_id_1 ^a <x> ^b <y> ^c <x> )
    (pat_id_2 ^a <y> ^b  3          )
    (pat_id_3        ^b <z> ^c <z> )
-->
    (make (fact_id ^d <x> ^e <z>))
    (modify 1 -(^b <y>))
)
```

Figure 7-17. An OPS5 rule.

```
/* pat_id_1 = 1; pat_id_2 = 2; pat_id_3 = 3; */
 andfor xx in pat_id_1 .eq. fact_id[$] .and.
                  a[$] .eq. c[$]
   andif yy in pat_id_2 .eq. fact_id[$] .and.
               b[xx] .eq. a[$]        .and.
               b[$]  .eq. 3
     andif zz in pat_id_3 .eq. fact_id[$] .and.
                     b[$] .eq. c[$]
     andthen zz
       rr[$] = 0;
       for qq in them[$]
         allocate pp in bi[$]
           e[pp] = c[qq];
           rr[$] = rr[$] .or. pp[$];
         endallocate pp;
       endfor qq;
     endandif zz;
   andthen yy
   endandif yy;
 andthen xx
   setscope rr[$]
     d[$] = a[xx]; /* note c[xx] = a[xx]  */
   endsetscope;
   allocate pp in bi[$]
     a[pp] = a[xx];
     c[pp] = c[xx];
   emdallocate pp;
 endandfor xx;
```

Figure 7-18. An associative pattern implementation.

and 5), setting the scope as shown in Fig. 7-19a. After the *zz*s are set to zero in the body of the **andthen**, the **for** *qq* statement is executed. The **them** keyword in the **for** *qq* statement refers to the current setting of the responders (flagged by *xx*). The **allocate** statement nested in the **for** *qq* will allocate two new cells (one for each iteration of the flags in them) and generate the *e* values for the entries shown in Fig. 7-19b flagged by *rr*. No action is specified for the first **andif**. The action portion of the **andfor** statement fetches the *a* attribute value (2) of the entry flagged by *xx* and stores it in parallel into the *d* attributes of the two new facts flagged by *rr*.

Finally, the second **allocate** in the body of the **andthen** portion of the **andfor** implements the $-(\hat{}\text{b}\ \langle \text{y} \rangle)^{-2}$ action. It gets a new entry and flags it with *pp*. The non-*b* attributes of the fact flagged by *xx* are moved to *pp*.

7.6. Flow of Control for And Constructs

The syntax for the **andcons, andfor**, and **andif** is shown in Fig. 7-15. The **andcons** statement is required for technical reasons and is discussed last. The control structures for **andif** and **andfor** are illustrated in Figs. 7-20 and 7-21, respectively. The figures show that the action portion (i.e., statement_block) of the statement is at the end, after any nested **andfor**s or **andif**s (i.e., the and_block).

fact_id	^a	^b	^c	^d	^e	tt	scope	xx	rr	pp
1	3	5	3			1		1		
3	17	5	5			2	1			
2	4	3	14			3				
1	2	4	2			4		1		
3	12	9	9			5	1			
1	3	8	2			6				

a - Original Facts

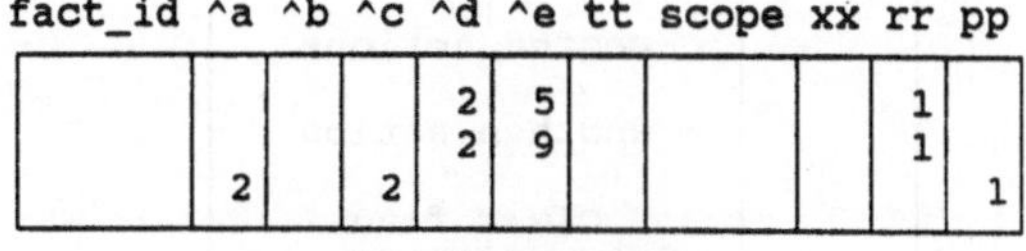

fact_id	^a	^b	^c	^d	^e	tt	scope	xx	rr	pp
				2	5				1	
				2	9				1	
	2		2							1

b - New Facts

Figure 7-19. A fact base.

This is to ensure that the action is executed only if there is a successful search for all constructs combined. Only **andfors** and **andifs** may be nested in the optional and_block. The and_block is empty for the bottom level of nesting. Any failure in any of the nested constructs exits the code via the fail path. Successful searches exit through the success path.

The control structure for the **andfor** shown in Fig. 7-21 is made slightly more complicated than the **andif**, in order to accommodate its iterative nature. The complication of the construct is due to the fact that the **andfor** must select a binding for the index variable, which may then be used by nested **and** constructs in their searches. If any of these subsequent nested searches fail, control must return to the present **andfor** so that the next binding can be tried.

If there are no responders to the initial search of an **andfor**, the fail path is taken. Otherwise, a flag is set which will be cleared only if one or more of the

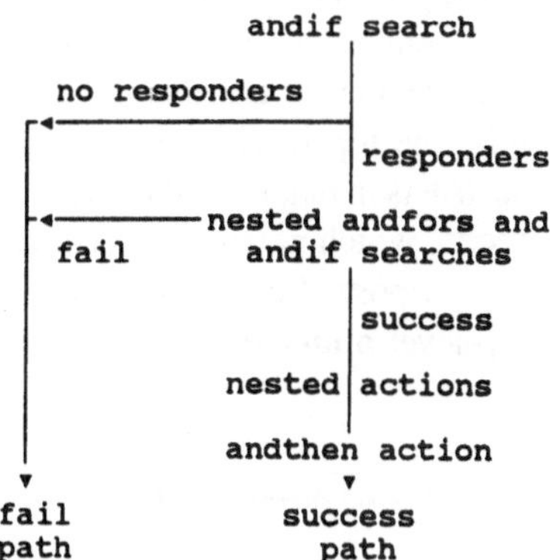

Figure 7-20. Andif control logic.

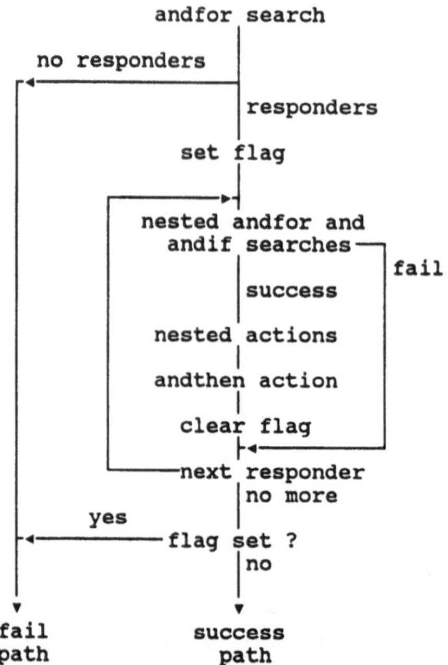

Figure 7-21. Andfor control logic.

andfor's index-variable bindings is successful. That is, since **andfor** is an "OR node," only one of the initial responders needs to be on a success path in order for the **andfor** construct to be successful.

Note that when nested **andfors** are used, the index variable binding is valid throughout the entire body of the construct so that it may be used in all of the action and search portions of nested constructs.

In a conventional parallel **if**, the fail exit and the success exit join at the bottom of the construct. However, with **and** constructs it is necessary to keep the fail and success exits separate so that a failure can exit the entire nested **and** construct instead of just the statement the failure occurred in. This means that an exit label must be provided to the nested **andifs** and **andfors** by the higher-level **and** construct. Consequently, the top level **and** construct is different from the nested **andif** and **andfor** constructs in that it must provide its own global exit label. A top level statement, **andcons**, which performs no computation, only control of structure, is supplied for this purpose. Figure 7-22 shows a six-level nested **and** construct bracketed by a top-level **andcons**.

7.7. Conclusion

As shown in the initial examples, there is a strong relationship between rule matching and **and** constructs. A matching rule can be expressed in an associative

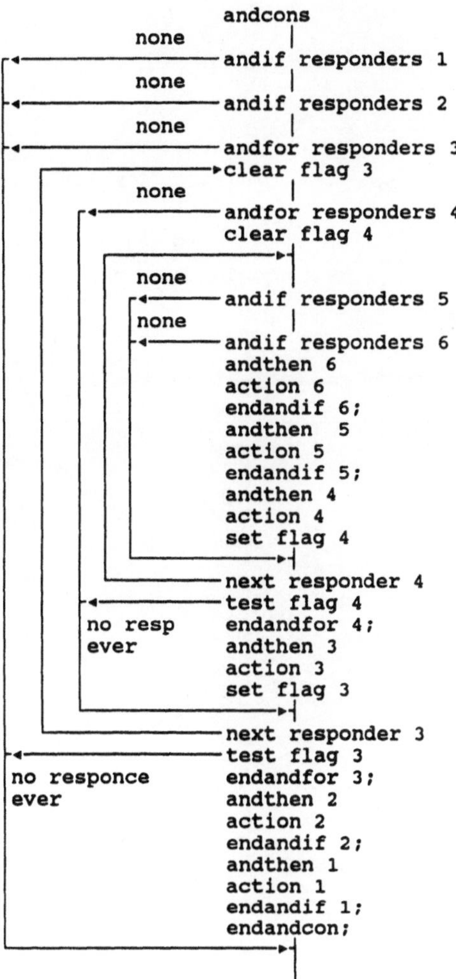

Figure 7-22. Nested **andifs** and **andfors**.

parallel form using ASC **andif** and **andfor** statements. The parallel searching capabilities of ASC have been used to compile context-sensitive rules of the form shown in Fig. 7-16 into **andif** and **andfor** constructs (Asthagiri [1986]); see Chapter 8. The nested **andif** and **andfor** constructs can be envisioned as tree searches to a fixed depth, with different search and action specifications at every level.

8

Context-Sensitive Compilation*

This chapter describes a procedure for compiling production rules into an equivalent parallel-procedural sequence of ASC **andif** and **andfor** statements. Since the compiler is written in ASC, this also provides a nontrivial example of the use of ASC.

First, the context-sensitive nature of rule-based languages and their associated databases is discussed. Then a brief overview of the basic approach to rule compilation is given. Next is a more detailed section on the conversion of a rule from a context-sensitive viewpoint. Finally, an example of the execution of a compiled production rule is given. (See section 7.1 for a brief review of the OPS5 rule format.)

8.1. Context Sensitivity

Context sensitivity is present in most high-level languages. In particular, consider rule-based languages which use variables. For example, Fig. 8-1a shows seven variables in the LHS patterns of an OPS5† rule. Variable $\langle m \rangle$ is a local variable because it occurs only in the pattern $n1$. Although variable $\langle z \rangle$ occurs twice in pattern $n2$, it is also a local variable, since it occurs only in $n2$. Variable $\langle x \rangle$ is a global variable since it occurs in both patterns $n1$ and $n3$. The local/global determination of variables is central to the compilation of these patterns into an executable sequence of code and is obviously context sensitive.

The context sensitivity of OPS5 rules is used to determine how to process them. A data-broadcast mechanism is used for processing patterns without global variables, and a rule-broadcast mechanism is used for processing patterns with

*Co-authored by Chandra R. Asthagiri.

†This research was performed using OPS5 (Forgy [1981]); however, the principles are general and are applicable to other rule-based languages such as Prolog or DATALOG.

```
(p r1
   ( n1 ^a1  <x>  ^a3 5   ^a15 <m> ^a20 <i>)
   ( n2 ^a4  <z>  ^a5 bob ^a16 <z>)
   ( n3 ^a7  cons ^a6 <x> ^a8 <y>  ^a19 <i> ^a9  <y> ^a2 <w>
        ^a13 <n>)
   ( n4 ^a10 <y>  ^a12 <w>)
   ( n5 ^a11 <n>)
   -->
   ( modify 1 ^a3  nil ^a1 5)
   ( remove 2)
   ( modify 3 ^a6  55)
   ( modify 4 ^a10 mom)
   ( remove 5)
)
```

a - An OPS5 Rule

```
(n1 ^a1 10 ^a3 5 ^a4 2 ^a8 8 ^a9 8 ^a10 dad ^a20 20)
```

b - An OPS5 Working Memory Element

Figure 8-1. OPS5 rules and data.

global variables. In the data-broadcast mode, the rules are compiled into associative data structures as described in section 7.2. The data items (see Fig. 8-1b for an OPS5 datum or WME) are broadcast in one parallel step to all of the rule patterns stored in the PEs. The success or failure of each test and its associated bindings are saved in the appropriate PEs. In the rule-broadcast mode, each rule with a global variable constraint is compiled into an ASC **and** construct, which is executed at run time. The global tests for a rule are executed whenever a fact which is being added to the database successfully matches the local tests of the rule. The **and** construct broadcasts the global requirements of the rule to all of the data structures testing all of the facts in the database in parallel. This approach to rule-based processing requires the use of context-sensitive analysis to separate local from global variables and a context-sensitive grammar to compile global rules into a program.

Selecting which pattern to compile first is also context sensitive. The compiled **and** construct executes more efficiently if parallel **andif** statements are executed first and last. If any test in the **andif** construct fails, the entire **and** construct fails. Thus, when an outer test fails, the inner, more complex global-interaction variable consistency tests can be skipped. Selecting a pattern without global variables so that an **andif** construct can be compiled at the top level is context sensitive. Notice that the second LHS pattern of Fig. 8-1a has no global variables and would be compiled first.

8.2. A Brief Overview

The patterns used in this chapter are intentionally simple to minimize the impact of the details of rule-based systems on the topics of this section. For the sake of generality and simplicity, this chapter describes how a complete rule, including the local and global patterns, can be compiled into a single sequence of code. Faster execution is achieved, however, if the rule is divided into local and global portions. All of the local patterns are compiled into one data structure, as described in sections 7.1 and 7.2. The global patterns are compiled into executable code as described in this chapter. When a new fact is added to or deleted from the data base, it is broadcast to the local patterns in parallel. Patterns which are successfully matched are identified, and the global pattern tests associated with them are executed. In this way, the local pattern testing which is done in parallel for all rules in the program acts as a filter minimizing the number and complexity of the global rules that must be run. For more information on rule-based processing in associative computers, the interested reader is referred to Haston [1987] and Potter *et al.* [1987b].

The semantics of the ASC **and** constructs allows them to be chained together to effect a complete OPS5 rule pattern test. LHS patterns map onto **andifs** and **andfors**. **Andifs** basically search the fact database in parallel for constant matches. That is, as a first-order approximation, if an OPS5 pattern or class has only constant values in its attribute–value pairs, then it is compiled into an **andif** construct. The ANDing of the class patterns into a rule is achieved by nesting **andifs**—one **andif** for each pattern. Just as all patterns in a rule must be true for the rule to fire, all nested **andifs** must be true before any of their statement bodies are executed.

In the same way as **andifs** handle constant attribute–value matching, **andfors** handle variable attribute–value bindings and matching. **Andfors** iterate on all possible consistent fact bindings. **Andfors** may be nested within **andifs** and **andfors** and execute in an environment determined by the values of the surrounding **andfor** bindings. With nested **andifs** and **andfors**, if any inner nested **andif** or **andfor** fails, the entire nested substructure fails and the next **andfor** iteration is bound and tested. This preserves the basic production-rule concept that a rule takes effect only when all of the LHS conditions are simultaneously true. Under some conditions, discussed later, some constant tests may be incorporated into **andfors**. This in effect combines an **andif** with an **andfor**, resulting in a simpler, more efficient construct that in no way alters the execution of the rule.

OPS5, as shown in Fig. 8-1a, treats the class or pattern names (*n*1, *n*2, . . .) as special items. However, in associative computing there is no need to do so, and in fact rule transformation is much simpler if the rule and pattern names are treated like any other attribute–value pairs. Figure 8-2 gives the associative version of the rule shown in Fig. 8-1a. Note that in this form, the class name attribute is ^*cn* and

```
(^rn rl
 (^cn nl ^al <x> ^a3 5 ^a15 <m> ^a20 <i>)
 (^cn n2 ^a4 <z> ^a5 bob ^a16 <z>)
 (^cn n3 ^a7 cons ^a6 <x> ^a8 <y> ^a19 <i>
         ^a9 <y> ^a2 <w> ^a13 <n>)
 (^cn n4 ^a10 <y> ^a12 <w>)
 (^cn n5 ^a11 <n>)
-->
```

Figure 8-2. An associative version of the rule.

the value is the ASCII name of the pattern or class. The ASC code which follows assumes the input is in conventional OPS5 form, but it produces code for the internal associative form.

8.3. Context-Sensitive Compilation

Section 8.3.2 describes the context-sensitive rules used to translate production rules into ASC procedures. First, however, section 8.3.1 discusses the order in which the context-sensitive rules need to be applied, the order in which the LHS patterns need to be compiled, and the order in which RHS patterns need to be compiled. Section 8.4 gives an example of compiling a production rule into an equivalent procedure and the execution of the procedural rule.

LHS patterns can be classified into the following types:

1. A pattern is a local pattern if it does not contain any global variables. For example, pattern *n*2 (class *n*2) in Fig. 8-1a is a local pattern.
2. A pattern is a global pattern if it contains at least one global variable. For example, all patterns except *n*2 in Fig. 8-1a are global patterns.
3. The first global pattern in a rule is the global pattern which is not preceded by any other global pattern. Thus pattern *n*l in Fig. 8-1a is the first global pattern.
4. A global variable is said to be a distinct global variable (DGV) for a pattern if that pattern is the first one to contain it. For example, in Fig. 8-1a, ⟨*x*⟩ and ⟨*i*⟩ are DGVs for pattern *n*l but not for pattern *n*3. Similarly, ⟨*y*⟩, ⟨*w*⟩, and ⟨*n*⟩ are DGVs for pattern *n*3, but not for *n*4 or *n*5. Nonfirst global patterns can be divided into two types: those with one or more DGVs and those without any. Accordingly, *n*3 is a DGV pattern but *n*4 and *n*5 are non-DGV (NDGV) patterns.

The tn variables (i.e., *t*l, *t*2, and so on) in Fig. 8-3 following the **andif** and **andfor** keywords are one-bit temporary parallel-index variables. For each **andfor** and **andif** statement, a unique tn is used to flag the responders to the tests of the associated LHS-pattern. The index variable from a previous **andfor** statement flags the responders to the tests of a previous pattern, which contained a global

```
/* Pattern matching tests for local pattern n2 */
andif t1 in cn[$] .eq. n2                                          a
    .and  a5[$] .eq. bob                                           aa
    .and. a4[$] .eq. a16                                          aaa
/* Pattern matching tests for first global pattern n1 */
andfor t2 in cn[$] .eq. n1                                         b
       .and. a3[$] .eq. 5                                          bb
/* Pattern matching tests for dgv global pattern n3 */
andfor t3 in cn[$] .eq. n3 .and. a1[t2] .eq. a6[$]                 c
       .and. a20[t2] .eq. a19[$] .and.                             cc
       .and. a7[$] .eq. cons .and. a8[$] .eq. a9[$]               ccc
/* Pattern matching tests for non-dgv patterns n4 and n5         */
andif t4 in cn[$] .eq. n4 .and. a8[t3] .eq. a10[$]                 d
       .and.  a2[t3] .eq. a12[$]                                   dd
andif t5 in cn[$] .eq. n5 .and. a13[t3] .eq. a11[$]                e

andthen t5
  cn[$] = NIL ;                            /*code for RHS pattern 5*/
endandif t5 ;
andthen t4
  a10[$] = mom ;                           /*code for RHS pattern 4*/
endandif t4 ;
andthen t3
  a6[T3] = 55 ;                            /*code for RHS pattern 3*/
endandfor T3 ;
andthen t2
  a3[t2] = NIL ;                           /*code for RHS pattern 1*/
  a1[t2] = 5 ;
endandfor t2 ;
andthen t1
  a4[$] = NIL ;                            /*code for RHS pattern 2*/
endandif t1 ;
```

Figure 8-3. An ASC **and** construct.

variable, and is used to restrict the binding of that global variable in the current pattern. Thus *t*2, in line *b* of Fig. 8-3, flags the responders of the constant tests from the first pattern in Fig. 8-1. Since pattern *n*1 has variable ⟨*x*⟩ associated with attribute *a*1, *t*2 is used to restrict the binding of ⟨*x*⟩ in the third pattern (attribute *a*6 of pattern *n*3 in Fig. 8-1) to those WMEs which passed the constant tests of the first pattern (*n*1), i.e.,

a1[t2] .eq. a6[$]

in line *c* of Fig. 8-3. Index variables used in this manner are referred to as *restricting index variables*.

8.3.1. Order of Execution

The purpose of rule compilation is to increase the executional efficiency of a production system by using the associative parallelism in the ASC **and** constructs. The **and** constructs can be used to the fullest extent when LHS patterns of a production rule are compiled into a proper sequence of **andif/andfor**s. Figure 8-4 shows the relationship between the type (local, first global, DGV, or NDGV) of an LHS pattern and the context-sensitive rule sequence to be applied to it. The left

Order of Compilation	Pattern Type	Pattern	Rules in sequence Order of Compilation →	Type of **and** construct
I	local	n2	1, 6*, 7*	**andif**
II	first global	n1	2, 6*, 7*	**andfor**
III	dgv	n3	3, 5+, 6*, 7*	**andfor**
IV ▼	non-dgv	n4,n5	4, 5+, 6*, 7*	**andif**
			* = closure + = positive closure	

Figure 8-4. The relationship among LHS patterns, context-sensitive rules, and ASP **and** constructs.

column shows the order of compilation of the LHS pattern types (from I to IV). The third column gives an example of the pattern type from Fig. 8-1. Each row in the fourth column gives the order of application (from left to right) of the context-sensitive rules during the compilation of the LHS patterns. The far-right column shows what type of **and** construct is generated for the patterns.

Tests for local patterns are less complex than those for global patterns. The tests are mostly constant tests or intraelement-variable tests which can be accomplished at all PEs in parallel with the use of only their local memories. So, first, all the local patterns are compiled to generate the top (outer) level **andif**s (row I in Fig. 8-4). Then the first global pattern (row II) and then all the patterns with at least one DGV are compiled to **andfor**s (row III). Finally, all of the remaining global LHS patterns are compiled to generate the bottom (innermost) level **andif**s (row IV).

After compiling all of the LHS patterns of a rule into an equivalent set of pattern-matching tests of **andif**s and **andfor**s, the RHS actions associated with the LHS patterns are compiled in reverse order, since the statements are nested and the action of the innermost nested statement must be executed before the outermost (see Fig. 8-3). Note that the action for **andif**s is executed in data-parallel mode, while the action for **andfor**s is restricted by the index variable.

The rationale behind this order of construction is that when an outer test fails in a rule, all global-interaction and/or binding-consistency tests can be skipped. Thus the simpler local tests filter the data items reducing the number of times the more complex global tests must be executed. In addition, the bottom-level tests are parallel **andif**s if possible, thus maximizing the computational efficiency of the innermost nested statements.

8.3.2. The Rules of Compilation

This section describes the context-sensitive rules used to generate the **andif** and **andfor** constructs. The first four rules describe the action for the four basic pattern types described above and shown in Fig. 8-4. The next three rules are applicable to two or more of the pattern types. Rules 6 and 7 for example, are applied to all pattern types and attach the local tests of the pattern to the previous

andif or **andfor** generated by rule 1, 2, 3, or 4. Note that the order of description in this section is not the order of application as shown in Fig. 8-4. That is, once a pattern is found and rule 1, 2, 3, or 4 is applied, rules 6 and 7 are applied to the pattern to complete its processing before the next pattern is selected and processed. After the rules are explained in this section, the next section gives an example of how the rule of Fig. 8-la is converted to the code of Fig. 8-3.

8.3.2.1. Compiler Overview

As the transformation rules are discussed below, the ASC code that implements them will be given. In order that this code may be meaningful, this section will briefly outline the flow of control and the data associations of the rule-compilation program.

The source code is input using the **scin** input function, producing a nested LISP list representation. Figure 8-5 shows the LHS association in three columns in order to save space. In the associative computer, the data is in a single column for maximum parallelism.

After the code is input, it is associatively scanned to flag variables, constants, operators, etc., as shown in Fig. 8-6. Figure 8-7 gives the main program. As shown, the data is searched next to detect local and global variables and to determine the pattern types using subroutine lgvar shown in Fig. 8-8. Since a local variable may appear more than once, but only within the same pattern, the searching is performed on a pattern-by-pattern basis. Once the property of a variable has been determined, it is flagged wherever it appears so that it will not be processed again.

Subroutine lgvar loops until all patterns have been processed. Since the first global pattern must be determined, the patterns are processed in order by structure

psc[$]	pel[$]	pid[$]	psc[$] (continued)	pel[$]	pid[$]	psc[$] (continued)	pel[$]	pid[$]
100000	p	0	460000	^a16	2	5f0000	<n>	3
200000	r1	0	470000	<z>	2	610000	n4	4
310000	n1	1	510000	n3	3	620000	^a10	4
320000	^a1	1	520000	^a7	3	630000	<y>	4
330000	<x>	1	530000	cons	3	640000	^a12	4
340000	^a3	1	540000	^a6	3	650000	<w>	4
350000	5	1	550000	<x>	3	710000	n5	5
360000	^a15	1	560000	^a8	3	720000	^a11	5
370000	<m>	1	570000	<y>	3	730000	<n>	5
380000	^a20	1	580000	^a19	3		:	
390000	<i>	1	590000	<i>	3		:	
410000	n2	2	5a0000	^a9	3			
420000	^a4	2	5b0000	<y>	3			
430000	<z>	2	5c0000	^a2	3			
440000	^a5	2	5d0000	<w>	3			
450000	bob	2	5e0000	^a13	3			

Figure 8-5. Structure codes for an OPS5 LHS.

```
subroutine scanner

defvar(char, pel);
char parallel pel:64[$], char:8[$,8];

define(CARAT, x'5E');    /* ^ */
define(MULOP, x'2A');    /* * */
define(ZERO, x'30');     /* 0 */
define(NINE, x'39');     /* 9 */

if char[$,0] .eq. CARAT then attribute[$] = TRUE; endif;
if char[$,0] .eq. MULOP then  operator[$] = MULT; endif;
if char[$,0] .ge. ZERO  .and.
   char[$,0] .le. NINE  then  constant[$] = TRUE; endif;
     :
if .not. (attribute[$] .or. constant[$] .or.
         (operator[$] .ne. 0) ...) then
   atom[$] = TRUE;
endif;

end;
```

Figure 8-6. Scanner subroutine.

```
main cops5

scin(pel[$], psc[$], pbi[$]);
call scanner;
/* mark fstglo, local, dgv and ndgv patterns */
call lgvar;
tn = x't0';
level = 0;
offset = 0;
unprocessed[$] = TRUE;
/* compile local patterns - rule 1 */
while yy in pbi[$] .and. local[$]
  pat[$] = pid[yy] .eq. pid[$];
  call rule1 tn<nxttn;
  nxttn = nxttn+1;
  call rule6;
  call rule7;
  release pat[$] from unprocessed[$];
endwhile yy;
/* process first global pattern - rule 2 */
get zz in  sbi[$]
  get yy in savvr[zz] .eq. pel[$] .and. fstglo[$]
    pat[$] = fstglo[$];
    call rule2 tn<savtn[yy] ni<savat[yy];
    nxttn = nxttn+1;
    call rule6;
    call rule7;
    release pat[$] from unprocessed[$];
  endget yy;
endget zz;
call dgv;  /* rule 3 */
call ndgv; /* rule 4 */
scot(oel[$], osc[$], obi[$]);
end;
```

Figure 8-7. The main program.

```
subroutine lgvar
fstc = TRUE;/* first clause */  fstr = TRUE;/* first rule */
if psc[$] .gt. x'200000' .and. pbi[$] then
  unprocessed[$] = TRUE;
endif;
loop                                                                g
  if unprocessed[$] then                                            a
    if pid[$] .eq. pid[mindex(psc[$])] then pat[$] = TRUE;          a
  endif; endif;                                                     a
  any unprocessed[$] .and. variable[$] .and. pat[$]                 b
   while yy in unprocessed[$] .and. variable[$] .and. pat[$]        c
     if pel[yy] .eq. pel[$] then                                    d
       any .not. pat[$]
         setscope pbi[$]
           if fstr then                                             e
             if fstc then
               fstglo[$] = pat[$]; fstc =  FALSE;
             endif;
           else dgv[$] = pat[$];                                    ee
           endif;                                                   e
         endsetscope;
         global[$] = TRUE; /* must be outside setscope */
       elsenany
         setscope pbi[$] local[$] = pat[$]; endsetscope;
       endany;
       unprocessed[$] = FALSE;
     endif;
   endwhile yy;                                                     c
   if .not. fstc then
     fstr = FALSE; fstc = TRUE;
   endif;
  elsenany                                                          bb
   any global[$] .and. variable[$] .and. pat[$]
     global[$] = pat[$];
     ndgv[$] = pat[$];
   elsenany
     local[$] = pat[$];
  endany; endany;                                                   b
  /* if one or more global variables, flag entire pattern */
  any pat[$] .and. .not. (global[$] .or. local[$] .or.              f
        fstglo[$] .or. dgv[$] .or. ndgv[$])
     any pat[$] .and. global[$]
     global[$] = pat[$]; elsenany local[$] = pat[$];
  endany; endany;                                                   f
  release pat[$] from unprocessed[$];
  until nany unprocessed[$]
  endloop;
end;
```

Figure 8-8. The local–global detection subroutine.

code. Thus the first two **if** statements on lines *a* in Fig. 8-8 select the (first) unprocessed pattern (i.e., smallest structure code) and flag it with pat[$].

The **any** statement of lines *b* looks for unprocessed variables in the pattern. If none are found (line *bb*), either the pattern contains one or more global variables that have already been processed and flagged or it contains no variables at all. In the former case, the pattern is NDGV. In the latter case it is local.

The **while** statement (lines *c*) in the **any** part of the **any** statement processes the variables iteratively. First, scope is restricted to all like variables in the rule by an **if** statement (line *d*). If there are responders which are not in the current pattern (i.e., not flagged with pat[$]), a global variable is being processed and, as a result, a global pattern. The scalar **if** statements (lines *e*) are true if this is the first global pattern. In that case the fstglo[$] flag is set for the pattern and fstc is set to FALSE. Since the first global–DGV determination is mutually exclusive and the determination is inside a double loop (**while** *yy*, line *c*, and loop, line *g*), two flags (fstr and fstc) are required.

If this is not the first pattern (line *ee*) and the pattern contains an as-yet-unprocessed variable, then the pattern is flagged as DGV. Note that in order to flag the entire pattern, a **setscope** has to be used to override the parallel **if** (line *d*) that restricts the scope to just the responding global variables. After the pattern type has been determined, the scope of the parallel **if** is restored so that the responding variables can be flagged as global or local and not unprocessed. The bottom **any** statement, lines *f*, catches any patterns not previously classified. If the pattern contains one or more variable flagged as global, the entire pattern is flagged as global. Otherwise, the pattern is flagged as local.

As shown in Fig. 8-7, the local patterns are compiled next. The flow of control of the main program simply calls the subroutines for the rules in the order shown in the fourth column of Fig. 8-4. The subroutines for processing DGV and NDGV patterns are shown in Figs. 8-9 and 8-10, respectively.

The rule subroutines shown in Figs. 8-11 and 8-12 are mostly used to call the code-generation subroutines, Fig. 8-13, in the correct order. The output is generated using structure codes and the output association (oel[$], osc[$], obi[$]). The output code is output by routine **scot8**, which outputs new lines and tabs in place of parentheses resulting in indented-block structured code. The templates of

```
subroutine dgv;

/* process all dgv patterns */
while zz in dgv[$] .and. sbi[$]                                    a
 /*pick rule with global var*/
 while yy in dgv[$] .and. pbi[$] .and. unprocessed[$] .and.
             pel[$] .eq. savvr[zz]
 savit[$] = them[$];                   /* save for rule5 */
 pat[$] = pid[yy] .eq. pid[$];
 unprocessed[$] = pat[$];
 setscope pat[$]                       /* set class name */
   cn = pel[mindex(psc[$])];
 endsetscope;
    call rule3;
    nxttn = nxttn+1;
    call rule5;
    call rule6;
    call rule7;
    release pat[$] from unprocessed[$];
 endwhile yy;
endwhile zz;

end;
```

Figure 8-9. The DGV subroutine.

```
subroutine ndgv

/* process all remaining ndgv patterns */
while zz in .not. dgv[$] .and. sbi[$]                               a
 while yy in dgv[$] .and. pbi[$] .and. unprocessed[$] .and.
            pel[$] .eq. savvr[zz]
 savit[$] = them[$]; /* save for rule5 */
 pat[$] = pid[yy] .eq. pid[$];
 unprocessed[$] = pat[$];
 setscope pat[$]
   cn = pel[mindex(psc[$])]; /*save class name*/
 endsetscope;
    call rule4;
    nxttn = nxttn+1;
    call rule5;
    call rule6;
    call rule7;
    release pat[$] from unprocessed[$];
 endwhile yy;
endwhile zz;

end;
```

Figure 8-10. Subroutine NDGV.

the **andif** and **andfor** statements are generated by **scst** functions. The **scst** routine, like **scin**, returns a field flagging the newly created association entry. The structure codes generated by the copy statement are origined at the specified level and offset, where level specifies the starting (leftmost) structure code digit and offset specifies the initial value of the structure code. The subroutine incroff (not shown) adds the value specified in *i* to the rightmost nonzero digit of the offset.

Normally, the **scst** functions would be in a separate initialization subroutine that is executed only once. They are shown in the generation routines for convenience only. The sequence of code generated by the routines is shown at the beginning of each. The copy function used in these routines returns a flag of the newly created entries.

8.3.2.2. Local-Pattern Rule

The local-pattern rule, given in rule 1 below and coded in Fig. 8-11, initiates an **andif** construct for each local pattern.

Rule 1: If an LHS pattern, nm, does not contain any global variables, then generate

andif tn in cn[$] .eq. nm . . .

where . . . represents the local-interaction tests of the pattern.

The local interaction tests are generated by rules 6 and 7, described in section 8.3.2.6, below. Since pattern *n*2 in Fig. 8-1a is a local pattern,

```
subroutine rule1
if pat[$] then
   call genif;
   unprocessed[mindex(psc[$])] = FALSE;
endif;
end;

subroutine rule2
   call genfor;
   call savelink;
   unprocessed[mindex(psc[$])] = FALSE;
end;

subroutine rule3
   call genfor;
   call savelink;
   unprocessed[mindex(psc[$])] = FALSE;
   call augment pan<savat[zz] ptn<savtn[zz]
                am<pel[prvdex(psc[yy])];
   unprocessed[yy] = FALSE;
end;

subroutine rule4
   call genif;
   unprocessed[mindex(psc[$])] = FALSE;
   call augment pan<savat[zz] ptn<savtn[zz]
                am<pel[prvdex(psc[yy])];
   unprocessed[yy] = FALSE;
end;


subroutine savelink
  for xx in global[$] .and. variable[$]
          .and. unprocessed[$] .and. pat[$]
    allocate qq in sbi[$]
      savat[qq] = pel[prvdex(psc[xx])];/* attribute*/
      savvr[qq] = pel[xx];              /* value */
      savtn[qq] = tn;                   /* restrict index */
      savdgv[qq] = dgv[xx];             /* dgv status */
    endallocate qq;
  endfor xx;
end;
```

Figure 8-11. Routines for rules 1–4.

andif t1 in cn[$] .eq. n2

is generated as shown on line *a* of Fig. 8-3. All of the local patterns of a rewrite rule are processed first.

8.3.2.3. First Global-Pattern Rule

The first global-pattern rule, rule 2 below, initiates the first **andfor** construct for the first global pattern. The first global pattern has at least one global variable to be correlated with subsequent patterns. The correlation requires that the restricting index variable and the global variable with its associated attribute name be passed to rule 3 or 4 via the savelink subroutine. The global variable name and

```
subroutine rule5
while nn in savit[$] .and. unprocessed[$] .and. pat[$]
    .and. variable[$]
  get xx in pel[nn] .eq. savvn[$]
     call augment pan<savat[xx] ptn<savtn[xx]
                  am<pel[prvdex(psc[nn])];
  endget xx;
  unprocessed[nn] = FALSE;
endwhile nn;
end;

subroutine rule6  /* .and. at [$] .eq. val */
andplate[$] = scst(tel[$], tsc[$], tbi[$], "(.and., [$] .eq.,);
atplate[$] = scst(tel[$], tsc[$], tbi[$], "(, at,,,);
valplate[$] = scst(tel[$], tsc[$], tbi[$], "(,,,, val);
while nn in pat[$] .and. (atom[$] .or. constant[$]) .and.
            unprocessed[$]
  copy(tbi[$], level, offset, andplate[$],
             oel[$], osc[$], obi[$]);
  oel[copy(tbi[$], level, offset, atplate[$],
             oel[$], osc[$], obi[$])]
    = pel[prvdex(psc[nn]);
  oel[copy(tbi[$], level, offset, valplate[$], obi[$])]
    = pel[nn];
  call incroff i < 5  off<offset;
  unprocessed[nn] = FALSE;
endwhile nn;
end;

subroutine rule7   /* .and. an[$] .eq. am[$] */
define(DOLLAR, x'24');
ptn = DOLLAR;
while nn in pat[$] .and. variable[$] .and.
            local[$] .and. unprocessed[$]
  pan = pel[prvdex(psc[nn])];
  while mm in them[$] .and. .not. nn[$]
      call augment am<pel[prvdex(psc[mm])];
      unprocessed[mm] = FALSE;
  endwhile mm;
  unprocessed[nn] = FALSE;
endwhile nn;
end;
```

Figure 8-12. Code for rules 5–7.

attribute name are required by rules 3 and 4 for proper processing. Since processing the responding WMEs requires iteration, an **andfor** construct is generated.

Rule 2: If a LHS pattern, nm, is the first global pattern, then generate

andfor tn in cn[$] .eq. nm . . .

where . . . represents the local interaction tests of the pattern generated by rules 6 and 7.

By applying rule 2 (see Fig. 8-12) to pattern *n*1 in Fig. 8-1,

andfor t2 in cn[$] .eq. n1

```
/* routine to generate: "andif tn in cn[$] .eq. ni"  */
subroutine genif  /* tn<..  ni<.. */
ifplate[$] = scst(tel[$], tsc[$], tbi[$],
                  "(andif, in cn[$] .eq.,)");
tnplate[$] = scst(tel[$], tsc[$], tbi[$], "(, tn ,,,,)");
cnplate[$] = scst(tel[$], tsc[$], tbi[$], "(,,,,, ni)");
copy(tbi[$], level, offset, ifplate[$], oel[$],
     osc[$], obi[$]);
oel[copy(tbi[$], level, offset, tnplate[$], oel[$],
         osc[$], obi[$])] = tn;
oel[copy(tbi[$], level, offset, cnplate[$], oel[$],
         osc[$], obi[$])] = ni;
call incroff i<6;
end;

/* routine to generate: "andfor tn in cn[$] .eq. ni"  */
subroutine genfor   /* tn<..  ni<.. */
forplate[$] = scst(tel[$], tsc[$], tbi[$],
                   "(andfor, in cn[$] .eq.,)");
tnplate[$]  = scst(tel[$], tsc[$], tbi[$], "(, tn ,,,,)");
cnplate[$]  = scst(tel[$], tsc[$], tbi[$], "(,,,,, ni)");
copy(tbi[$], level, offset, forplate[$], obi[$]);
oel[copy(tbi[$], level, offset, tnplate[$], oel[$],
         osc[$], obi[$])] = tn;
oel[copy(tbi[$], level, offset, cnplate[$], oel[$],
         osc[$], obi[$])] = ni;
call incroff i<6;
end;

/* routine to generate: ".and. pan[ptn] .eq. am[$]"  */
subroutine augment  /* pan<savat[xx] ptn<savtn[xx]
                       am<pel[prvdex(psc[nn])] */
augplate[$] =
    scst(tel[$], tsc[$], tbi[$], "(.and., [ , ] .eq., [$])");
panplate[$] = scst(tel[$], tsc[$], tbi[$], "(, pan ,,,,,,)");
ptnplate[$] = scst(tel[$], tsc[$], tbi[$], "(,,, ptn ,,,,)");
amplate[$]  = scst(tel[$], tsc[$], tbi[$], "(,,,,,,, am,)");
copy(tbi[$], level, offset, augplate[$], oel[$],
     osc[$], obi[$]);
oel[copy(tbi[$], level, offset, panplate[$], oel[$],
         osc[$], obi[$])] = pan;
oel[copy(tbi[$], level, offset, ptnplate[$], oel[$],
         osc[$], obi[$])] = ptn;
oel[copy(tbi[$], level, offset, amplate[$], oel[$],
         osc[$],  obi[$])] = am;
call incroff i<8;
end;
```

Figure 8-13. The code-generation subroutines.

is generated in Fig. 8-3, line *b*. Note that the restricting index *t*2 used in rule 2, the attribute name *a*1, and the variable name ⟨*x*⟩ are saved.

8.3.2.4. Global-Interaction Rules

The global-interaction rules are used to chain the global patterns into an **and** construct. The global-interaction rules generate code which tests for consistent global bindings. That is, when processing a LHS pattern *p*, with a global variable ⟨*b*⟩, if there is a LHS pattern *q* that occurs after *p* and has the same global variable

$\langle b \rangle$, then it is necessary to check for the consistency of the binding of $\langle b \rangle$ in the WMEs that match patterns p and q.

The WMEs and thus the binding of $\langle b \rangle$ matching pattern p may be further restricted by other tests in p. The WMEs which satisfy all of the restrictions are flagged by a parallel index variable. That is, the index variable is used to restrict the binding of $\langle b \rangle$ in pattern q to the WMEs that are consistent with the binding for $\langle b \rangle$ in p. Since this restriction is limited to one binding value at a time, an **andfor** is used to iterate through all possible bindings. Thus, for example, let p be $n1$, $\langle b \rangle$ be $\langle x \rangle$, and q be $n3$; then

```
andfor t3 in cn[$] .eq. n3 .and. a1[t2] .eq. a6[$] . . .
```

is needed in Fig. 8-3 (line c). *T2* is a restricting-index variable since it flags the logically ANDed result of all tests of pattern $n1$. This global-interaction test looks for consistent bindings of $\langle x \rangle$ associated with $a1$ in the first pattern and $\langle x \rangle$ associated with $a6$ in the third pattern. The result of this test and all of the other tests of the third LHS pattern of Fig. 8-1 are logically ANDed and flagged by the new restricting index variable $t3$. Thus global interaction patterns generate chains of tests.

The chaining is organized by the savelink association (savat[$], savvr[$], savtn[$], and savdgv[$] (see Fig. 8-12). That is, rules 3 and 4 are called inside **while** statements (see Figs. 8-9 and 8-10, lines *a*) that selects savelink association entries. The global-variable name associated with the entry is used to search for the patterns to be processed by rule 3 or 4. Rule 3 processes DGV patterns and rule 4 processed NDGV patterns. Note that rule 3 consumes and generates savem entries, but rule 3 just consumes them.

Rule 3: If there is an LHS pattern p, with restricting index variable tj associated with a global variable $\langle v \rangle$ and attribute am, and there is another LHS pattern q occurring after p with the same global variable $\langle b \rangle$ associated with attribute an, and q has at least one DGV that does not occur in p, then generate

```
andfor tk in cn[$] .eq. q .and. am[tj] .eq. an[$] . . .
```

where . . . represents rule 5 followed by the local interaction tests for pattern q.

The example above is for rule 3. An example for rule 4 follows. See Fig. 8-12 for the ASC code for rules 3 and 4.

Rule 4: If there is an LHS pattern p with restricting index variable tj associated with a global variable $\langle b \rangle$ and attribute am, and there is another LHS pattern q occurring after p with the same global variable $\langle b \rangle$ associated with attribute an, and q has no DGVs, then generate

```
andif tk in cn[$] .eq. q .and. am[tj] .eq. an[$] . . .
```

where . . . represents rule 5 and the local interaction tests of pattern q.

For example, in Fig. 8-1a, the pattern *n*3 (*p*) has the variable ⟨*y*⟩ associated with the attribute *A*8 and the fourth pattern *n*4 (*q*) has variable ⟨*y*⟩ associated with attribute *a*10. The fourth pattern has another global variable ⟨*w*⟩ which is also present in the third pattern. The fourth pattern does not have any DGV. Attributes *a*8 of the third pattern and *a*10 of the fourth pattern are linked by the common variable ⟨*y*⟩. So the restricting index variable *t*3 of the previous pattern is used to restrict the matches in this case; as a result,

andif t4 in cn[$] .eq. n4 .and. a8[t3] .eq. a10[$] . . .

is generated in Fig. 8-3 (line *d*). Similarly, attributes *a*13 of the third pattern and *a*11 of the fifth pattern are linked by the common variable ⟨*n*⟩, and the fifth pattern has no DGV. So

andif t5 in cn [$] .eq. n5 .and. a13[t3] .eq. a11[$]

is generated in line *e* of Fig. 8-3 for the first global variable of the fifth pattern that is shared with the third pattern.

8.3.2.5. The Augmentation Rule

Rules 3 and 4 process only the first global interaction variable in patterns *p* and *q*. A test must be generated for each variable pair shared by patterns *p* and *q*. This test is presented in rule 5, which is applied repeatedly after rules 3 and 4 generate the initial **and** construct until it can no longer apply.

Rule 5: If LHS pattern *q* has an additional variable ⟨*c*⟩, associated with attribute *an*, and the same variable ⟨*c*⟩ is associated with attribute *am* of pattern *p*, and *p*'s restricting index variable is *tj*, then generate the augment
.and. am[tj] .eq. an[$]

Note in Fig. 8-1a that rule 3 is applied to the variable ⟨*x*⟩, which is shared by both the first and the third patterns. The third pattern has an additional variable ⟨*i*⟩ shared by the first pattern. So, on applying rule 5,

.and. a20[t2] .eq. a19[$]

is generated for the third DGV global pattern in Fig. 8-3 (line *cc*). Similarly, the variable ⟨*n*⟩, being shared by the third and fourth patterns, is compiled by rule 4. So, on applying rule 5 (see Fig. 8-12) for the additional shared variable ⟨*w*⟩,

.and. a2[t3] .eq. a12[$]

is generated for the fourth (NDGV global) pattern in Fig. 8-3 (line *dd*).

8.3.2.6. Local-Interaction Rules

The local interaction rules generate tests to append to the local and global patterns to incorporate the local aspects of each LHS pattern. The ASC code for local interaction rules 6 and 7 is shown in Fig. 8-13.

Constant Rule. The constant rule is applied when there is an attribute–value pair in an LHS pattern with an attribute *an* and a constant value *vn*. The entire attribute field *an* in WM must be searched for the value *vn* at execution time.

Rule 6: If the pattern contains an attribute *an* with a constant value *vn*, then generate

.and. an[$] .eq. vn

Each constant test is logically ANDed with the previous constant test in the same LHS pattern. Thus, from the first and the second patterns of Fig. 8-1a,

.and. cn[$] .eq. nl
.and. a3[$] .eq. 5

and

.and. cn[$] .eq. n2
.and. a5[$] .eq. bob

are generated in Fig. 8-3.

Intraelement-Variable Rule. If a variable, local or global, occurs more than once in an LHS pattern, then it needs to be checked for consistent bindings within the matching WME. For example, consider an LHS pattern (^al ⟨b⟩ . . . ^an ⟨b⟩ . . . ^ap ⟨b⟩) with three occurrences of the variable ⟨*b*⟩. Assume WM has seven instances of facts with *a*l having values 1,2,8,5,11,3,4, *an* having 4,2,8,5,0,3,4, and *ap* having 11,2,4,5,9,3,8, as shown in Fig. 8-14, then ⟨*b*⟩ must be restricted to one of the values in the set {2,5,3}, since these three values are the only consistently bound values for variable ⟨*b*⟩. So

.and. al[$] .eq. an[$]
.and. al[$] .eq. ap[$]

must be generated. This will allow all three facts with consistent ⟨*b*⟩ bindings to be found and processed in parallel. This case is embodied in rule 7.

cn	a1	a2	a3	a4	a5	a6	a7	a8	a9	a10	a11	a12	a13	a16	a19	a20
n1	-	-	8	7	-	-	-	2	2	-	-	-	-	7	-	-
n3	-	-	-	5	-	5	-	1	1	-	-	-	-	5	-	-
n2	-	-	-	**nil**	bob	-	-	2	2	-	-	-	-	3	-	-
n3	-	2	-	1	-	55	**10**	8	8	-	-	-	13	1	20	-
n1	**5**	-	**nil**	2	-	-	-	8	8	-	-	-	-	2	-	20
n5	-	-	-	4	-	-	-	8	8	-	-	-	-	4	-	-
n3	-	-	-	8	-	10	-	6	6	-	-	-	-	8	20	20
n4	-	-	-	1	-	-	-	5	5	**mom**	-	2	-	1	-	-
n2	-	-	-	3	tom	-	-	4	4	-	-	-	-	3	-	-
n1	8	-	5	2	-	-	-	3	3	-	-	-	-	2	-	-
n4	-	-	-	1	-	-	-	2	2	**mom**	-	2	-	1	-	-
nil	-	-	-	2	-	-	-	1	1	-	13	-	-	2	-	-

Figure 8-14. Consistently bound ⟨*b*⟩.

Rule 7: If the LHS pattern has a variable ⟨*b*⟩ associated with attribute *am* and with attribute *an*, where *an* occurs after *am*, then generate
.and. am[$] .eq. an[$].

For example, the second pattern of the input rule in Fig. 8-1a has the variable ⟨*z*⟩ occurring twice. So

.and. a4[$] .eq. a16[$]

is generated in Fig. 8-3. If a variable occurs *n* times in an LHS pattern, then this rule needs to be applied ($n - 1$) times. Thus

.and. am[$] .eq. an[$]
.and. am[$] .eq. ap[$]
.and. as[$] .eq. at[$]

will be generated for the pattern

(. . . ^am ⟨b⟩ . . . ^an ⟨b⟩ . . . ^as ⟨C⟩ . . . ^ap ⟨b⟩ . . . ^at ⟨C⟩ . . .).

8.4. Execution of a Procedural Rule

This section describes how a compiled procedural rule executes, giving the same results as its equivalent production rule. Figure 8-15 is the associative form of WM (Fig. 8-16), on which the ASC procedural rule (Fig. 8-3) is applied to obtain the modified WM (Fig. 8-17). Figures 8-18a through 8-19b show the responders for every individual test of the **andif/andfor** construct of Fig. 8-3 on the WM shown in Fig. 8-15. The *ti* shown are the ANDed results of the individual tests. Figure 8-19c is a collective picture of all five **and** tests.

For a production rule to fire, all the tests in all its LHS patterns must be true. Thus, a procedural rule (Fig. 8-3) equivalent to a production rule (Fig. 8-1a) fires only when the following requirements are met at run time:

cn	a1	a2	a3	a4	a5	a6	a7	a8	a9	a10	a11	a12	a13	a16	a19	a20
n1	~	~	8	7	~	~	~	2	2	~	~	~	~	7	~	~
n3	~	~	~	5	~	5	~	1	1	~	~	~	~	5	~	~
n2	~	~	~	**3**	bob	~	~	2	2	~	~	~	~	3	~	~
n3	~	2	~	1	~	**10**	**cons**	8	8	~	~	~	13	1	20	~
n1	**10**	~	**5**	2	~	~	~	8	8	~	~	~	~	2	~	20
n5	~	~	~	4	~	~	~	8	8	~	~	~	~	4	~	~
n3	~	~	~	8	~	10	~	6	6	~	~	~	~	8	20	~
n4	~	~	~	1	~	~	~	5	5	**8**	~	2	~	1	~	~
n2	~	~	~	3	tom	~	~	4	4	~	~	~	~	3	~	~
n1	8	~	5	2	~	~	~	3	3	~	~	~	~	2	~	~
n4	~	~	~	1	~	~	~	2	2	**8**	~	2	~	1	~	~
n5	~	~	~	2	~	~	~	1	1	~	**13**	~	~	2	~	~

Figure 8-15. Associative form of WM.

```
n1 ^a3  8  ^a4  7   ^a8  2 ^a9  2    ^a16 7
n3 ^a4  5  ^a6  5   ^a8  1 ^a9  1    ^a16 5
n2 ^a4  3  ^a5 bob ^a8  2 ^a9  2    ^a16 3
n3 ^a2  2  ^a4  1   ^a6 10 ^a7 cons ^a8  8 ^a9 8  ^a13 13
   ^a16 1  ^a19 20
n1 ^a1 10  ^a3  5   ^a4  2 ^a8  8     ^a9 8 ^a16 2 ^a20 20
n5 ^a4  4  ^a8  8   ^a9  8 ^a16 4
n3 ^a4  8  ^a6 10   ^a8  6 ^a9  6    ^a16 8 ^a19 20
n4 ^a4  1  ^a8  5   ^a9  5 ^a10 8    ^a12 2 ^a16 1
n2 ^a4  3  ^a5 tom ^a8  4 ^a9  4    ^a16 3
n1 ^a1  8  ^a3  5   ^a4  2 ^a8  3    ^a9  3 ^a16 2
n4 ^a4  1  ^a8  2   ^a9  2 ^a10 8    ^a12 2 ^a16 1
n5 ^a4  2  ^a8  1   ^a9  1 ^a11 13   ^a16 2
```

Figure 8-16. A sample WM.

1. *t*1 is not nil.
2. Suppose *t*2 has *m* responders and *t*3 has *n* responders, where *m*, *n* are positive integers. Then there must be at least one iteration among the $m * n$ inner iteractions for which *t*4 and *t*5 are not nil.

If these requirements are not met, then the rule will not fire.

With the given WM, *t*1 is nonempty, with the third entry on, as shown in Fig. 8-18a. *t*2 has two responders (Fig. 8-18b), and *t*3 has one, as shown in Fig. 8-18c. There may at most two $(2 * 1)$ inner iterations. For the value of the first *t*2 responder, *t*3 gets flagged on the fourth entry, and for this *t*3, *t*4 has two responders (Fig. 8-19a) and *t*5 has one responder (see Fig. 8-19b). For the second responder of *t*2, the test *a*l[*t*2] .eq. *a*.6[$] fails for the value 8 of *a*l[*t*2]. Thus, there is no responder in *t*3 on the second iteration.

There is at least one iteration for which both *t*4 and *t*5 are true, and all five tests are simultaneously TRUE as shown in Fig. 8-19c. Hence the rule gets fired and the sample WM (Fig. 8-16) is changed, as shown in Fig. 8-17.

Suppose *t*l (Fig. 8-18a) is all zeros. This implies that all the tests in the outermost **andif** statement fail. The exit logic of the **andif** statement causes an immediate exit of control from the entire **and** construct. Consequently the rule does not fire. The same is true whenever *t*2, *t*3, *t*4, and *t*5 are nil initially.

al	an	ap	and responders
1	4	11	0
2	2	2	1
8	8	4	0
5	5	5	1
11	0	9	0
3	3	3	1
4	4	8	0

Figure 8-17. Modified WM.

cn[$] .eq. n2	a5[$] .eq. bob	a4[$] .eq. a16[$]	t1
0	0	1	0
0	0	1	0
1	1	1	1
0	0	1	0
0	0	1	0
0	0	1	0
0	0	1	0
0	0	1	0
1	0	1	0
0	0	1	0
0	0	1	0
0	0	1	0

a - Responders for T1 andif Tests

cn[$] .eq. n1	a3[$] .eq. 5	t2
1	0	0
0	0	0
0	0	0
0	0	0
1	1	1
0	0	0
0	0	0
0	0	0
0	0	0
1	1	1
0	0	0
0	0	0

b - Responders for T2 andfor Tests

cn[$] .eq. n3	a1[t2] .eq. a6[$]	a20[t2] .eq. a19[$]	a7[$] .eq. cons	a8[$] .eq. a9[$]	t3
0	0	0	0	1	0
1	0	0	0	1	0
0	0	0	0	1	0
1	1	1	1	1	1
0	0	0	0	1	0
0	0	0	0	1	0
1	1	1	0	1	0
0	0	0	0	1	0
0	0	0	0	1	0
0	0	0	0	1	0
0	0	0	0	1	0
0	0	0	0	1	0

c - Iteration1: Responders for T3 andfor Tests

Figure 8-18. Responders to **and** construct tests.

cn[$] .eq. n4	a8[t3] .eq. a10[$]	a2[t3] .eq. a12[$]	t4
0	0	0	0
0	0	0	0
0	0	0	0
0	0	0	0
0	0	0	0
0	0	0	0
0	0	0	0
1	1	1	1
0	0	0	0
0	0	0	0
1	1	1	1
0	0	0	0

a - Iteration1: Responders for t4 **andif** Tests

cn[$] .eq. n5	a13[$] .eq. a11[$]	t5
0	0	0
0	0	0
0	0	0
0	0	0
0	0	0
1	0	0
0	0	0
0	0	0
0	0	0
0	0	0
0	0	0
1	1	1

b - Iteration1:Responders for t5 **andif** Tests

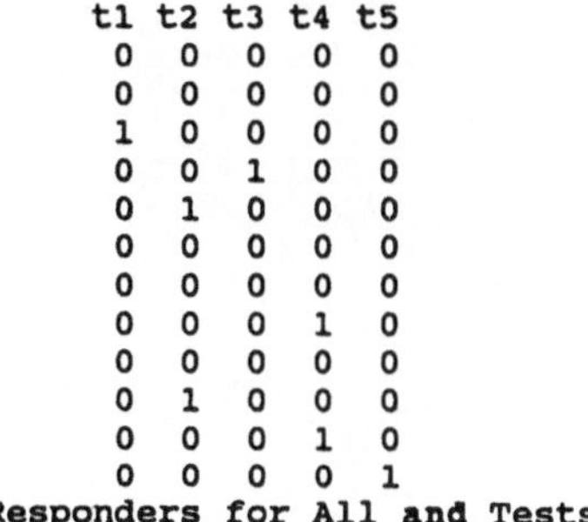

t1	t2	t3	t4	t5
0	0	0	0	0
0	0	0	0	0
1	0	0	0	0
0	0	1	0	0
0	1	0	0	0
0	0	0	0	0
0	0	0	0	0
0	0	0	1	0
0	0	0	0	0
0	1	0	0	0
0	0	0	1	0
0	0	0	0	1

c - Responders for All **and** Tests

Figure 8-19. Responders to **and** construct tests, continued.

8.5. Conclusion

A context-sensitive approach to compiling production rules into equivalent procedural rules has been described. A compiled procedural rule is a sequence of special parallel **andif** and **andfor** constructs. The context-sensitive rules have been used in a prototype OPS5 system (Haston [1987]) that obtains an estimated throughput of up to 6000 rules per second as opposed to 70 (Gupta [1984]) and 900 (Hilyer and Shaw [1986]) rules for SIMD approaches adhering to the sequential RETE algorithm (Forgy [1982]). The **and** constructs are useful for dealing with parallel AND/OR tree searching. This approach allows rules to be added, deleted, and modified at run time while one still reaps the speed benefits of executing compiled code. While each new rule must be compiled (estimated to be less than a second of CPU time) when added to the system, existing compiled rules are not touched.

c) Responders for A2 and Test3

Figure 8.13. Responses to and conflict tests, continued.

8.5. Conclusion

A context-sensitive approach to compiling production rules into equivalent procedural rules has been described. A compiled procedural rule is a sequence of special matcher [illegible] and [illegible]. The context-sensitive rules have been used in a prototype OPS5 system [illegible] that obtains an estimated throughput of up to [illegible] rule firings per second as compared to [illegible] and [illegible] (Hillyer and Shaw [illegible]) rules for SIMD approaches [illegible] for the [illegible] RETE algorithm (Forgy [illegible]). The two approaches are useful for dealing with parallel AND/OR tree searching. This approach allows rules to be added, deleted and modified at run-time while one still reaps the speed benefits of executing compiled code. When each new rule must be compiled (estimated to be less than a second of CPU time) when added to the system, existing compiled rules are not touched.

9

Associative Prolog*

This chapter presents the design and implementation of a simple Prolog interpreter. The intent is to introduce some associative computing concepts and illustrate them with a substantial program that performs a nontrivial task. A complete contrast between a conventional Prolog interpreter implementation and an associative implementation is instructive but beyond the scope of this book. Only the most important aspects, such as unification, variable binding, clause filtering, and AND/OR searching are discussed in detail.

This chapter begins with a background section on Prolog. It is assumed that the reader has a basic knowledge of rule-based languages, so that only the details of Prolog essential to the discussion here are given. The next four sections introduce unification, the binding association, searching, and the inference engine. The sixth and seventh sections describe how clause filtering and variable binding can be accomplished in a data-parallel manner on an associative computer. The next section describes the special Prolog **scinp** routine. The ninth section gives an example of a Prolog program and shows how it is processed by the previously described techniques and routines. The next-to-last section briefly discusses some remaining Prolog topics such as adding and deleting facts from the data base, the search-cut operator, and list searching and processing. The last section summarizes the chapter, presents estimated throughput results and lessons learned, and suggests future directions.

9.1. Background

Prolog is a rule-based language which uses predicate-calculus Horn clauses as its fundamental construction. The classic paper by Kowalski [1979] describes how various forms of Horn clauses can be interpreted as the program components

*Co-authored by Arvind Bansal.

in an interpretive inference system. Figure 9-1 gives examples of Prolog rules, goals, and facts. In Prolog, a variable starts with a capital letter, constant with a lower-case letter. The predicate name is always a constant. Clauses are symbolic and are frequently stored and manipulated as nested lists. Thus a LISP list form for the rule in Fig. 9-1a is shown in Fig. 9-2. The :- symbol is read as a left-facing arrow (i.e., ←). In a rule, :- states that the truth of the conjunction of the subgoals on the RHS of the arrow imply the truth of the goal on the LHS.

In a Prolog program, the rules are read backwards and are interpreted as stating that the answer to the question posed by the LHS (or *head* of the rule) can be answered by finding answers that are in agreement with each other (i.e., consistent) to the questions on the RHS. Answers to questions (i.e., goals) can be obtained by finding a matching fact in the data base or in a recursive manner by finding a rule head that matches the goal and then searching for answers to that rule. Two processes are fundamental to this operation: clause matching or unification and the AND/OR tree search of the fact and rule base.

```
a(X, Y) :- b(c, X), e(f, g(Y)).
```

a - A Prolog Rule (Clause)

```
:- b(c, X).
```

b - A Prolog Goal or Query

```
b(c, d).
```

c - A Prolog Fact

```
good_lecture(A_Lecturer) :-
  teacher(A_Lecturer, A_Day), in_time(A_Lecturer).
teacher(Lecturer, Day) :-
  course(Course, time(Day,Start,Finish), Lecturer, Location).
in_time(potter).
in_time(bansal).
course(parallel, time(monday,3,4), potter, 312).
course(logic, time(tuesday,2,5), bansal, 205).
```

d - A Prolog Program

```
<----------- clause ----------->
<head>   <------- body -------->
term         term          term
goal   :-  subgoal1, ... subgoaln.
```

e - Rule Terminology

Figure 9-1. Prolog Components.

```
((a X Y) (b c X) (e f (g Y)))
```

Figure 9-2. Lisp list form of a Prolog rule.

9.2. Unification

Matching two terms is known as unification. In the most general case, both terms may have variables as well as constants. A basic purpose of unification is to find a consistent set of bindings for the variables that allows the two terms to match. Implicit in this process is the understanding that constants must also match. This section will discuss unification from an associative point of view at a fundamental level. Readers not familiar with unification may want to consult an introductory artificial intelligence text (such as Rich [1983]) for a discussion of the conventional, recursive unification algorithm *after* reading this section. Consulting a conventional text before reading this section is likely to create confusion.

Someone who is asked to match two terms will do so in three steps. First, he or she will look at shape. That is, do the terms have the same number of arguments (arity) and do the arguments have the same degree of complexity (structure)? A single constant does not match a predicate with arguments. Figure 9-3 shows matching and nonmatching shapes. Both the Prolog and internal-nested-list representations are shown.

Second, he or she will match symbols or, more accurately, constants. Apples do not match oranges and $a \neq b$. This step is so natural and obvious that it would not seem to merit mentioning, but it must be done. Figure 9-4 gives examples.

If the first two steps have not eliminated the possibility of matching two terms, the third and most complex step is to match (or bind) the variables. In a completely general situation, variables may match other variables in addition to both constants and structure. Moreover, if a variable appears in more than one location (a shared variable), the items matched by the variable must agree. That is, the two or more items matched by the variable must be unifiable. (This step is the basis of the conventional recursive unification algorithm.)

Figure 9-5 gives a few examples of variable matching. Example 3 shows a predicate matching a variable. This is not allowed in conventional unification. But in an abstract unification algorithm, there is no reason for such a restriction.

```
a(b, c)  =  a(b, c)          (a b c)  =  (a b c)
         != a(b)                      != (a b)
         != a(b, c, d)                != (a b c d)
         != a(b, c(d))                != (a b (c d))
         != a(b(d), c)                != (a (b d) c)
```

Figure 9-3. Matching shape.

```
a(b, c)  =  a(b, c)        (a b c)  =  (a b c)
         !=  a(c, b)                 !=  (a c b)
         !=  a(b, d)                 !=  (a b d)
         !=  d(b, c)                 !=  (d b c)
```

Figure 9-4. Matching constants.

Examples 4, 8, 14, and 15 show shape matching. In 8, the terms match because they have the same tree (nested list) structure, as shown in Fig. 9-6b, but example 9 does not match (see Fig. 9-6c). That is, when structure is considered, a variable may match only one node. However, that node may represent any subtree, such as the leaf *b* in Fig. 9-6a or a subtree as illustrated in Fig. 9-6b. But a variable can not match two or more sibling nodes (Fig. 9-6c). The purpose of unification is to establish a consistent set of bindings of the variables in the terms. Traditionally, bindings are specified as sets of substitution pairs, as shown on the right in examples 11, 12, and 15 of Fig. 9-5.

9.3. The Binding Association

Variable bindings are maintained by two binding associations. The first association establishes a one-to-one binding between a variable and a constant, another variable, or a structure id. Bound structures are stored in the second association. Figure 9-7 shows the fields in the first binding association. The left field contains the variables being bound. The right and value fields contain the item to which the variable is bound. The initially bound item is saved in the right field. If it is a constant, the ra flag (right item is an atom) is set. If it is a variable, the rv flag (right item is a variable) is set. If the item is a structure, the structure id

```
1)  a(b, c)  = a(b, X)         (a b c)  = (a b X)
2)           = a(X, c)                  = (a X b)
3)           = X(b, c)                  = (X b d)
4)  a(Y, c)  = a(b, c)         (a Y c)  = (a b c)
5)           = a(b, X)                  = (a b X)
6)           = a(X, c)                  = (a X c)
7)           = X(b, c)                  = (X b c)
8)           = a(d(b), c)               = (a (d b) c)
9)          != a(b, c, d)              != (a b c d)
10) a(Y, Y) != a(b, c)         (a Y c) != (a b c)
11)          = a(b, X)                  = (a b X)
                                             {Y/X,b/Y}
12)          = a(X, c)                  = (a X c)
                                             {Y/X,c/Y}
13)         != a(b, d(c))              != (a b (d c))
14)          = a(d(c), d(c))            = (a (d c) (d c))
15)          = a(d(c), X)               = (a (d c) X)
                                             {Y/X,d(c)/Y}
```

Figure 9-5. Clause matching.

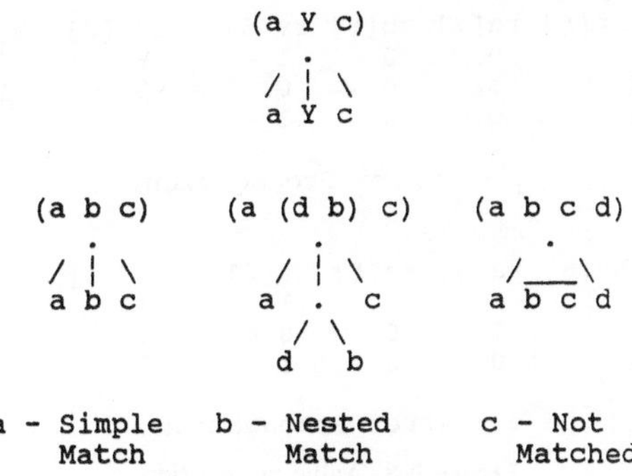

Figure 9-6. Matching trees.

is stored in the field and the rb flag (right is a binding) is set. The va flag is set if the value is an atom. Figure 9-7 gives some examples of binding entries.

Two-element fields, right and value, are required in the binding association to allow efficient consistency checking. Whenever a constant is ultimately bound to a variable, the constant is saved in the value field for easy reference. Consider Fig. 9-8. Variable *X* is first bound to *Y*, but *Y* is as yet unbound. Next, *Z* is bound to 3. Finally, variable *Y* is bound to *Z*. This is the state shown in Fig. 9-8a. At this point, the value 3, bound to *Z*, is propagated to variables *Y* and *X*. After the process is complete, as shown in Fig. 9-8b, the binding table provides a complete history of the bindings. Thus during subsequent consistency checks for the variable *X*, it can be determined that it was initially bound to variable *Y* but that it is now bound to constant 3. The final binding value can be determined immediately without having to follow the path from *X* to *Y* to *Z* to 3.

The second binding association is the structure association. It is shown in Fig. 9-9b. Field bno contains the structure id number corresponding to the id number in the right field in the binding association. The field atom contains the data elements of the structure. Flag ap is set if the element is an atom (constant). Flag vp is set if the element is a variable. Field ssc contains associated normalized structure codes obtained by subtracting the structure code of the variable from the structure code of the data elements. Normalizing the structure code allows the entry in the structure association bound to *X* to be identical even though *X* appears in two different locations in the pattern. Thus the pattern *r*(*X X*) matches *r*(*q*(*b*) *q*(*b*)) with *X*:*q*(*b*) (See Fig. 9-10).

left[$]	right[$]	ra[$]	rb[$]	rv[$]	value[$]	va[$]	bsc[$]
Y	b	1	0	0	b	1	000000
Y	X	0	0	1	X	0	000000

Entries for {b/Y, X/Y}

Figure 9-7. Fields in the binding association.

left[$]	right[$]	ra[$]	rb[$]	rv[$]	value[$]	va[$]	bsc[$]
X	Y	0	0	1	Y	0	000000
Z	3	1	0	0	3	1	000000
Y	Z	0	0	1	Z	0	000000

a - Before Propagation

left[$]	right[$]	ra[$]	rb[$]	rv[$]	value[$]	va[$]	bsc[$]
X	Y	0	0	1	3	1	000000
Z	3	1	0	0	3	1	000000
Y	Z	0	0	1	3	1	000000

b - After Propagation

Figure 9-8. Value propagation.

9.4. Search Organization

The AND/OR tree search of the Prolog inference engine depends on the associative implementation of three basic concepts. These items, associative AND/OR tree searching, associative backtracking, and associative stacks are described below.

9.4.1. Associative-Search Tree

In general, a goal may be matched by many facts and rule heads. The order in which the alternatives are explored must be controlled in some manner. The standard method is to view the search as an AND/OR tree search.

An AND/OR tree is composed of alternating levels of AND and OR nodes. AND nodes are generated when a rule head is matched and it is expanded into a conjunction of the subgoals on the RHS, as illustrated in Fig. 9-11a. Fig. 9-11b shows two OR nodes. An OR node is generated when a goal can be matched by any of several different facts, at the top of Fig. 9-11b, or any of several different rules, as shown at the bottom. It is possible (even probable) that a goal is matched by both facts and rules so that an OR node may have descendants of both types. By convention (and in order to terminate a search as quickly as possible), if

left[$]	right[$]	ra[$]	rb[$]	rv[$]	value[$]	va[$]	bsc[$]
X	2	0	1	0		0	000000

a - Binding Association

bno[$]	atom[$]	ap[$]	vp[$]	ssc[$]
2	q	1	0	000000
2	b	1	0	100000

b - Structure Association

Figure 9-9. The binding entries for $\{Y/q(b)\}$.

```
 constant            variable           normalized
structure code     structure code     structure code

pel[$]  sc[$]      pel[$]   sc[$]          ssc[$]
  r     100000       r      100000
  q     210000       X      200000         010000
  b     220000                             020000
  q     310000       X      300000         010000
  b     320000                             020000
```

Figure 9-10. Structure–code normalization.

both facts and rules are present at a node, facts are processed first. When all facts have been tried, the rules are tried in the order specified in the original program.

An answer or solution to the original goal is found when a tree has been expanded to all leaf nodes (facts) and the facts are consistent. The search of the AND/OR tree is commonly controlled by using stacks. In associative computing, structure codes can be used for the same purpose.

For example, the initial goal node is assigned structure code 000000. When a goal matches a rule head and the rule is invoked, the node associated with the goal is expanded. A descendant node is generated for every subgoal in the body (RHS) of the rule, and one additional node is generated as a terminator, which is assigned the nil term as its goal. An expansion is illustrated in Fig. 9-12. The structure code manipulation functions are used to generate the descendant and sibling codes. Fig. 9-12b shows the association for the tree in Fig. 9-12a.

9.4.2. Backtracking

A crucial feature of the tree search is the ability to backtrack. That is, when all of the alternatives at a node have been tried, a mechanism is required to backtrack to the previous node. The **prvcd** function provides a method to move

```
          a(X, d) :- b(X), c(e, X).

               a(X, d)  is true
                 /    \
     if   b(X)   AND   c(e X)     are true

               a - An AND Node


                     b(X)
                   /     \
               b(a) OR ...b(z)

                    c(e X)
           /                          \
c(e, X) :- d(X) OR ... c(e, X)  :- f(X), g(X)

                 b - OR Nodes
```

Figure 9-11. AND and OR nodes.

```
c(e, X) :- f(X), g(X).
```

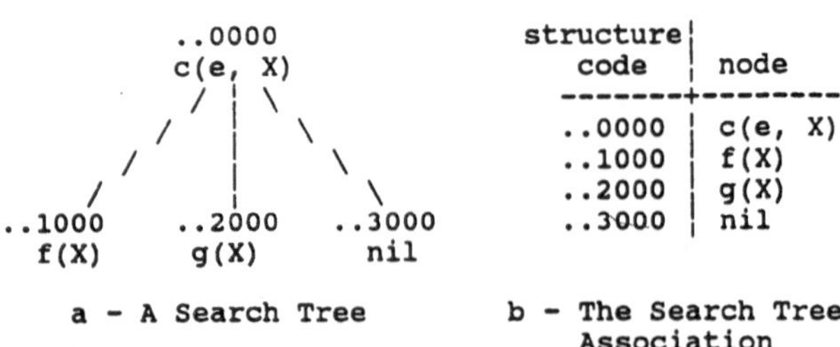

Figure 9-12. An AND node expansion.

from one node to a previous sibling, but in a tree structure, the previous node is not always a sibling. Figure 9-13 shows three examples. Figure 9-13a shows the simplest case where the **prvcd** function provides the correct node code. In Fig. 9-13b, **prvcd** provides the correct code also, but it is only by coincidence that the **prvcd** of the first sibling is the parent node.

Figure 9-13c illustrates the case in which the current node is not leftmost and the left sibling is not a leaf node. The **prvcd** function will find the correct sibling

```
                    100000
                   /      \
            110000          120000
            /    \          /    \
      111000   112000   121000   122000 <-- current node
                          |
                          └prvcd(122000)

                 a - Sibling Backtrack


                    100000
                   /      \
            110000          120000     <-- prvcd(121000)
            /    \          /
      111000   112000   121000   <-- current

                 b - Parent Backtrack


                  100000
  prvcd          /      \
  (120000) --> 110000      120000    <-- current
               /    \
proper --> 111000   112000   <-- largest node less
backtrack                        than current (but nil goal
node                             to mark end of ANDed clauses)

                 c - Non-leaf Sibling
```

Figure 9-13. Using **prvcd** for backtracking.

family, but not the lowest-level leaf node. The **prvval** function is needed to find the largest structure code less than the one specified, which is the rightmost leaf of the left sibling. But, as mentioned above, the rightmost sibling node always has a nil goal. Thus the **prvval** function must be applied again to find the rightmost node with a non-nil goal. Since **prvval** can be used in the first two cases also, the ASC code in Fig. 9-14 loops on **prvval** until a non-nil goal node is found or the root of the tree is reached.

9.4.3. Associative Stacks

Figure 9-15 illustrates the use of an associative stack to store goals. An associative stack is more permanent than a conventional stack. As a search progresses, considerable work is performed to establish the environment when a node is expanded. If the search backtracks through the node and then later re-expands it, and if a conventional stack is used, all of the environmental data specific to the node is lost when it is popped off the stack and must be regenerated when it is pushed back on.

In an associative stack, all of the node's data is saved in arrays, and a common index is saved in an association which can be searched by the structure code representing the node's position in the search tree. The example in Fig. 9-15 shows the indices in essentially sequential order, but remember that the order of entry depends on how the search tree is originally expanded and is completely immaterial as to efficiency. When backtracking occurs, only the structure code of the current node changes; none of the environmental data associated with the popped node is lost. When the node is revisited, its indexx[$] value can be obtained by an associative search and all of the previously generated environment data can be accessed. This example of an associative stack is an extension of the data structure discussed in section 4.2.

Figure 9-15 just shows goal[$] as being on the stack. As described in the following section, many different variables may be on the stack and, indeed, new variables are easily added to the stack simply by declaring them as multidimensional arrays and using the stack index to access them.

```
subroutine backtrack

loop
  cnode = prvval(code[$], cnode);
  until cnode .eq. 0
  until goal[$,indexx[cnode .eq. code[$]]
endloop;

end;
```

Figure 9-14. Associative backtrack.

```
code[$] indexx[$]
100000     0
110000     1
120000     2
111100     3
112000     4
121000     5
```

goal[$,0]	goal[$,1]	...	goal[$,5]	...	goal[$,n]
goal flag for node 100000	goal flag for node 110000		goal flag for node 121000		

Figure 9-15. An associative stack for storing goals.

9.5. Inference Engine

The influence engine uses an associative stack and looping to achieve the effect of recursion. A road map of the engine is given in Fig. 9-16. To start, the data is input and variables initialized. The current node value is set to zero (the root), and the expand routine is used to put the initial goal on the stack. Then the basic loop of the engine is entered. The test for stopping is at the top of loop (1). The root node has structure code 000000. After initialization, it is reached only after backtracking out of the entire tree. In this situation, the search is over and all successful solutions have been printed.

When a goal node in the search tree is first reached (2), there will be no previously calculated responders. The goal is used to filter (search) the entire data base for matching facts and rule heads (3). All responders are saved on the associative stack. On subsequent revisits to this goal node, as a result of backtracking, the unprocessed filtered responders are still flagged (5) and processing can continue from where it left off.

Filtering (3) is accomplished in two phases. The first phase is based on constants and shape, and the results do not change for the duration of the program. The second phase is based on consistent bindings. That is, the facts and rules that remain after the first filter phase are filtered again to eliminate responders that do not agree with the current bindings. If there are no fact or rule responders (4) after filtering, this goal has failed, and the system backtracks to a previous goal. Otherwise control passes to the unification loop (7).

If there are responders on the stack at the top of the loop (5), the fact or rule that was just processed is still present and the responders and associative stack must be updated. After updating (6), if there are no more responders, then the last fact (or rule) alternative for this node under the current set of bindings has been processed and the system backtracks. Otherwise, control passes to the unification loop (7).

At entry to the unification loop (7), one or more matching facts or rules have

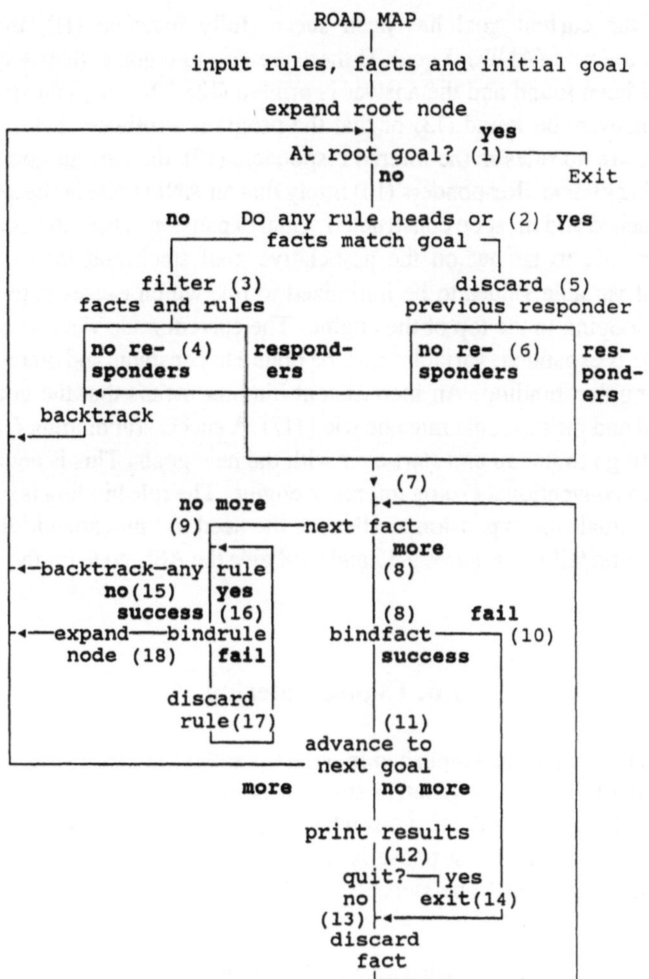

Figure 9-16. The inference-engine road map.

been found for the current goal. The system stays in the unification loop until all facts matching the goal have been processed (8). When a fact is successfully matched and more goals remain, the current status is "stacked" (11) and the next goal processed. After all facts have been processed, the first filtered rule, if any, will be selected (9) and the node expanded.

When a fact is matched (8), the variables in the fact are processed. Variables which appear in the fact and have been previously bound are consistent with the existing bindings or this fact would have been eliminated by the second phase of filtering. Unbound variables are bound and the bindings are checked for inconsistencies. If any inconsistencies are found, this fact fails and it is discarded (10).

When the current goal has been successfully matched (11), the system advances to the next (ANDed) goal. If there are no more goals, then a successful solution has been found and the answer is printed (12). The user can specify that additional answers be found (13) or that the program terminate (14).

If there are no rules in the filtered responders (15), the current goal fails and the system backtracks. Responders (16) imply that an AND node in the search tree has been reached and must be constructed. Goal expansion causes the goals on the RHS of the rule to be put on the associative goal stack and the associative-environment variable values to be initialized to nil, which causes path (3) to be taken upon looping to the top of the engine. The current node value is advanced. When a node is expanded, variables may be bound to constants and other variables just as during fact binding. An inconsistent binding means that the goal-to-rule match failed and the next rule must be tried (17). A successful binding (18) causes the system to go to its top and start over with the new goals. This is equivalent to recursion in a conventional Prolog inference engine. The rule binding is performed prior to the actual rule expansion to alleviate the need to "un-expand" the rule in case of a binding failure. Figures 9-17 and 9-18 give the ASC code for the inference engine.

9.6. Clause Filtering

Clause filtering is accomplished in a data-parallel manner. When a goal first appears on the top of the associative stack, it is used to filter all of the database facts and rule heads to eliminate items which can not match. Clause filtering takes place in two phases. The first phase is static and has three steps. The second is dynamic but contains just one step.

9.6.1. Static Filtering

The first phase searches for all facts and rules which match the pattern (goal). Potential bindings discovered during filtering are saved in the associative stack for retrieval when (or if) the fact or rule is bound to the goal. Since this filtering is based on constants and structure, the results are constant throughout the duration of the program. These results could be calculated at the very beginning of the program for every possible goal. However, this process is time consuming and is performed only when necessary, as, for example, when a goal first appears on top of the stack. Once it is performed, the results are saved in the associative environment stack for the remainder of the program.

The basic approach to pattern matching used in phase one is to match components on an element-by-element basis and then flag those that match. After matching, the flags are checked to see if all of the elements of a fact or rule are flagged. During the first phase the first two steps, cmes and cames, flag the

```
main main
#include pengine.h

call input;
call init;
call expand jj[$]<pid[$] .eq. 1  tcode<cnode;
loop
until cnode .eq. 0
  cindex = indexx[cnode .eq. code[$]];
  any facts[$,cindex] .or. rules[$,cindex]
    call discard;
    any facts[$,cindex] .or. rules[$,cindex]
    elsenany
      call backtrack;
    endany;
  elsenany
    any filters[$,cindex]
       /* variables initialized in the elsenany section */
       call bfilt cover[$]<filters[$,cindex]
               /* pattern[$] < goal[$,cindex] */;
       call mames qq[$]<cover[$] .and. (fact[$] .or. head[$])
               tempid[$]<pid[$];
       facts[$,cindex] = match[$] .and. fact[$];
       rules[$,cindex] = match[$] .and. head[$];
    elsenany
       call filter   pattern[$] < goal[$,cindex];
       /* sets facts[$], rules[$], filters[$], mat..[$] */
    endany;
    any facts[$,cindex] .or. rules[$,cindex]
    elsenany
       call discard;
       call backtrack;
    endany;
  call unification_loop;
  endany;

endloop;
end;
```

Figure 9-17. The Prolog inference engine.

matched elements and the third step, mames, checks to see if all of the elements are flagged. These steps are controlled by the filter routine shown in Fig. 9-19.

Table 9-1 shows the match flags for all of the possible cases of matching pattern elements. A pattern constant can match only a like constant or a variable, but a pattern variable may match a constant, a variable, or a structure. Since structures may contain variables, all of the elements in variable-structure matches have two flags: one for variable–structure, the other for the variable–constant or variable–variable indication. Finally, pattern structures can be matched by data variables and are flagged accordingly. All of the flags shown are saved in the associative stack using variables matcc[$], matcv[$], etc.

9.6.1.1. Constant Filtering

The first step in the first phase is based on constant matching and is shown in Fig. 9-20, lines *a*. The constant atoms in the goal flagged by mes are used to filter

```
subroutine unification_loop
 expanded = FALSE;
 while zz in facts[$,cindex]
   cnflctvs = FALSE;
   call bindfact vv[$,cindex]<pid[zz] .eq. pid[$] .and. fact[$]
                  vaa[$] < va[$]
                  vaa[$] > bindva[$,cindex]
                  qqq[$] > bind[$,cindex];
   if cnflctvs then
     call discard;
   else
     call nextnode;
     any goal[$,ncindex]
        cindex = ncindex;
        call initastack;
        cnode = nxtcd(tcode);
        expanded = TRUE;
     elsenany
        msg "The bindings are:";
        call dumpbind;
        call discard;
         cnode = prevcd(cnode);
     endany;
   endif;
 endwhile zz;
 while xxx in rules[$,cindex] .and. .not. expanded
   cnflctvs = FALSE;
   call bindfact vv[$,cindex]<pid[xxx] .eq. pid[$] .and. head[$]
                  vaa[$] < va[$]
                  vaa[$] > bindva[$,cindex]
                  qqq[$] > bind[$,cindex];
   if cnflctvs then
     call discard;
   else
     cnode = fstcd(cnode);
     call expand tcode<cnode
          jj[$]<pel[xxx] .eq. dhead[$] .and.
                pid[xxx] .eq. pid[$];
     cindex = indexx[cnode .eq. code[$]];
     expanded = TRUE;
   endif;
 endwhile xxx;
end;
```

Figure 9-18. The Prolog inference engine, continued.

the facts and rule heads using two tests. A goal constant matches a fact constant if and only if the element values and structure-code values are equal. Requiring equivalent structure codes allows the matching to be done in parallel with no fear that a constant in one location of a fact will falsely match the same element value in a different location. For example, in Fig. 9-21, the element being tested, *b*, matches the equivalent element in fact 1 even though they are not in the same order in the association. On the other hand, it does not match either element in fact 2 because either the structure code or the element value does not match.

The second test, lines *b* in Fig. 9-20, allows variables in the facts to be matched. That is, a pattern constant matches a fact or rule variable if the fact or rule variable's structure code matches the pattern's constant structure code. Since the variables are data parallel—i.e., there may be several instances of the same or

```
subroutine filter /* pattern[$] < goal[$,cindex] */
#include pengine.h

matcc[$,cindex] = 0;
matvc[$,cindex] = 0;
matcv[$,cindex] = 0;
matvv[$,cindex] = 0;
matvs[$,cindex] = 0;
matsv[$,cindex] = 0;
patv[$,cindex] = 32;   /* space */
patsc[$,cindex] = 0;

call cmes mes[$] < ptyp[$] .eq. CONSTANT .and. pattern[$] ;
call cames mes[$] < ptyp[$] .eq. VARIABLE .and. pattern[$] ;
filters[$,cindex] = matcc[$,cindex] .or. matcv[$,cindex] .or.
                    matvc[$,cindex] .or. matvv[$,cindex] .or.
                    matsv[$,cindex];
call bfilt cover[$]<filters[$,cindex]
        /* pattern[$] < goal[$,cindex] */;
call mames qq[$]<cover[$] .and. (fact[$] .or. head[$])
           tempid[$]<pid[$];
facts[$,cindex] = match[$] .and. fact[$];
rules[$,cindex] = match[$] .and. head[$];

end;
```

Figure 9-19. The filter routine.

different variables in the same or different facts in the data base that may be matched by the constant (pattern) value—the constant value is saved with each data element so that if (or when) the fact or rule is bound the appropriate binding value can be readily retrieved. Figure 9-22 shows how the value is saved with the variable in a data parallel manner. These values are stored in patv on the associative stack.

9.6.1.2. Variable Filtering

The second step in filtering is based on variables in the pattern. The structure code of every variable is considered a node in a tree and is used to search for all

Table 9-1. Element Matching Combinations

Pattern Element	Fact Element	Matching Type	Match Flags
a	a	Constant to constant	matcc
a	Y	Constant to variable	matcv
X	a	Variable to constant	matvc
X	Y	Variable to variable	matvv
X	a(b)	Variable to structure	matvs; vc, vc
X	a(Y)	Variable to structure	matvs; vc, vv
a(b)	Y	Structure to variable	matsv; cv, cv
a(X)	Y	Structure to variable	matsv; cv, vv

```
subroutine cmes
      /* mes[$] < pattern[$] .and. ptyp[$] .eq. CONSTANT */

 for xx in mes[$]
   setscope pbi[$] .and. pid[xx] .ne. pid[$]
     if psc[$] .ge. psc[xx] .and.
        psc[$] .lt. nxtcd(psc[xx])
        .and. .not. (functor[$] .xor. functor[xx]) then
       if psc[xx] .eq. psc[$] then                          a
         if pel[xx] .eq. pel[$] then                        a
            matcc[$,cindex] = TRUE;                         a
         endif;                                             a
         if ptyp[$] .eq. VARIABLE then                      a
            matcv[$,cindex] = TRUE;                         a
            patv[$,cindex] = pel[xx];                       a
         endif;
       else                                                 b
         if psc[xx] .eq. psc[$] .and.                       b
            ptyp[$] .eq. VARIABLE then                      b
           for zz in them[$]                                b
             setscope pid[xx] .eq. pid[$]                   b
               any pel[zz] .eq. pel[$]                      b
               elsenany                                     b
                 matsv[zz,cindex] = TRUE;                   b
               endany;                                      b
             endsetscope;                                   b
           endfor zz;                                       b
         endif;                                             b
       endif;
     endif;
   endsetscope;
 endfor xx;

end;
```

Figure 9-20. The cmes routine.

```
                  clause  a(b c)

                          100000  a
            testing --> 200000  b
                          300000  c


                  fact 1  a(b c)

                          100000  a
                          300000  c
            matches --> 200000  b


                  fact 2  a(c b)

                          100000  a
        not matched --> 200000  c
        not matched --> 300000  b
```

Figure 9-21. Cmes matching.

```
          clause  a(b c)

                  100000  a
      testing --> 200000  b
                  300000  c

          fact 1  a(X c)
                                patv[$,cindex]
                  100000  a
                  300000  c
      matches --> 200000  X          b

          fact 2  a(Y c)
                                patv[$,cindex]
                  100000  a
      matches --> 200000  Y          b
                  300000  c
```

Figure 9-22. A constant–variable match.

matching subtrees (see lines *a* in Fig. 9-23; the pattern variables are flagged by mes[$]). Leaf nodes are eliminated by accepting only subtrees with more than one element (line *b*). If the subtree is nontrivial, all of the responders are flagged as being a variable–structure match in the associative stack (line *c*). Each element of the structure is further subcategorized and flagged as being a variable (line *d*) or a

```
subroutine cames
    /* mes[$] < pattern[$] .and. ptyp[$] .eq. VARIABLE */

  for xx in mes[$]
    setscope pbi[$] .and. pid[xx] .ne. pid[$]
      if psc[$] .ge. psc[xx] .and.                            a
         psc[$] .lt. nxtcd(psc[xx]) .and.                     a
         (fact[$] .or. head[$])  then                         a
        for yyy  in them[$]
          if pid[yyy] .eq. pid[$] then
            if count(them[$]) .eq. 1 then                     b
            else
              matvs[$,cindex] = TRUE;                         c
            endif;
            if ptyp[$] .eq. VARIABLE then
              matvv[$,cindex] = TRUE;                         d
            else
              matvc[$,cindex] = TRUE;                         e
            endif;
            patsc[$,cindex] = psc[xx];                        f
            patv[$,cindex] = pel[xx];                         f
          endif;
        endfor yyy;
      endif;
    endsetscope;
  endfor xx;
end;
```

Figure 9-23. The cover-augmented MES routine.

constant (line *e*). Just as the constant value is saved for a constant–variable match in cmes, the variable name is saved for a variable structure match in cames and, in addition, the variable's structure code (i.e., the structure code of the node at the root of the matching subtree) is saved on the associative stack (lines *f*). Figure 9-24 shows examples of cames matches as well as the associative stack entries.

9.6.1.3. Cover Verification

The third step is to check for facts and rules that have every element covered. (An element is said to be *covered* if any of its match flags, such as matvc[$], matvv[$], etc., have been set.) This step is performed by the mames routine (see Fig. 9-25). The flag field *qq*[$] is set to TRUE for all elements that were flagged by matcc[$], matcv[$], matvc[$], matvv[$], or matvs[$] in cmes or cames. An element of *qq*[$] is picked at random (line *a*), and the scope is set to all elements with the same id (line *b*). That is, every element in the fact or rule head is flagged. If there are any such elements that are not in *qq*[$], then every element of the fact was not covered by cmes or cames, and thus the fact was not matched by the goal (line *c*). Otherwise, the entire fact is flagged as matched, and the just-tested fact is

```
        clause  a(X c)

                100000  a
    testing --> 200000  X
                300000  c


         fact 1  a(b c)
                                      vs vv vc    sc   patv
                 100000  a
     matches --> 200000  b             0  0  1 200000   X
                 300000  c

         fact 2  a(Y c)
                                      vs vv vc    sc   patv
                 100000  a
     matches --> 200000  Y             0  1  0 200000   X
                 300000  c


         fact 3  a(b(d) c)
                                      vs vv vc    sc   patv
                 100000  a
     matches --> 210000  b             1  0  1 200000   X
     matches --> 220000  c             1  0  1 200000   X
                 300000  c


         fact 4  a(b(Y) c)
                                      vs vv vc    sc   patv
                 100000  a
     matches --> 210000  b             1  0  1 200000   X
     matches --> 220000  Y             1  1  0 200000   X
                 300000  c
```

Figure 9-24. Cames matches.

```
subroutine mames /* tempid[$] < pid[$] */
                 /* qq[$] < filter[$,cindex] */
match[$] = FALSE;
if fact[$] .or. head[$] then
  while xx in qq[$]                                          a
    if tempid[xx] .eq. tempid[$] then                        b
       saveit[$] = them[$];
       any .not. qq[$]                                       c
       elsenany
          match[$] = TRUE;
       endany;
       release saveit[$] from qq[$];
    endif;
      saveit[$] = 0;
  endwhile xx;
endif;

end;
```

Figure 9-25. The mames routine.

released from *qq*[$]. This process is repeated until all cmes and cames responders have been processed.

9.6.2. Dynamic Filtering

The second phase of filtering is embodied in subroutine bfilt. Bfilt filters facts based on the current status of the variable bindings. Statically filtered facts are dynamically filtered by bfilt when a goal is first established. In addition, when a goal node is re-entered from above, the static facts must be refiltered since the variable bindings may have changed.

The binding filter routine, Figs. 9-26 and 9-27, assumes that the statically filtered facts are consistent (i.e., cover[$] is true for all elements). It then processes every variable in the goal. If a fact is found with a binding inconsistent with a goal variable's current binding, it is uncovered.

The routine proceeds by iterating on every variable in the pattern. If an entry with an atomic binding is found in the binding association, the constant (atomic) value and associated normalized structure code are extracted and used to check all filtered facts and rules in a data-parallel manner. In particular, all constant entries with the same structure code as that in the binding table must have the same constant value. If not, they are uncovered (lines *a* in Fig. 9-26). Figure 9-28 illustrates the case where *X* is bound to the constant *c*.

If an entry with a structure binding is found (line *b*, Fig. 9-26), then the structure id number is extracted from the right field and used to identify the structure in the structure binding association. Each entry in the structure is processed in turn (line *c*, Fig. 9-26). If the entry is an atom, it is used as above to uncover data items that do not match both value and structure (lines *d*, Fig. 9-26). Figure 9-29 shows an example in which the variable *X* is bound to the structure *q*(*r*) with only constants.

```
subroutine bfilt /* cover$<filters[$,cindex] */
 for xx in pattern[$] .and. ptyp[$] .eq. VARIABLE
   for yy in pel[xx] .eq. left[$] .and. bbi[$]
     if va[yy] then
        if cover[$] .and. ptyp[$] .eq. CONSTANT .and.       a
           psc[$] - psc[xx] .eq. bsc[yy] .and.              a
           pel[$] .ne. value[yy] then                       a
             cover[$] = FALSE;                              a
        endif;
     else
        if rb[yy] then                                      b
           for ww in right[yy] .eq. bno[$]                  c
             if ap[ww] then
               if cover[$] .and. ptyp[$] .eq. CONSTANT .and. d
                   psc[$]-psc[xx] .eq. ssc[ww] .and.        d
                   pel[$] .ne. atom[ww]  then               d
                     cover[$] = FALSE;                      d
                endif;
             else if vp[ww] then /* X:a(Y) */
               if cover[$] .and. ptyp[$] .eq. VARIABLE .and. e
                   psc[$]-psc[xx] .eq. ssc[ww] .and.        e
                   pel[XX] .ne. left[yy]  then              e
                          cover[$] = FALSE;                 e
                 endif; endif;
             endif;
           endfor ww;
        endif;
     endif;
   endfor yy;
 endfor xx;
```

Figure 9-26. The binding filter (bfilt) routine.

If the entry is a variable, facts with structures which contain the same variable are uncovered, as this represents an illegal variable recursion (line *e*, Fig. 9-26). Figure 9-30 illustrates this case.

The second half of bfilt, shown in Fig. 9-27, is the same as the first half except that it processes the variables in the facts.

9.7. Binding Variables

The entries in the binding associations described in section 9.3 are made by bindfact and five binding routines. There is a separate routine for each of the binding combinations shown in Table 9-1. The routines check to verify that the variable has not already been bound. If not, they make a new binding association entry. Figures 9-31 and 9-32 show typical variable–constant and variable–variable binding routines. Figure 9-33 is the makeentry routine used by all of the binding routines.

Since bound variables are always stored in field left[$], bindvc checks to see if a current binding exists. If so, the va[$] flag is checked (line *a*, Fig. 9-31). If an atom value is present, it is compared with the element being bound. If they are the same, it is a consistent but redundant binding and no action is taken. If they are

```
unprocessed[$] = cover[$];
while zz in unprocessed[$] .and. ptyp[$] .eq. VARIABLE
  get qq in pel[zz] .eq. left[$] .and. bbi[$]
    if va[qq] then
       if pattern[$] .and. ptyp[$] .eq. CONSTANT .and.
          psc[$]-psc[zz] .eq. bsc[qq] .and.
          pel[$] .ne. value[qq] then
          setscope pel[zz] .eq. pel[$] .and. cover[$]
            cover[$] = FALSE;
            unprocessed[$] = FALSE;
          endsetscope;
       endif;
    else
      if rb[qq] then
         for ww in right[qq] .eq. bno[$]
           if ap[ww] then
              if pattern[$] .and.
                 ptyp[$] .eq. CONSTANT .and.
                 psc[$]-psc[zz] .eq. ssc[ww] .and.
                 pel[$] .ne. atom[ww]  then
                   setscope pel[zz] .eq. pel[$]
                            .and. cover[$]
                     cover[$] = FALSE;
                     unprocessed[$] = FALSE;
                   endsetscope;
              endif;
           else
              if vp[ww] then /* X:a(Y) */
                 if pel[xx] .eq. atom[ww] then
                   cover[$] = FALSE;
           endif; endif; endif;
         endfor ww;
      endif;
    endif;
  endget qq;
endwhile zz;
end;
```

Figure 9-27. The binding filter (bfilt) routine, continued.

different, the bindings are inconsistent and the cnflctvs flag is set to FALSE. If va[$] is not set but rb[$] is (line *b*, Fig. 9-31), then the variable is already bound to a structure. Since the shapes of a constant and a structure are not compatible, the cnflctvs flag is set to FALSE. Otherwise, a new entry is made in the binding association. In addition to setting left[$], right[$], and value[$], va[$] is set to TRUE, vb[$] to FALSE, and vv[$] to TRUE.

pattern	binding	pid	pel	cover		fact
		1	p	1		p(a c)
		1	a	1		
p(a,X)	X:c	1	c	1	<-- matched	
		2	p	1		
		2	a	1		p(a b)
		2	b	0	<-- unmatched	

Figure 9-28. A variable-to-constant binding.

```
pattern          binding          pid pel cover              fact
                                   1   p    1
              X:q(r)               1   a    1                p(a,q(r))
p(a,X)     left[$] right[$]        1   q    1 <-- matched
              X        1           1   r    1 <-- matched
                                   2   p    1
           bno[$]   atom[$]        2   a    1                p(a,q(s))
             1        q            2   q    1 <-- matched
             1        r            2   s    0 <-- unmatched
```

Figure 9-29. A variable bound to a structure without a variable.

After all of the variables in a goal have been bound, the propagation routine shown in Figs. 9-34 and 9-35 is called to propagate the binding's right[$] and values[$] fields and check for inconsistencies. Propagate iterates on the newly created entries flagged by seed[$]. Each iteration consists of two phases. The first phase is a loop, which sets a flag vector (mask[$]) for every appearance of the new entry's variable in left[$], right[$], or value[$] of the binding association. This phase is incorporated into the proploop routine of Fig. 9-35. In order to minimize computation, in Fig. 9-35 many flags are used, resulting in code that looks more complicated than it is. The flags are used to keep track of the need to search in the left[$], right[$], or value[$] fields depending on whether a left or right variable is currently being propagated. The basic loop allows the detection of chained bindings as shown in Fig. 9-8 and will set the mask flag so that the value field will be updated in parallel to the common variable or atom during the second phase (lines *b*, Fig. 9-34).

9.8. Prolog I/O

A special **scio** routine was developed for Prolog input. The routine **scinp** understands the syntax of Prolog rules and facts and sets various flag parameters to facilitate the processing of the Prolog terms. For example, the subroutine call

```
pattern          binding          pid pel cover              fact
                                   1   p    1
              X:q(Y)               1   a    1                p(a,q(Z))
           left[$] right[$]        1   q    1 <-- matched
              X        1           1   Z    1 <-- matched
p(a,X)                             2   p    1
           bno[$]   atom[$]        2   a    1                p(a,q(X))
             1        q            2   q    1 <-- matched
             1        Y            2   X    0 <-- illegal
                                   3   p    1
                                   3   a    1                p(a,q(Y))
                                   3   q    1 <-- matched
                                   3   Y    1 <-- matched
```

Figure 9-30. A variable bound to a structure with a variable.

```
subroutine bindvc    /* case i  */
#include pengine.h

 for xx in vv[$,cindex] .and.
     matvc[$,cindex] .and. .not. matvs[$,cindex]
   if patv[xx,cindex] .eq. left[$] .and. bbi[$]
      if va[$]                                                 a
         any pel[xx] .eq. value[$])
         elsenany
            cnflctvs = TRUE;
         endany;
     else any rb[$]                                            b
             cnflctvs = TRUE;
          elsenany
             call makeentry leftval<patv[xx,cindex]
                            rightval<pel[xx]
                            raval = TRUE
                            rbval = FALSE
                            rvval = FALSE;
          endany;
     endif;
   elsenany
     call makevcentry;
   endif;
 endfor xx;

end;
```

Figure 9-31. Binding a variable to a constant.

```
subroutine bindvv
#include pengine.h

for xx in vv[$,cindex] .and.
  matvv[$,cindex] .and. .not.  matvs[$,cindex]
  yy[$] = patv[xx,cindex] .eq. left[$] .and. bbi[$]
  any yy[$]
    any yy[$] .and. pel[xx] .eq. right[$]
    elsenany
       any pel[xx] .eq. left[$]
       elsenany
          call makeentry
               leftval<pel[xx]
               rightval<patv[xx,cindex]
               raval<FALSE
               rbval<FALSE
               rvval<TRUE;
           endany;
        endany;
   elsenany
     call makeentry
          leftval<patv[xx,cindex]
          rightval<pel[xx]
          raval<FALSE
          rbval<FALSE
          rvval<TRUE;
   endany;
endfor xx;

end;
```

Figure 9-32. Binding a variable to a variable.

```
subroutine makeentry /*leftval rightval raval rbval rvval*/
#include pengine.h

 allocate qqt in bbi[$]
   left[qqt] = leftval;
   right[qqt] = rightval;
   ra[qqt] = raval;
   rb[qqt] = rbval;
   rv[qqt] = rvval;
   value[qqt] = rightval;
   va[qqt] = TRUE;
   bsc[qqt] = psc[xx] - patsc[xx,cindex];
   bid[qqt] = timtag;
   qt[qqt] = TRUE;
 endallocate qqt;

end;
```

Figure 9-33. Making binding-table entry.

```
subroutine propigate
  /* seed[$]<binding[$] mask[$] > prop[$,cindex]
     pstat > cnflctvs  */
#include pengine.h

ww[$] = 0;
pstat = SUCCESS;
for yy in seed[$]
arr[$] = yy[$];
arl[$] = 0;
alr[$] = 0;
all[$] = 0;
mask[$] = 0;
todor[$] = 0;
call proploop;
mask[$] = mask[$] .and. bbi[$] .and. .not. yy[$];
if mask[$] then                                          b
   any ra[$] .or. rb[$]                                  b
      cnflctvs = TRUE;                                   b
   elsenany                                              b
      if rb[yy]  then                                    b
         right[$] = right[yy];                           b
      else                                               b
         value[$] = right[yy];                           b
         va[$] = TRUE;                                   b
      endif;                                             b
      rv[$] = rv[yy];                                    b
      rb[$] = rb[yy];                                    b
      ra[$] = ra[yy];                                    b
      bsc[$] = bsc[yy];                                  b
   endany;                                               b
ww[$] = TRUE;
endif;
endfor yy;
mask[$] = ww[$];
end;
```

Figure 9-34. Binding propagation.

```
subroutine proploop
#include pengine.h

setscope bbi[$]
loop
  todol[$] = (arr[$] .or. alr[$]) .and. .not. mask[$];
  mask[$] = mask[$] .or. todol[$];
  arr[$] = 0;
  alr[$] = 0;
  until nany todol[$] .or. arl[$] .or. all[$]
  for xx in todol[$]
    id = left[xx];
    alr[$] =
        alr[$] .or. id .eq. right[$] .or. id .eq. value[$];
    all[$] = all[$] .or. id .eq. left[$];
  endfor xx;
  todor[$] = (all[$] .or. arl[$]) .and. .not. mask[$];
  mask[$] = mask[$] .or. todor[$];
  all[$] = 0;
  arl[$] = 0;
  until nany todor[$] .or. alr[$] .or. arr[$]
  for xx in todor[$]
    id = right[xx];
    arl[$] = arl[$] .or. id .eq. left[$];
    arr[$] =
        arr[$] .or. id .eq. right[$] .or. id .eq. value[$];
    id = value[xx];
    arl[$] = arl[$] .or. id .eq. left[$];
    arr[$] =
        arr[$] .or. id .eq. right[$] .or. id .eq. value[$];
  endfor xx;
endloop;
endsetscope;

end;
```

Figure 9-35. The propagation loop.

result[$] =
    scinp(pel[$], psc[$], pbi[$], pred[$], head_flag[$], tid[$], pred_flag[$]);

will give terms a unique id in the tid[$] field and flag predicate and rule-header elements. The pred field is set to the predicate of the header clause. Figure 9-36 shows how Prolog rules are handled by the above call.

Normally, Prolog output consists of facts, not program rules, so the **scot** routine can be used to print the results if nested-list notation is desired. **Scotp** will print the result using Prolog notation. Since the rule syntax is ignored, rules will be printed as a sequence of terms.

9.9. Example of a Prolog Program

The rules in Fig. 9-36 constitute a small sample program. The data base is shown in Fig. 9-37. The initial goal is good(X).

Initially, good(X) is used to filter the data and rule base. Only rule 1 remains

pel[$]	psc[$]	pid[$]	pred[$]	head_ flag[$]	tid[$]	pred_ flag[$]
good	100000	5	good	1	0	1
Alec	110000	5	good	1	0	0
teac	100000	5	good	0	1	1
Alec	110000	5	good	0	1	0
Aday	120000	5	good	0	1	0
inti	100000	5	good	0	2	1
Alec	110000	5	good	0	2	0
teac	100000	6	teac	1	0	1
Lect	110000	6	teac	1	0	0
Day	120000	6	teac	1	0	0
cour	100000	6	teac	0	1	1
Cour	110000	6	teac	0	1	0
time	120000	6	teac	0	1	1
Day	121000	6	teac	0	1	0
Star	122000	6	teac	0	1	0
Fini	123000	6	teac	0	1	0
Lect	130000	6	teac	0	1	0
Loca	140000	6	teac	0	1	0

```
good(Alec) :- teac(Alec Aday), inti(Alec).
teac(Lect Day) :- cour(Cour time(Day Star Fini) Lect Loca).
```

Figure 9-36. Prolog rule association.

after filtering. Thus *X* is bound to Alec, and rule 1 is expanded by flagging the individual subgoals on the goal stack as shown by indices 0, 1, and 2. The current node (cnode) is advanced to 100000, and cindex is set to 0 (see Fig. 9-38). Since this is the initial entry (location (2) on the road map in Fig. 9-16), the facts[$] and rules[$] entries on the stack are nil, so data and fact filtering is performed (path

pel[$]	psc[$]	pid[$]
good	100000	1
X	110000	1
cour	100000	2
logi	110000	2
time	120000	2
t	121000	2
3	122000	2
5	123000	2
arvi	130000	2
204	140000	2
cour	100000	3
para	110000	3
time	120000	3
m	121000	3
3	122000	3
4	123000	3
jerr	130000	3
312	140000	3
init	100000	4
jerr	110000	4

Figure 9-37. A sample data base.

```
pel[$] goal[$,cindex]
       0 1 2  3 4
good   0 0 0  0 0
Alec   0 0 0  0 0
teac   1 0 0  0 0
Alec   1 0 0  0 0
Aday   1 0 0  0 0
inti   0 1 0  0 0
Alec   0 1 0  0 0
teac   0 0 0  0 0
Lect   0 0 0  0 0
Day    0 0 0  0 0
cour   0 0 0  1 0
Cour   0 0 0  1 0
time   0 0 0  1 0
Day    0 0 0  1 0
Star   0 0 0  1 0
Fini   0 0 0  1 0
Lect   0 0 0  1 0
Loca   0 0 0  1 0
```

Figure 9-38. The associative stack (goal field only).

(3)) for the first goal (teac(Alec Aday)). No facts and only rule 2 pass the filter, resulting in the rule[$] and fact[$] stack entries shown for cindex zero. At the bottom of the engine loop, rule 2 is expanded since there are no facts to process resulting in the goal flags with indices 3 and 4, and the bindings Alec:Lect and Aday:Day. Cnode is set to 110000 and at the top of the engine, cindex is set to 3. Again, this is the first entry for this node, so path 3 is taken and the facts and rules are filtered. Facts 1 and 2 match and are processed in turn in the unification loop. First the bindings Course:logic, Day:t, Stat:3, Finish:5, Lect:arvind, and Loc:204 are established by bindfact. After propagation, the binding table is as shown in Fig. 9-39a. The associative stack flag bind[$] records the binding entries made for this node, and stack variable *vv*[$] records which fact of the responders is being bound.

Since node 110000 has been successfully matched, cnode is advanced to 120000 and cindex to 4 which signals the end of this AND node by a nil goal in goal[$,4]. The nextgoal routine (11) searches for a unprocessed goal on the previous level and finds cnode = 200000, cindex = 1, which flags the second goal of rule 1. Control advances to the top of the engine.

After the initial filtering at (3), only fact 3 remains, but bfilt discovers the inconsistent bindings Alec:arvind and Alect:jerr and eliminates it also. Since no consistent facts were found this goal fails and backtrack is called.

Backtracking causes node 110000 (with cindex = 3) to be revisited. At the top of the engine, since the facts[$,3] flag is not empty, this is recognized as not being an initial entry for this node. Thus *vv*[$,3], which flags the just-processed fact, is released from facts[$,3] and the binding entries associated with this fact, which are flagged by bind[$,3] and binds[$,3], are released from the binding association. Control advances to the unification loop.

left[$]	right[$]	ra[$]	rb[$]	rv[$]	value[$]	va[$]	bsc[$]
Alex	Lect	0	0	1	arvi	1	000000
Aday	Day	0	0	1	t	1	000000
Cour	logi	1	0	0	logi	1	000000
Day	t	1	0	0	t	1	000000
Star	3	1	0	0	3	1	000000
Fini	5	1	0	0	5	1	000000
Lect	arvi	1	0	0	arvi	1	000000
Loc	204	1	0	0	204	1	000000

a - Bindings after the First Match

left[$]	right[$]	ra[$]	rb[$]	rv[$]	value[$]	va[$]	bsc[$]
Alex	Lect	0	0	1	jerr	1	000000
Aday	Day	0	0	1	m	1	000000
Cour	para	1	0	0	para	1	000000
Day	m	1	0	0	m	1	000000
Star	3	1	0	0	3	1	000000
Fini	4	1	0	0	4	1	000000
Lect	jerr	1	0	0	jerr	1	000000
Loc	312	1	0	0	312	1	000000

b - Bindings after the Second Match

Figure 9-39. The bindings after the first and second matches.

The next fact (fact 2) flagged in fact[$,3] is bound, resulting in the bindings Course:para, Day:m, Star:3, Fini:4, Lect:jerr, and Loc:312. Since the *va*[$] flag has been released and the related value[$] entries cleared, propigate re-established atom bindings resulting in the binding association shown in Fig. 9-39b.

A successful binding of node 110000 causes the system to advance to node 120000, which has a nil goal, so the next unprocessed goal on the previous level (node 200000) is selected by logic at forward, and control passes to the top of the engine.

Since node 200000 has been previously processed, static filtering has been previously performed and filter is not called. However, bfilt must be re-executed to verify that the statically filtered facts (just inti(jerr) in this case) are consistent with the current bindings.

In the unification loop, fact 3 is bound. More accurately, variable Alec in the second goal of rule 1 is bound to jerr in fact 3 but variable Alec has already been bound to Lect by the first clause of rule 1 and Lect was bound to jerr when the first goal of rule 2 was matched with fact 2 and by propigate, jerr was bound to Alec at that time. So at this point all that is done is that the consistency of the binding Alec:jerr is verified.

After the successful verification, the nextgoal track searches for the next unprocessed node. There are none, so a successful solution has been found and the bindings are printed. If additional solutions are desired the last set of bindings are released and the system backtracks. This process is repeated until all solutions have been found.

9.10 Additional Details

The inference engine described in this chapter outlines the basic associative approach to Prolog. However, there are several additional facets of Prolog that need to be addressed. Namely, adding facts (inferences) to the data base at run time, deleting facts from the data base at run time, the cut control operator and list processing. These items are discussed in turn below.

9.10.1. Logical Inferences

When a new fact is added to the data base, all goals which have been previously processed by filter need to be updated. This is accomplished in a data-parallel manner, similar to cmes and cames except that the role of matcher and matched are reversed. That is, the new fact is matched against all goals as opposed to a goal being matched against all facts. Since all goals and facts are stored in the same association, the process is exactly the same except for which individual elements are selected, matched, and covered.

Once the matching goals have been found, the facts[$] and filtered[$] flags of the corresponding entries in the associative stack must be updated. This is accomplished simply by searching every goal[$] entry in the associative stack for a match (i.e., the responders to the filter process are ANDed with the entries of the stack. A non-nil response means that the goal represented by the entry on the stack has been matched.) The stack index is used to access and update the filter's element on the stack. No special action is needed for search-tree nodes established after a fact is asserted.

9.10.2. Logical Dereferencing

When a fact is removed from the data base, it must also be erased from the filters[$] entries on the associative stack. A fact is removed by simply releasing (resetting) its association busy/idle flag entries. Since a release operation takes no action if the items were not allocated, a deleted fact can simply be removed from the associative stack by releasing it from every filters[$] flag in the stack.

9.10.3. The Cut Operator

The cut operator in Prolog simply prevents additional alternatives for a node from being tried. Since after filtering, all possible alternatives for a node are saved in the rules[$] and facts[$] flags on the associative stack, the cut operator simply clears these flags for the appropriate node.

9.10.4. List Processing

A common technique in Prolog is to organize data as a list and then search it in a typical LISP recursive manner. As has been explained elsewhere, recursion does not take advantage of associative parallelism and should be avoided. Accordingly, even though the specialized Prolog list functors ([|]) have been implemented and typical Prolog list recursion has been tested and debugged, this is not the correct approach.

The basic approach in associative Prolog is to treat a list as a type of vector data structure and to process vector data structures in parallel. At the time of writing this book, this approach is being explored but no definitive results have been obtained.

9.11. Conclusion

The results of the current associative Prolog research are quite encouraging. Currently speeds of up to 2000 logical inferences per second on data bases with 16,000 or more facts have been estimated. As indicated in section 9.10, research is still being conducted on some aspects of implementing the interpreter. Additional research is being conducted on compiling Prolog rules into executable code in a manner similar to the OPS5 rule-compilation process discussed in Chapter 8.

10

An Associative Processor Design

The previous chapters of this book have presented an abstract associative computer model, a programming language based on that model which executes on massively parallel SIMD computers, and several examples of programs and algorithms using associative concepts. This chapter presents a computer design based on the experiences gained from implementing the associative language and developing the associative algorithms and programs.

A general-purpose computer must accommodate a large range of computing requirements. Many tasks require a wide range of computing complexity. For example, scene analysis includes both the relatively simple but very repetitive pixel-processing algorithms of image processing and the search-intensive task of rule-based recognition and analysis. This chapter proposes an architecture which allows associative computing to be applied to a wide range of tasks.

Not all computing tasks are complex in themselves. Some tasks are complex due to the large amounts of data involved. For example, the image-processing task of convolution discussed in Chapter 4 does not take long for one pixel (picture element), involving typically nine multiplication and eight additions. But if it is to be evaluated for three colors at each of the 512×512 pixels in an image and at TV rates of 30 frames/sec, it requires approximately 400 mops—substantial computing power. SIMD architectures have been shown to be effective for this type of number-crunching processing (Potter [1984]). Other tasks, however, such as syntactic-pattern recognition, expert systems, or similar rule-based techniques, are frequently based on nonarithmetic operations. And while there are a relatively small number of items to be processed (perhaps a few hundred versus millions of pixels), the problem is not simply processing items but determining which of the many (perhaps thousands) of rules are pertinent and therefore to be applied. The combinatorial explosion and the nature of non-numerical computation techniques make this type of processing as computationally intensive as the raw image-processing problems. Thus a general-purpose associative computer must have the ability to efficiently execute non-numerical operations as efficiently as arithmetic computations.

Because of the close relationship of the abstract associative computing model to its hardware realization, the description of the model is repeated here: In the associative model of computation, each datum has its own dedicated processor. The model consists of a cellular organized memory, an exclusive read/write, and a restricted concurrent-read capability. A cellularly organized memory means that memory locations are organized into memory cells consisting of from several hundred to thousands of bytes and a processing unit. Each cell contains only one datum. Only one word from a cell may be accessed at a time. All cells may be accessed concurrently. The exclusive read/write capability means that each memory cell can be accessed by only one processor at a time. The concurrent-read restriction means that only one memory word from a single memory cell may be read at a time. The restricted concurrent-read capability is equivalent to a global broadcast capability.

Associative computing uses massive parallel searching in place of address calculation, reducing programming complexity and eliminating the need for time-sharing a single central processing unit with a multitude of data elements. Associative computing exploits massive fine-grain parallelism in a natural way, thus avoiding the classic memory–CPU bottleneck.

Fortunately, the SIMD architecture basic to associative processing holds the potential for efficient parallel execution of searching and non-numerical processing in addition to its recognized ability to crunch numbers. The ability of SIMD architectures to perform searching effectively is widely recognized, as evidenced by a number of special architectures which have been proposed for information retrieval applications (Oliver [1979], Schuster *et al.* [1979], Su *et al.* [1979], to name just a few). However, the requirements for an associatively based computing system are different than for a general data-base or number-crunching system, and considerable efficiency can be gained from a SIMD architecture designed specifically for associative processing.

10.1. Design Rationale

The design of the associative processor proposed here is based on the fundamental natures of

1. many-item-computational intensive processing and
2. search-intensive non-numerical processing.

Because of the two-dimensional aspect of many computationally intensive tasks, it is often assumed that a two-dimensional array of processors is the best configuration for the problem. However, as discussed in section 2.12, the important consideration in an associative processor is the mapping between the natural configuration of the problem data and the processor array's *memory* configuration.

Moreover, a *one-dimensional* array of processors has a *two-dimensional* memory configuration. Finally, most computationally intensive computations in widespread use involve only a small neighborhood of operands (3×3 or 5×5 on up to perhaps at most 32×32); consequently, a modest fan-out broadcasting interconnection between the memories and processors is adequate instead of a complete global interconnection network. In addition, larger neighborhoods and more-complex mappings between the pixels and the processor can be accomplished by replicating data during I/O operations or by using the I/O hardware in an auxiliary mode.

Two fundamental aspects of non-numerical computation dominate how it is implemented on SIMD processors. First the data can be organized so that it is re-locatable or content addressable (Potter [1983]). That is, during a parallel search, it makes no difference which processor memory contains the data. Second, complex searches are such that only a portion of the processors are busy at any one time. These two aspects can be effectively exploited in an associative processor design.

Finally, to maintain the SIMD nature of programming even in a multitasking/multiuser environment, the number of control channels is limited to approximately 16. This number is based on the human ability to manage at most six to eight different tasks simultaneously and the experience that generally MIMD throughput decreases when more than 16 or so processors are used. Any excess channel capacity beyond the capability of the programmer to use would be used for operating-system functions. The exact best number of channels would have to be determined by research.

10.2. Re-locatable Data

The concept of mapping a datum to a memory address is so commonplace that it is often assumed to be the only method of storing and retrieving data. However, content-addressing techniques are viable in associative SIMD processors because they can search all of memory in parallel in one operation. In a content-addressable organization, all of the related items of a fact are explicitly stored as an associative datum. The associative datum can be stored in any memory location, and its meaning is still valid and retrievable. Moreover, the location of the datum can be changed dynamically at run time.

The search, process, retrieve (SPR) cycle is basic to associative computation. Figure 10-1 shows how the SPR cycle maps onto an abstract machine design. The search sequence is issued by the sequential controller. The single instructions are replicated by fan-out logic so that they are effectively broadcast to all associative cells in parallel. The cells execute the instructions to determine if they satisfy the search query, and if so become responders. During the process phase, the responding cells execute the broadcast instructions in parallel. But during the retrieve phase the responders must send the requested data to the sequential controller one at a time.

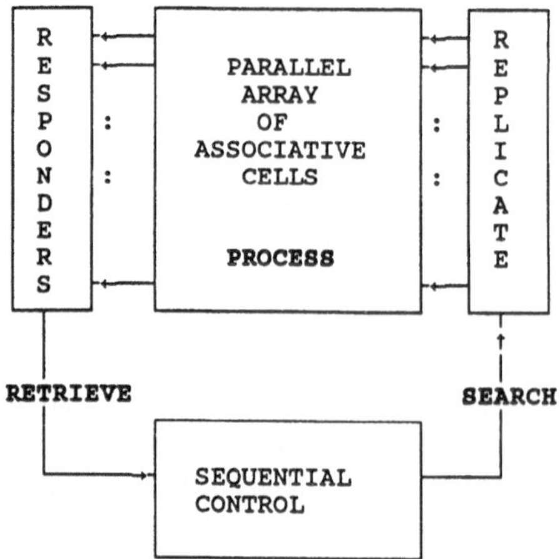

Figure 10-1. The SPR cycle.

Figure 10-2 shows a typical SIMD organization. Its topology is very similar to the SPR cycle diagram of Fig. 10-1. The search and process phases use the fan-out hardware of the sequential control/parallel array interface whereas the retrieve phase uses the fan-in. Most SIMD computers have an interconnection network as shown in Fig. 10-2. But there is no explicit process in the SPR cycle model that requires this component. However, it is useful for the parallel transfer of data between processors when data reorganization is desired or when multidimensional arrays of data are processed, as in convolution and other computationally intensive tasks.

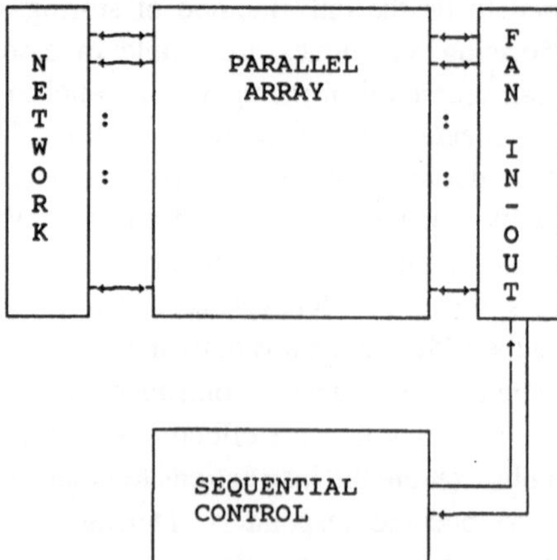

Figure 10-2. A typical SIMD processor.

The statements in the ASC language were designed to map the SPR cycle onto the basic SIMD hardware. Consider the **if** statement and the **for** statement, for example. The logical parallel expression of the **if** and **for** statements is the search phase of the SPR cycle and uses the fan-out hardware to broadcast the search to all processors in parallel. The statements in the body of the **if** statement also use the fan-out to broadcast the instructions to the entire array, but the action in these statements takes place only in those array cells that have responded to the search phase.

Since the fan-in circuitry in most SIMD processors is simply an ORing of all responses, only one cell at a time can use this circuitry to send data back to the sequential control. During the retrieval phase of the ASC **for** statement, the index-parallel variable controls which responder may use the path to the sequential control. A cell-to-sequential control communication is signaled in the body of the **for** statement by using the index-parallel variable in place of the execute-all index (i.e., [$]) in a parallel variable. Figure 10-3 illustrates how the data to be communicated is selected. Often the retrieved data is used in the search phase of a nested associative search statement.

10.3. Communication Paths

There are normally three communication paths within a SIMD processor. The first is the fan-out path shown in Fig. 10-2. The fan-out path is a broadcast mechanism from the single sequential controller to all of the array processors. In some SIMD architectures, such as PASM (Siegel *et al.* [1981]) and DADO (Stolfo and Miranker [1984]), this path is a binary tree with a processor at each node. In such configurations, the nodes are often complete processors and can perform computations on their own. In the associative model, there is only one sequential control and many array processors; consequently, the broadcast path does not have any computational components in it. Additional levels of programming control would destroy the simplicity and elegance of the associative model and add considerable programming and hardware complexity without adding any substantial computing power or flexibility.

The second communication path, shown as fan-in in Fig. 10-2, is the retrieve

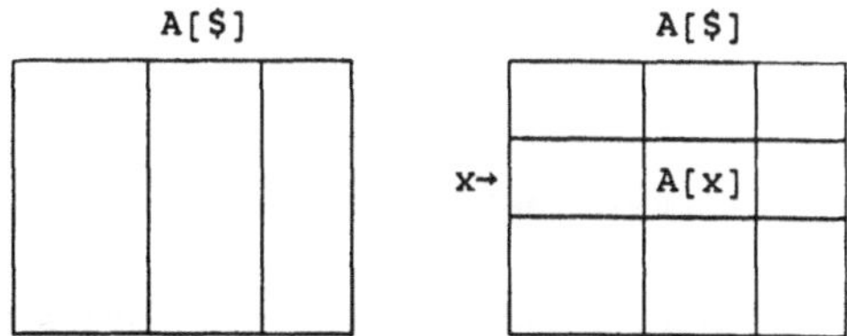

Figure 10-3. Index parallel variable selects one word.

data path. This is the path the data takes from the array to the sequential control. In most conventional SIMD designs, the importance of this data path is underestimated and as a consequence the path is underdeveloped. As a result, this path is frequently implemented using the inverse of the broadcast-data path. Thus in architectures in which the fan-out has no active component, the retrieve data path consists of a simple parallel fan-in sum–or circuit. In machines with a tree fan-out, the tree structure also serves as the fan-in circuitry.

In either design, the retrieve data path is a computational bottleneck for the associative model. At any one time, only one of the many cells may be sending data to the sequential control on the retrieve data path. The tree-structure architecture does have data parallelism at the lower levels of the fan-in tree, but the additional program control required to utilize it and the data bottleneck at the top of the tree make it of little more value than a sum–or circuit.

The third type of communication is the array interprocessor communication path shown as the network in Fig. 10-2. This is one of the main distinguishing characteristics of SIMD processors. Some SIMDs, such as the MPP and DAP, have a two-dimensional grid or mesh interconnection. Others such as the STARAN and the ASPRO have a one-dimensional flip network. The Connection Machine has a hypercube network. The MasPar has a multistage crossbar network and a mesh. The Wavetracer has a three-dimensional mesh. The intent of this communication path is to allow any data item in one array cell to be communicated to any other array processor. This path is assumed to be critical to supplying the communication needs of a SIMD processor. It is designed to allow maximal parallel communication so that a large-memory PE bandwidth can be obtained. Because of the perceived importance of this path, as much as 25–30% of a SIMD's hardware may be dedicated to it.

However, a fourth communication path is the most important. It is the random-access memory associated with each PE in a cell. That is, if a data item needs to be send to a PE frequently, it should be stored in the PE's memory. The hardware memory path supports the most active data interactions. In the associative model there are, by definition, interactions between items in an association entry. That is, two or more items, such as age, social-security number, and name, are organized into an association so that the age value of an entry can be efficiently obtained if the location of the cell that contains the name is known. Note that this data path is the most massively parallel path in the computer. If there are 64K processors in the associative processor, then the memory/PE communication path is 64K bits wide.

10.4. The Basic Design

One of the general complaints about SIMD parallelism is that unless a large amount of data is being processed, there is low PE utilization. A second problem is the fan-in bottleneck. The retrieval hardware is designed to allow only one PE to respond at a time. The basic design of the bit-serial SIMD architecture shown in Fig. 10-4 has been enhanced with seven features to address these and other problems. These enhancements are

1. byte-serial arithmetic,
2. parallel indexing,
3. an I/O stack,
4. parallel fan-in,
5. parallel comparison,
6. adequate local memory, and
7. bimodal interprocessor communication.

Each of these items is discussed below.

10.4.1. Byte-Serial Arithmetic

Most massively parallel SIMD processors use a bit-serial architecture to achieve a large number of parallel processors. The penalty that must be paid is a slower execution for each operation than in a word-serial design. That is, the addition of two *n*-bit numbers takes approximately 8*n* instructions in bit-serial mode but only three instructions in bit-parallel mode. One advantage to the bit-serial approach is that field sizes can be declared to fit the range of data to be stored in them. Thus, if only values of 1000 or less are to be processed, the field can be limited to ten bits. The overall net effect is a more efficient utilization of resources.

In applications, however, there is very little need for field sizes of two, three, five, or seven bits. And in fact, except for one-bit fields used as flags, very little

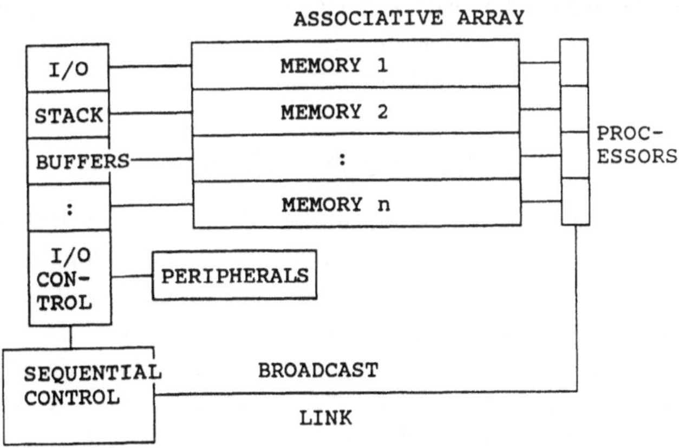

Figure 10-4. A basic associative processor.

efficiency would be lost if fields were limited to multiples of eight. The advantage of a byte-sized PE design are many.

First, integer arithmetic operations would execute approximately eight times faster with little decrease in efficiency. The fact that a massively parallel 64K machine is now a less-massive 8K machine is compensated for by the fact that it runs eight times faster in general and, for problems that need only 8K parallelism, it executes much more efficiently.

Second, floating-point arithmetic is easier to accommodate when floating-point hardware is not included because of cost considerations. The floating-point number representation can be broken into subfields whose sizes are multiples (or near-multiples) of eight bits. Seven- and eight-bit exponents can be conveniently and effectively processed using byte-parallel operations, while 24-bit mantissas can be efficiently processed using byte-serial arithmetic.

In spite of the advantages of byte- and word-serial arithmetic, two aspects of the basic operation of an associative processor demand bit-serial processing. First is the concept of bit flags for control of flow. Second is the associative numeric search functions as explained in section 2.8.3. One approach that would satisfy both worlds would be to fetch and store a byte's worth of data at a time. A special register in the PE would hold all eight bits and allow instructions to specifically address the bit desired. Thus for flag fields there would be, in effect, eight mask registers which could be selected instead of always defaulting to a specific one. For numeric searching, the specified bit of the register would be output to the sum–or circuitry for the responder/no-responder test required by these operations.

The proposed byte-serial design is a judgment call on the mixture of massive data-parallel number crunching and non-numerical associative computation. There is no reason why a nibble-serial (as is the MasPar) or word-serial design could not be built. In fact, one of the advantages of associative computing and the ASC language is that an entire range of parallel-associative computers from bit-serial, to nibble-serial, to byte- and word-serial can be built. The specific architecture selection can be made on the tradeoffs between the anticipated mix of algorithms and the amount of parallelism desired. In any case, the same ASC program would work on a machine of any size.

10.4.2. Parallel Indexing

One of the major limitations of bit-serial SIMD design is the inability to allow indexing, as would be used for table lookup, at each PE. Supporting parallel indexing means that the common address field broadcast by the sequential controller would have to be modified at each PE's memory. This would require much more circuitry to accomplish than exists in an entire bit-serial PE. However, when a processor is eight bits wide, the tradeoff is more favorable, and if certain tricks are used—such as requiring the eight rightmost bits of the address to be zero and ORing in the index instead of adding it—considerable computational advantage can be gained at reasonable cost.

10.4.3. The I/O Stack

Adequate I/O bandwidth is one of the major design considerations of a SIMD machine. In general-purpose associative processing, two distinct types of I/O are required. The first is for re-locatable associative data. The second is for spatially related data, such as imagery, which would be stored in a multidimensional data structure. An I/O stack can be designed to meet both of these needs. The name of the described device comes from its logical organization and operation. Its physical realization may be quite different, using buses, a multisorted memory, or an interconnection network instead of stacks, for example.

In some designs, the operation of the stack could be implemented using ASC **for** statements. However, it should be kept in mind that speed is of the utmost priority; thus, the emphasis should be on putting as much functionality into the hardware as is economically feasible. Generally speaking, an order-of-magnitude or more speedup can be gained by adopting a hardware rather than a software implementation.

The I/O stack shown in Fig. 10-4 must be capable of handling both the bulk transfers required for large data arrays and the selective I/O needed for re-locatable data. Figure 10-4 shows that each associative cell has its own I/O stack buffer in the I/O stack. The buffers are connected directly to the associative cell memories, and data can move in parallel from every associative cell memory to its associated stack buffer. In addition, the buffers are connected to each other to form a stack. Data can move from a lower stack buffer to a higher buffer (or vice versa) in parallel to achieve the fastest transfer rates. In reality, as mentioned above, the hardware may be quite different, but it will be designed to maximize data transfer rates for I/O and other stack functions and minimize interconnection (hardware) costs.

Note that the two-dimensional interconnections of the stack perform a corner-turning operation. That is, data is input and output from the bottom of the stack in byte-parallel mode. It is moved in parallel from the buffers to the array memories in byte-serial mode.

The I/O control shown in Fig. 10-4 retrieves files from disks and other peripherals and stores them in a memory buffer. When requested it moves the data to the I/O stack. The sequential control allocates the array cells, calculates the cells' memories' field addresses, and transfers data between the I/O stack buffers and the cells' memories. The cells involved in the I/O process are flagged by the I/O mask register.

10.4.3.1. Block I/O Transfers

The block data I/O needed for large data arrays is a very regular (synchronous) process where each associative cell memory receives a fixed amount of data in a fixed order (from one or two bytes per item, for example, up to, say, 128 bytes per item). During the first step of this mode of operation (see Fig. 10-5), the

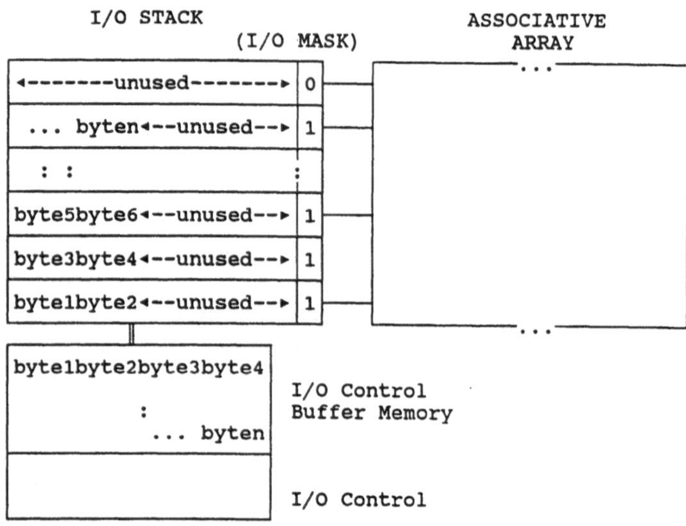

Figure 10-5. Bulk I/O for two bytes per item. First step.

I/O control determines the number of bytes in a data item and provides that information to the stack. The I/O control then sends data in the proper order so that the first item is accepted by I/O stack buffer 1. When the first stack buffer has received the specified number of bytes of data, the I/O stack terminates the buffer entry. Subsequent data is passed on to stack buffer 2 by buffer 1. Stack buffer 2 accepts data until it has received the specified number of bytes. Then the data is passed on to the next stack buffer, and so on. When an entire column of items has been input, the second step, shown in Fig. 10-6, is executed. The main program in the sequential control is interrupted, and the sequential control broadcasts the array-memory address and transfers the data in parallel from the I/O stack buffers to the associated array memories.

On output, the process is reversed. The main program, in the sequential control, determines the number of bytes and the address of the items in the associative array memories to be output. It sets the I/O mask to flag the appropriate cells and then transfers the data from the array memories to the stack buffers. The I/O control is signaled. It then starts to read the data from the first I/O stack buffer and stores it in the I/O control-buffer memory. As it reads the data, data from the other stack buffers trickles down until all stack buffers are emptied. On both input and output, the I/O mask is set to select a contiguous block of cells, thus preserving the implicit two-dimensional character of the data.

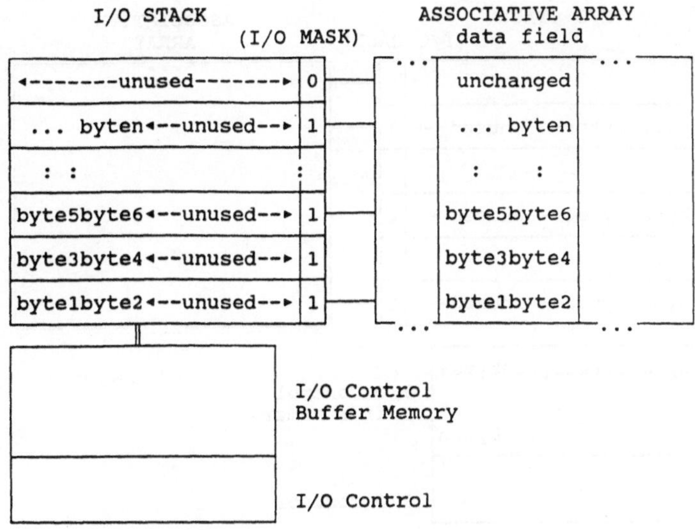

Figure 10-6. Bulk I/O for two bytes per item. Second step.

10.4.3.2. Re-locatable I/O Transfers

The I/O for data arrays is very regular, while that for non-numerical systems tends to be random. Associative non-numerical I/O can be characterized in two ways. First, the data can be organized so that it is re-locatable. That is, during a parallel search, it makes no difference which processor memory contains the data. Second, complex searches are such that only a portion of the processors are busy at any one time. These two aspects can be exploited by the I/O stack to achieve an effective I/O scheme (see Fig. 10-7). First, the sequential control interrogates the associative array's busy/idle flags to determine which cells are idle and sets the I/O mask accordingly. Then the I/O control sends re-locatable data to the stack. It trickles up (away from the I/O control) until an idle buffer flagged by a 1 in the I/O mask is found. When the first association item has been input, the buffer's I/O mask bit is cleared, and subsequent items pass over it, trickling up the stack until a buffer with a 1 in its I/O mask is found. When the entire data-association file has been input, the I/O stack control interrupts sequential control. Sequential control then sets the I/O mask to flag the cells with new data by an exclusive OR of the current I/O mask with the original mask, broadcasts instructions to move the stack-buffer data into the array memory, and updates the appropriate busy/idle flags in array memory (see Fig. 10-8).

The output process is basically the reverse of input. Data is moved, in parallel, from the memory of the array cells flagged by the I/O mask to the associated I/O stack buffers. The data then trickles down the stack until it reaches

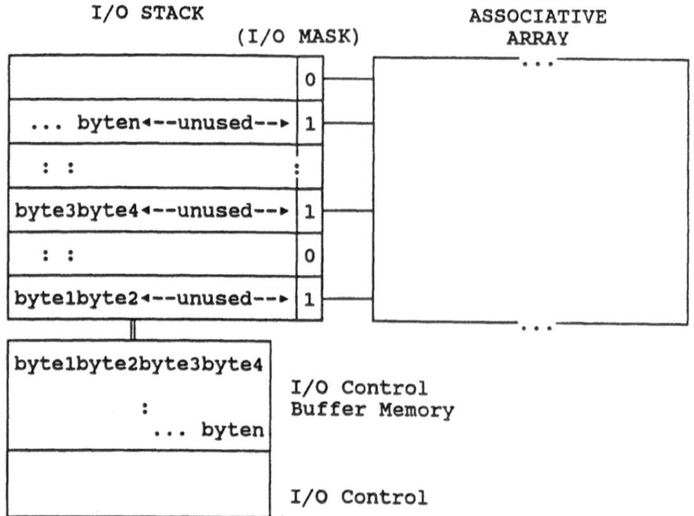

First Step: Move Data from I/O Control to Stack

Figure 10-7. Re-locatable I/O for two bytes per item. First step.

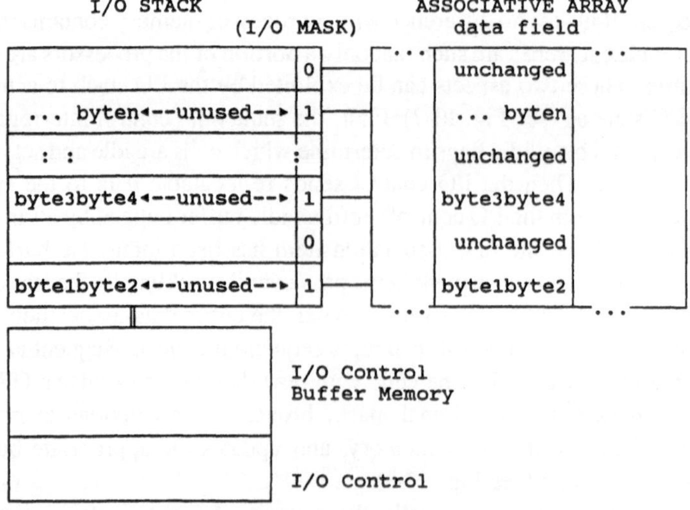

Second Step: Move Data from Stack to Array Field

Figure 10-8. Re-locatable I/O for two bytes per item. Second step.

the full part of the stack. As the I/O processor takes data from the bottom of the stack, the remaining data in the stack moves down to replace it. The I/O processor formats the data into blocks and writes it out on the disks or other peripherals.

In general, the processing elements become idle in a random order; thus, data will not necessarily be kept in memory in the same order as it was input. However, the re-locatable aspect of the data makes this acceptable.

Note that, if the sequential control allocates a consecutive block of cells, a block I/O transfer is effected. If the sequential control specifies a random set of cells, a re-locatable transfer is accomplished. Except for the pattern of the initial selection of cells, both I/O processes are identical.

10.4.3.3. Miscellaneous I/O Stack Functions

In addition to the high-speed I/O utility of the I/O stack, it performs certain miscellaneous but important functions. The corner-turning function has already been mentioned. The trickle-down/trickle-up feature allows data reorganization and compaction. A **collapse** operation uses trickle down to move data from random locations in the stack into a contiguous block of data, as shown in Fig. 10-9. **Collapse** is very useful in converting data from the re-locatable format to the block-mode format. In addition, it can be used to prepare data for medium-grain parallelism by moving data items of the same class into contiguous regions to allow simultaneous parallel data broadcasting.

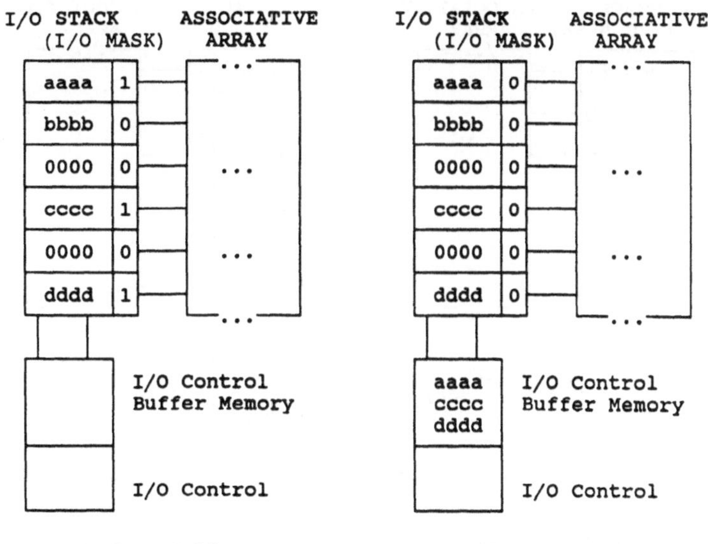

Figure 10-9. Effects of a **collapse**.

The inverse of the **collapse** operation is **expand**. It starts with all the data in the I/O control-buffer memory. The idle cells, possibly containing garbage, are flagged by a 1 in the I/O mask. The data trickles up the stack, filling the idle entries until all of the data has been distributed, as shown in Fig. 10-10. The two operations together in a **collapse–expand** sequence allow re-locatable data to be moved efficiently from one set of random cells to another.

Two dimensions of data replication are essential for efficient general-purpose associative processing. The normal parallel memory-to-memory (i.e., field *a* to field *b*) move provides one dimension of data replication. The I/O stack provides the second by a **collapse–expand** sequence.

Collapse and **expand** use the I/O mask to flag the source PEs for the **collapse** operation and the destination PEs for **expand**. These operations are used in the block and re-locatable modes of I/O simply by setting the I/O mask bits in a contiguous block for the block mode or by allocating the next available cells for the re-locatable mode. Obviously, these operations can support random–random, random–block, block–block, and block–random reorganizations, depending on the configurations of the I/O mask.

The I/O stack hardware can select a random responder in one step. The selection process allows the data in the selected I/O buffer to be transferred to or from the I/O control-buffer memory in one step, using a **read** or **write** operation bypassing the trickle down/up process. Two forms of the selection instruction are needed. The first only selects the I/O buffer to be transferred. The second form not

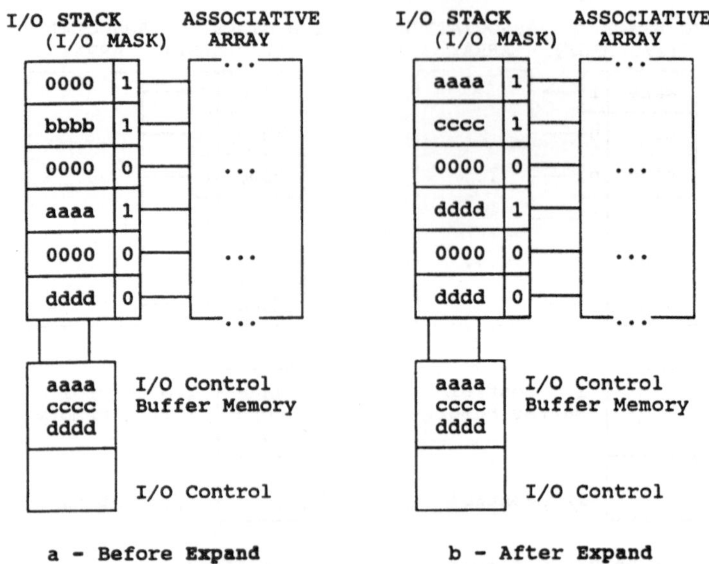

Figure 10-10. Effects of an **expand**.

only selects the buffer but clears the buffer's I/O mask flag so that it will not be selected again (until the I/O mask is reset by an external operation).

After stack-buffer selection, a **read** moves data directly from the stack buffer to the I/O control-buffer memory. The inverse operation is to **write** from the I/O control-buffer memory to the selected stack buffer. Figures 10-11, 10-12, and 10-13 illustrate a **first/read**, a **next/read**, and a **first/write** sequence, respectively.

A second selection capability exists to specify the desired stack buffer by the id number of the associated cell. Once it is specified, either a **read** or **write** may be executed.

Another miscellaneous I/O stack function is the ability to sum the contents of all the I/O buffers flagged by the I/O mask. Since the I/O buffer is quite wide (on the order of 256 bits), different fields of, say, 32 bits each can be loaded with data corresponding to different conditions and the entire buffer summed to give a histogram of the responses, as illustrated in Fig. 10-14. The numbers flagged by the I/O mask are summed. The remaining numbers are ignored. When the I/O mask is included as a field, a count of the responders is produced.

10.4.4. Parallel Fan-in

Figure 10-4 shows that the I/O control has a data path to the sequential control. This means that the second data path (array fan-in), which is sequential and very slow in conventional SIMD designs, can be replaced by a much faster

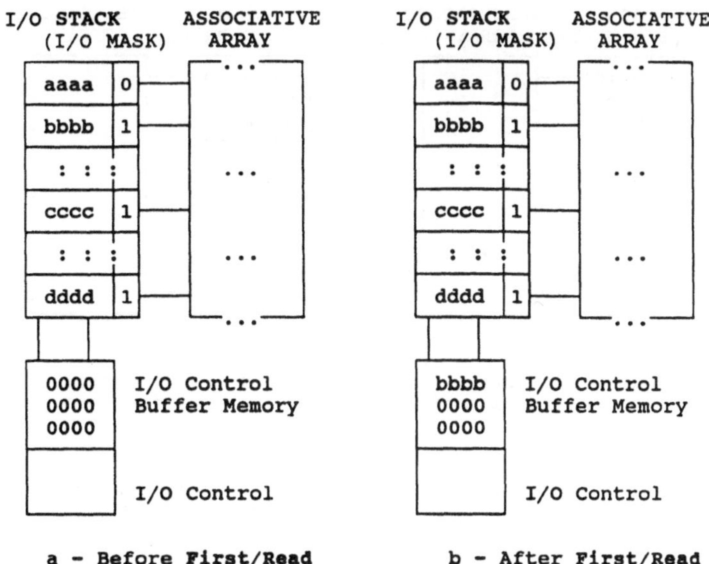

Figure 10-11. Effects of a **first/read**.

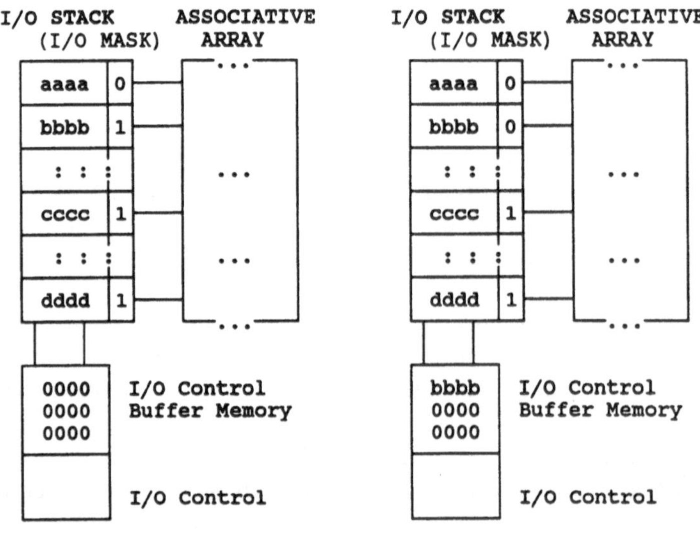

Figure 10-12. Effects of **next/read**.

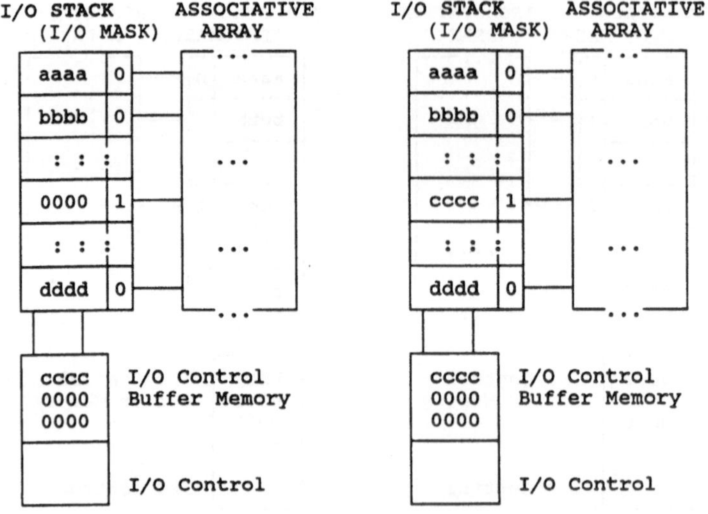

Figure 10-13. The effects of **first/write**.

```
◄──────────────I/O STACK──────────────►
Field 1  Field 2  ...  Field n  IOMASK
```

Field 1	Field 2	...	Field n	IOMASK
3	19		7	1
2	15		22	1
1	5		8	0
4	29		13	0
7	9		19	1
16	7		3	0
15	2		6	1
4	9		11	0
27	45		54	4

Figure 10-14. The effects of a stack sum.

parallel path via the I/O stack. This allows the retrieve phase of the SPR cycle to be executed much faster.

For example, consider the ASC **for** statement. The body of a **for** statement is executed once for each responder to the conditional expression. In a typical **for** statement, many items may be retrieved from the association cells flagged by the parallel index variable. For example, a[xx], b[xx], and c[xx] in Fig. 10-15a will be retrieved. The code in the body of the **for** loop is executed sequentially for each responder. However, the ASC compiler can reorder the field transfers to the beginning of the loop, as shown in Fig. 10-15b. Since all of the responders are

```
for xx in .........
   if a[xx] .eq. 3 then
     :
   endif;
      for yy in b[xx] .gt. 9
          dd[yy] = c[xx] + 3;
      endfor yy;
endfor xx;

      a -  Original Source
```

```
for xx in ...
move a[xx], b[xx], c[xx] via I/O
stack to I/O control buffer memory
"real time break"
   if a[xx] .eq. 3 then
     :
   endif;
      for yy in b[xx] .gt. 9
          dd[yy] = c[xx] + 3;
      endfor yy;
endfor xx;

     b - Rearranged Retrieves
```

Figure 10-15. Code organization for a parallel retrieval.

known at the beginning of the loop, all of the responders' fields specified in the body of the loop can be transferred in parallel to the I/O stack. A **collapse** operation then moves the data to the I/O control buffer memory, where it is available to the sequential controller as needed. This mode of operation allows the retrieve phase of the SPR cycle to be speeded up considerably. The only delay is in the time required for the data from the first responder to reach the I/O control buffer and then the sequential control. The trickle-down time of the remaining entries can overlap the **for** loop iteration. In effect, the I/O stack provides a parallel peripheral fan-in circuit.

10.4.5. Parallel Comparison

The basic associative computer design includes a status and a test register in each PE. Thus all comparisons as described in section 7.2 would be performed in parallel. The desired test for each PE would be specified in the PE's test register. A **compare** instruction would cause the data items to be compared and the results stored in the status register of each PE. It would then cause the test register to be ANDed on a bit-by-bit basis with the status register. The resulting bits would be ORed into one bit, which would be stored in the status-summary register. As illustrated in Fig. 10-16, a 1 in the summary register indicates that the test was successful; a 0 indicates that it failed.

10.4.6. Local Memory

Each PE would be supplied with at least 128 bytes of on-chip memory. This memory acts as local registers and would considerably speed up arithmetic and logical computations. The specific number of bytes on the chip would be engineered considering speed/cost tradeoffs. Since the ASC compiler object code is optimized, a large on-chip memory is not required for efficient operation. However, there is always a need for more, faster memory.

10.4.7. Bimodal Interprocessor Communication

The associative computing model combines computationally intensive data-parallel computations, which require intensive local interprocessor communications, with associative searching for general-purpose computation, which requires a global communication capability.

```
 test    status and  or summary
eq 010    001   000  0    0
le 110    100   100  1    1
gt 001    001   001  1    1
```

Figure 10-16. Parallel comparison.

Thus the basic design assumes a need for bimodal interprocessor communication, as illustrated in Fig. 10-17. The assumed communication pattern is quite different from that assumed by other massively parallel designs. A common assumption is that the father away the data in terms of the number n of intervening PEs, the less need for communication (or more accurately, the more expensive the cost of communication). For example, in a grid the cost is linear in n; in a hypercube, the cost is a function of $\log n$. In a crossbar, the cost is constant in time but expensive in dollars.

10.5. VLSI Organization

The proposed design is well suited for VLSI technology in that it does not place great emphasis on global interconnections and is scalable. Thus if the I/O stack buffer, memory, PE, and memory/PE interconnect are organized as shown in Figs. 10-18 and 10-19, the number of leads on/off a chip remains constant regardless of the number of associative cells on the chip. The off-chip lead requirements are

1. I/O data leads,
2. memory address leads,
3. PE instruction leads,
4. memory PE fan-out leads for the PEs at the edge of the chip, and
5. sum–or/responder–no responder lead.

The PE interconnection capability is designed to meet the anticipated needs. The design assumes that communications are bimodal. That is, many data-intensive calculations require only nearest-neighbor communication; the rest span large distances. Thus the five-lead memory-to-PE fan-out allows convolution and other spatial data-intensive computations (with up to a 5×5 weight matrix) to be achieved without any communication overhead. (Only a three-lead fan-out is shown in Fig. 10-19.) Longer distances can be achieved with minimal overhead. For example, a 9×9 convolution would require a total of only 18 units of overhead out of 161 operations.

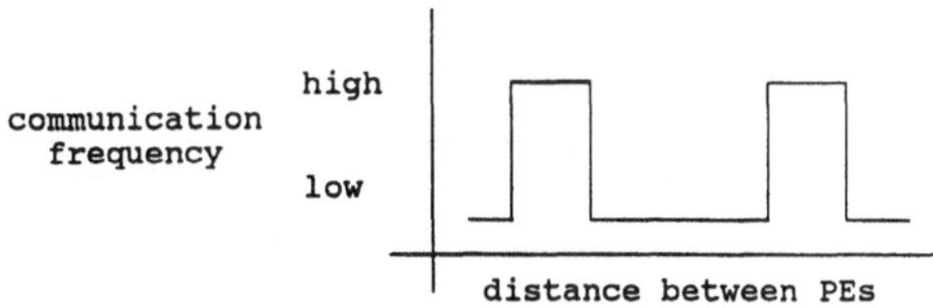

Figure 10-17. Bimodal intercommunication.

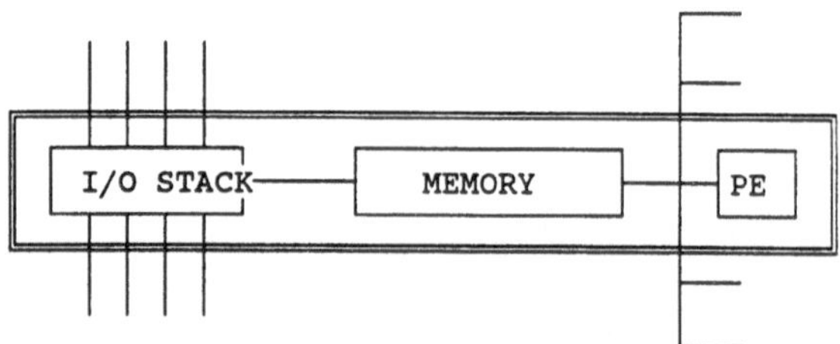

Figure 10-18. One PE per chip.

10.6. Associative Multitasking/Multiuser Parallelism

10.6.1. Associative Multitasking

Several proposals have been made to produce MIMD/SIMD machines: for example, Siegel *et al.* [1981] and Shaw [1982]. The proposal here is a multitasking, multiuser SIMD using the associative model of computation. All current approaches to multitasking parallelism in SIMD processors in fact consist basically of MIMD parallelism with SIMD components. They all depend on conventional MIMD programming techniques to divide the PE array into predefined physical pieces. It is difficult to dynamically modify the number of physical PEs assigned to a problem at run time. Certain other restrictions also exist, such as the requirement that the PEs assigned to a task must be physically adjacent or the number of processors assigned to a task must be a power of 2. The basic concept is that there are a number of MIMD tasks that can execute in parallel. Each of these tasks may include SIMD components. There is no attempt to partition SIMD tasks into parallel components.

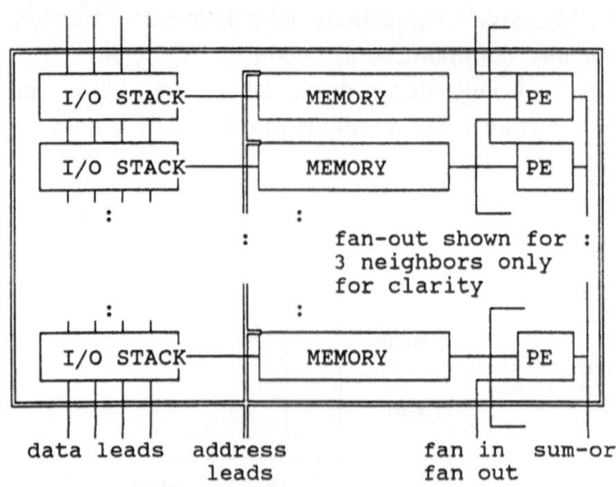

Figure 10-19. *n* PEs per chip.

10.6.2. Multiple Associative Instruction Streams

A more dynamic and flexible approach to SIMD parallelism is to use multiple parallel associative instruction streams. The streams would be broadcast on a single time-shared instruction bus. Time sharing of the instruction stream allows parallelism at the PE level because the broadcast instructions would be in a high-level assembly language which would require fifty or more PE microinstructions per assembly instruction. Each cell PE would be capable of accepting instructions from up to 16 instruction streams or channels. In a straightforward extension of the masking or activity bit, the PEs would select their channels as a function of their local data content. Figure 10-20 illustrates that associative cells would be organized by job and task id fields. PEs with the same job or task id do not need to be contiguous. PEs with the same job id may be executing different instruction streams, while PEs with the same job and task id would execute the same instruction stream.

This approach is a straightforward extension of the mask register and context flag of conventional SIMD processors such as the MPP and the Connection Machine. Instead of a single context bit, however, each PE would have a channel register of four bits. Each PE would listen to the instruction stream specified by the channel register. If a search were false for a PE it would be masked out by assigning the channel register to a channel which would broadcast no-ops.

One of the most powerful aspects of associative computers is their global parallel-searching capability. Special hardware can be included to find the first responder of a search or to detect if there are any responders. This hardware would be implemented on a channel-by-channel basis. Thus, if a PE is listening to the

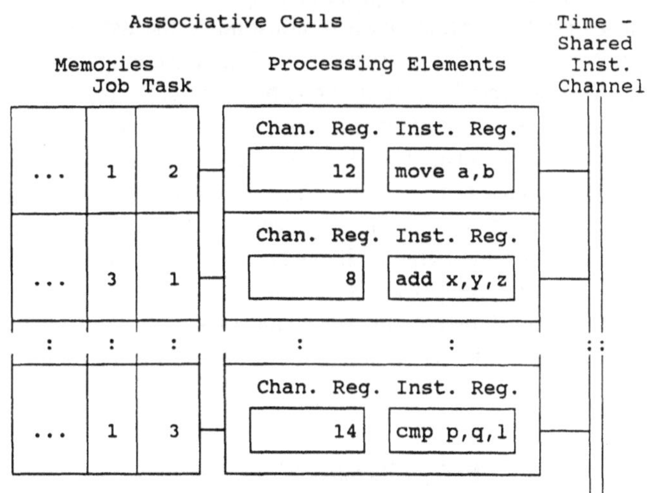

Figure 10-20. Cell partitioning by job and task ID.

instructions on time slot n, it would respond to queries on responder time slot n. This is a control channel, not a data channel. This channel would be limited to responders/no-responders signals only.

With this basic design, it is a simple, straightforward task to use ASC to write an operating system which would allow multiuser and multitasking computation. At the SIMD multitasking level of parallelism, there is no distinction between the tasks of a single user and the tasks of multiple users. Both types of parallelism are served by assuring that the PEs with the proper data are listening to the channels with the proper instruction streams. In a multiuser environment, each cell must contain its job id. The control channels can be shared between jobs, since the cells can be identified associatively as belonging to a specific job by their id. Multiuser parallelism adds a coarse level of parallelism to the system. Thus the addition of a multichannel instruction stream supports associative simultaneous coarse-, medium-, and fine-grain parallelism, overcoming the low-PE-utilization complaint of SIMD computers.

Since there are no hardware differences between the channels, the control channel may be any channel selected by the operating system at run time. If there is more than one program executing in parallel, more than one control channel may be designated.

10.6.3. Multiuser Interprocessor Communication

If the PEs of a task are not contiguous, certain communication functions such as the NEWS grid configuration may not be possible. When this kind of communication is desired, the user can specify that the job may not run until a block with the minimal number of PEs is available. If the grid communication is needed for only a short time, the various tasks of the program may be started and then the I/O stack **collapse** and **expand** operations used to consolidate the data into a contiguous block just prior to execution of the section requiring the contiguous block. If most of the program's tasks require a contiguous block of cells, the operating system would delay the entire job until such a block was available.

As is true of all the design specifications described in this chapter, the exact operation of the I/O stack can not be finalized until it has been emulated. But the initial design would specify that the I/O stack mechanism be time shared in a multiuser mode among the various channels. That is, if an instruction channel required an I/O function, the channel's sequential control would request the use of the I/O stack. When available, the I/O stack control would respond to the channel's request. The channel would maintain control of the I/O stack until the I/O process was complete.

10.6.4. Parallel Ifs and Fors

As an example of associative multitasking, assume that a parallel **if** is broadcast to all PEs listening to channel 5. The instruction sequence would direct the false responders to listen to an alternative channel, say channel 2. Then, in parallel, channel 5 would broadcast instructions for the **then** body to the true responders, and channel 2 would broadcast instructions for the **else** body to the false responders. Case constructs would be handled in a similar manner, except that there would be one channel for each of the different cases.

Under certain circumstances, **for** iteration can be parallelized. Given a parallel broadcasting (i.e., multitasking) capability, an associative architecture can achieve medium-grain parallelism, if the responders of the **for** condition partition the data into mutually exclusive subsections. In a single-instruction-stream environment, the body must be executed iteratively, once for each responder. In a multitasking associative processor, all of the **for** responders would be retrieved in parallel by the I/O stack, as described in section 10.4.4, and delivered to the parallel sequential controls. These controls would execute the **for** body in parallel, each control with a different set of retrieved data. Since fine-grain parallelism is used to process nested SPR cycles in the **for** body in parallel, simultaneous medium-grain and fine-grain parallelism would be achieved.

10.6.5. Associative Synchronism

In general, the instruction stream segments on the different channels will be of different lengths, so some method of gathering together the cell subsets that are listening to different channels must be devised. A straightforward approach is to tell the cell subsets to listen to a control channel when they are done executing their code. When the last group of cells has been switched to the control channel, the channel assignments for the next set of tasks would be initialized by a control instruction sequence that says, in essence, "All PEs working on Task *A* of Job *B* switch to channel *n*." Channel *n* then would begin broadcasting the instruction sequence for Task *A* of Job *B*.

Control stream synchronism would be achieved by parallel searching. When each task of a job was completed, it would branch to an operating-system rendezvous routine. This routine would assign the just-released PEs to a specified rendezvous channel. It then would search for all PEs with the same job id. It knows what channels the job is using and would simply broadcast on all of the assigned channels for the PEs to respond TRUE if they are not listening to the assigned rendezvous channel. Any responder from any of the assigned channels would indicate that not all segments are complete. If there were responders, the rendezvous routine would exit. When the last task of a job executed the rendezvous routine, there would be no responders to the rendezvous query and the routine would then assign all of the PEs on the rendezvous channel to the next task in the job sequence.

10.6.6. Advantages of Associative Multitasking

There are a number of advantages to SIMD associative multitasking. Normally, in large programs where parallelism is desirable for rapid execution, there is considerably more data than code. In conventional MIMD computers, the data from one task must be communicated from one processor to another before the spawned program segment may begin to execute. Even in shared-memory MIMD machines, problems may arise when many processors try to simultaneously access the data in the same memory bank. However, in associative multitasking, each datum has its own processor, so no data movement is necessary, and the program is stored in a common program memory accessible to all program sequencers. Thus virtually all delay is eliminated.

Another advantage of associative multitasking is simple synchronism. For example, assume that a task has two parallel sub-tasks. Under conventional MIMD approaches, a rendezvous must be arranged to coordinate the tasks, since the amount of data processed often varies from one run to the next, and therefore the lengths of execution of the tasks may be vastly different. In associative multitasking, however, the execution time is a function of the length of the code—which, once compiled, never changes. It takes the same amount of time regardless of the amount of data, since more processors are assigned if more data is present. Consequently, the forking and joining processes are deterministic and easier to synchronize.

10.7. The Basic Associative Intermediate Level Instruction Set

Perhaps the most effective way of specifying a specific concept behind an architecture or computational model is to define the instruction set it would execute. This section defines an instruction set at an intermediate level which provides an efficient bridge between the higher-level constructs of ASC and the lower-level instructions of an actual machine.

The Basic Associative Intermediate Level (BAIL) instruction set is organized into three components. The first component is scalar, the second is parallel, and the third contains instructions common to both the scalar and parallel parts of the architecture. Instructions in the common component have both scalar and parallel arguments. Triple-address intermediate-level instructions (or quadruples) will be used to describe the instruction set, since they are quite general and can easily be converted into and generated from an intermediate code tree representation. The basic form of a quadruple is:

```
opcode        input1, input2, result
```

Thus an assignment statement of the form

$$a = b \text{ op } c$$

is mapped into

```
op b,c,a
```

Moves and unary operations such as

a = b

and

a = −b

are mapped into

move b, a

and

minus b, a

respectively. Conditional and unconditional branches put the target of the branch in the last position, giving

branch label

and

branch_on_true test, label

In an extension of the convention of naming a quadruple operator according to the type of operands it takes (i.e., integer add, floating add, etc.), the quadruple names also include the scalar/parallel type designation of the operands. Thus an operator that adds fixed-integer parallel operands would be labeled addfxppp. Figure 10-21 shows the taxonomy of the different quadruple names. It shows that common quadruples have both a common left (cl) type when the scalar (the common variable to be broadcast to the parallel variables) is in the first argument and a common right (cr) type when the scalar is in the second position.

It is common for the field specification of a parallel field to include an address and a length component. In order to assure compatibility between the scalar and parallel quadruples, BAIL requires address and length for scalar variables also.

10.7.1. The Scalar Instruction Set

Column 1 of Table 10-1 gives the scalar instruction set. As can be seen, it is essentially equivalent to a conventional scalar-computer instruction set. This is the instruction set used for scalar arithmetic, comparisons, and the control of program flow based on scalar variables.

10.7.2. The Parallel Instruction Set

Column 2 of Table 10-1 gives the parallel instruction set. It too looks like the instruction set for a conventional computer, but all instructions are executed in parallel in each associative cell. The instructions are implicitly masked. That is,

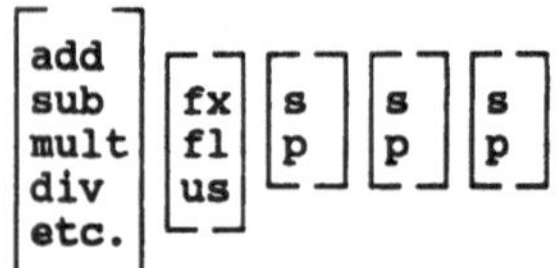

a - BAIL Operator Taxonomy

quadruple	BAIL Component
addfxsss	scalar
addfxspp	common left
addfxpsp	common right
addfxps	common(reduction)
addfxppp	parallel

b - A Declension of Integer Add

Key: fx - fixed point signed integer
fl - floating point
us - unsigned integer
s - scalar
p - parallel

Figure 10-21. Quadruple taxonomy.

the instructions are executed in all processors for which the mask flag is set to TRUE.

The move instructions represented by the parallel move operators in row 4 are more complex than the scalar moves due to variable length fields. Thus moves include resizing when a field of one size is moved to a field of a different size. Resizing has several variations (i.e., sign extend, zero fill) to accommodate the different data types. The shift of a field is also achieved by a move.

Note that in the fifth and sixth row, a branch on responders capability (b_rs and b_nr) replaces the branch on scalar value. These tests form the basis for iteration in an associative computer.

There are three additional classes of parallel instructions. The communications rows include additional types of move quadruples for the hardware interconnection network. The first move quadruple assumes a simple, *n*-dimensional grid, in which case a shift direction and amount are given in addition to the address of the fields to be moved. The second move instruction is for general interconnection networks where the address of the PE as well as the address of the field must be specified.

The associative quadruples in rows 11 and 12 are unique in parallel computing. They, in conjunction with the data control of flow quadruples, provide the associative model with its most powerful capabilities. The **find** quadruple selects the first PE flagged by a 1 in the specified parallel field. The common **reduce**

Table 10-1. The BAIL Instruction Set

	Scalar Quads		Parallel Quad		Common Quads	
Arithmetic & logical & move	tai	sc,sc,sc	tai	pa,pa,pa	tai	pa,sc,pa
	dai	sc,sc	dai	pa,pa	tai	sc,pa,pa
	sai	sc	sai	pa	dai	sc,pa
	move	sc,sc	pmv	pa,pa	move	pa,sc
Data control	b_t	sc,label	b_rs	pa,label		
	b_f	sc,label	b_nr	pa,label		
Program control	br	label				
	call	label				
Communications			move	sh,pa,pa		
			move	ppa,ppa		
Associative			find	pa		
			dex	pa		
I/O			collapse			
			expand			

key:
sc = scalar variable specifier = address, length
pa = parallel field specifier = address, length
br = branch, b_t = branch_on_true, b_f = branch_on_false
b_rs = branch_if_responders, b_nr = branch_if_no_responders
sh = communications grid shift = direction,amount
ppa = PE and parallel field address = PE,address,length
triple address operators
tai = add ¦ subtract ¦ multiply ¦ divide
¦ equal ¦ non_equal ¦ less_than ¦ greater _than
¦ less_than_or_equal ¦ greater_than_or_equal
¦ and ¦ or ¦ xor (logical operators)
¦ and ¦ or ¦ xor (bitwise operators)
double address operators
dai = minus ¦ move ¦ not (logical)
single address operators
sai = pop ¦ push
associative operators
dex = maxdex ¦ mindex ¦ sibdex
parallel move operators
pmv = resize ¦ move ¦ shift

instruction described below uses **find** to select the PE that responds to the command.

The last rows contain the two I/O quadruples that incorporate the corner-turning feature required by bit-serial SIMD arrays.

10.7.3. The Common Instruction Set

Column 3 of Table 10-1 gives the common quadruples. The common instructions combine scalar and parallel arguments. When the result is parallel, the instruction acts as a broadcast instruction. When the result is scalar, the instruction performs a reduction selection—the only primitive reduction operation. A reduction operation requires a previous **find** operation to set the mask register. The only processor that responds to a parallel-to-scalar move is the one selected by the previous **find** quadruple.

10.7.4. The Associative Environment

The proposed instruction set assumes that, normally, all parallel instructions are implicitly masked. That is, there is a hardware register which contains a mask bit for each PE which determines which processors are active. This register can be specified as the result address of a move or a parallel compare quadruple. Some implementations may choose to implement a stack of mask registers. The top level of the stack represents the current mask register value. The mask register would be updated to the top of the stack as the various quadruples manipulate the stack.

An equally viable alternative protocol would be to affix a new field to all parallel instructions and require that a mask field be explicitly specified for every operation. These and additional implementation details, such as which instructions are unmasked, are left to the hardware and high-level-language designers.

Most current SIMD architectures would map the scalar instruction set onto the host machine and the parallel instruction set onto the parallel array, while the third instruction set would be mapped onto the hardware interface between the two computers. But keep in mind that most (perhaps all) current SIMD designs envision the host as the master and the parallel array as the slave. Associative computing envisions the opposite. That is, the parallel array is the master computer and the host is the slave, performing I/O and providing a link to the sequential peripherals.

An associative computer (parallel array) could have its own internal scalar processor, independent of the host. Thus the scalar instruction set could be implemented in the SIMD array. In fact, in conventional configurations with a host and parallel array "add on," where the host–array communication path may be quite slow due to its being implemented over a general-purpose channel (i.e., SCSI interface), it may be most efficient to perform scalar operations in the parallel array, to avoid channel communication.

The BAIL instruction set makes no statement as to the degree of complexity of the underlying hardware. For example, the **collapse** and **expand** quadruples can easily be implemented using the other BAIL quadruples with the addition of only a corner-turning primitive. Thus on simpler, less expensive (and slower) machines, these quadruples could be achieved in software, but on more powerful, expensive machines they would be achieved in hardware. Figure 10-22 gives examples of how a **for** and a parallel **if** statement are implemented in the ASC emulator using BAIL quadruples.

```
move   (STACK,1), (MASK,1)           ;establish environment
 :          :                        ;logical parallel expression
b_nr   (responders,1), end_label
move   (responders,1), (MASK,1)
 :          :                        ;then body of if
not    (MASK,1), (MASK,1)
 :          :                        ;else body of if
label end_label
```

a - BAIL code for a parallel if statement

```
move   (STACK,1), (MASK,1)           ;establish environment
 :          :                        ;logical parallel expression
b_nr   (responders,1), end_label
label loop_label
next   (responders,1), (parallel_index,1)
 :          :                        ; body of for
b_rs   (responders,1), loop_label
label end_label
```

b - BAIL code for a for statement

Figure 10-22. For and if using BAIL.

10.8. Conclusion

This chapter presents the broad outline of the design of an associative computer. It briefly provides the rationale for the overall design and outlines how its objectives can be achieved. The design emphasizes the ability to search in parallel and shows how a multitasking/multiuser design is a straightforward extension of the basic associative computing concepts. Perhaps the most significant aspects of the design are the basic principles that

1. the parallel array is the main part of the computer
2. associative parallelism is the normal mode of operation
3. the sequential computer to which the array is connected is simply an I/O slave processor to which the conventional peripherals are connected, and
4. scalar operations are the exception in computing rather than the rule.

Appendix

ASC Tables

ASC Program Format

main program_name
define constants
define variables
variable declarations
association declarations
body
end;

Reserved Words

a/an	elsenany	endstack	maxval
allocate	end	for	msg
any	endandbody	fstcd	next
andbody	andandfor	get	nany
andif	endandif	if	nthdex
andfor	endany	ifany	nthval
andthen	endallocate	in	nxtcd
asmcode	endasm	include	parallel
associate	endfor	index	pa_perform
call	endget	int	perform
count	endif	its	prevcd
define	endifany	logical	print
deflog	endloop	loop	procedure
defvar	endnext	mindex	real
during	endrecursewhile	maxdex	recursewhile
else	endsetscope	minval	release

return
scalar
scin
sc_perform
scot
setscope
stack
stop
subroutine
the
their
them
then
trncd
trnacd
until
while
with
#include

Operators

Relational Operators

Less than	.lt.	<
Greater than	.gt.	>
Less than or equal to	.le.	<=
Greater than or equal to	.ge.	>=
Equal	.eq.	=
Not equal	.ne.	!=

Logical Operators

Not	.not.	!
Or	.or.	||
And	.and.	&&
Exclusive Or	.xor.	^^

Arithmetic Operators

Negation	−
Addition	+
Subtraction	−
Multiplication	*
Division	/

Functions

fstcd(code)	first structure code (leftmost child)
nxtcd(code)	next structure code (right sibling)
prvcd(code)	previous structure code (left sibling)
trncd(code)	truncate structure code (parent)
trnacd(code)	truncate all structure code (root)
maxdex(field)	index to maximum value of a field
mindex(field)	index to minimum value of a field
maxval(field)	maximum value of a field

minval(field)	minimum value of a field
nthval(field,*n*)	*n*th value of a field
nthdex(field,*n*)	*n*th index of a field
scin(atom,sc,bi)	structure code input (4 bit)
scin8(atom,sc,bi)	structure code input (8 bit)
scinl(atom,sc,bi)	structure code input (list)
scinp(atom,sc,bi,pred,head_flag,tid, pred_flag)	structure code input (Prolog)
scot(atom,sc,bi)	structure code output (4 bit)
scot8(atom,sc,bi)	structure code output (8 bit)
scotl(atom,sc,bi)	structure code output (list)
scotp(atom,sc,bi)	structure code output (Prolog)
scst(atom,sc,bi,list)	structure code constant (4 bit)
scst8(atom,sc,bi,list)	structure code constant (8 bit)
scstl(atom,sc,bi,list)	structure code constant (list)
scstp(atom,sc,bi,pred,head_flag,tid, pred_flag,list)	structure code constant (Prolog)

ASC Statements

```
[ int     ]
[ char    ]
[ logical ]
[ real    ]  [ scalar variable(:width)([,dimension,. . .]), . . ]
[ card    ]  [ parallel variable(:width)[$(,dimension,. . .)], . . ];
[ bin     ]
[ hex     ]
[ oct     ]
[ index   ]
```

```
allocate index_variable in association_name;
   statement_block
endallocate index_variable;
```

```
allocate n index_variable contiguously in association[$];
```

```
any conditional_expression
   statement_block1
(elseany
   statement_block2)
endany;
```

```
associate item1,item2,. . . with association_name;

call subroutine called_field1⟨calling_field1 . . .
                         calling_fieldn⟩called_fieldn;

deflog "("identifier, Boolean_constant")";

defvar "("identifier, ⎡decimal_constant                        ⎤")";
                      ⎣variable(⎡ + ⎤decimal_constant)⎦
                                ⎣ − ⎦

define "("identifier, constant")";

for index_variable in parallel_conditional_expression
   statement_block1
(elsenany
   statement_block2)
endfor index_variable;
get index_variable in parallel_conditional_expression
   statement_block1
(elsenany
   statement_block2)
endget index_variable;

if conditional_expression then

   statement_block1 (⎡else     ⎤ statement_block2)
                     ⎣elsenany⎦

endif;

(first
   statement_block)
loop

   ⎡until scalar_expression               ⎤
   ⎣until (nany) parallel_expression⎦

endloop;

msg delimitertextdelimiter variable_list;

next index_variable in parallel_variable
   statement_block1
(elsenany
   statement_block2)
endnext index_variable;

print "("handle")" itema[$] . . . itemn[$] in
logical_parallel_expression;
```

read “("handle“)” itema[$] . . . itemn[$] in association[$];

read “("handle“)” item[$] . . . contiguously in association[$];

readnl “("handle“)” itema[$] . . . itemn[$] in association[$];

release conditional_expression from association_name;
reread “("handle“)” itema[$] . . . itemn[$] in association[$];

setscope logical_parallel_expression
  statement_block
endsetscope;

while index_variable in parallel_conditional_expression
  statement_block
endwhile index_variable;

References

Aho, A., Sethi, R., and Ullman, J. [1986]. Compilers: Principles, Techniques, and Tools, Addision-Wesley, Reading, MA.

Asthagiri, C. [1986]. "Context Sensitive Parsing Using an Associative Processor," M.S. Thesis, Kent State University.

Asthagiri, C., and Potter, J. [1991]. "An Optimizing Parallel Algorithm for Evaluating Infix Operator Expressions on an Associative SIMD Computer," Technical Report CS9010-30, Kent State University.

Baase, S. [1978]. *Computer Algorithms: Introduction to Design and Analysis*, Addison-Wesley, Reading, MA.

Barnes, G., Brown, R., Kato, M., Kuck, D., Slotnick, D., and Stokes, R. [1968]. "The ILLIAC IV Computer," *IEEE Trans. Comput.* **17**, 746–757.

Batcher, K. [1976]. "STARAN Parallel Processor System Hardware," *Proc. NCC* **43**, 405-410.

Batcher, K. [1977]. "The Multidimensional Access Memory in STARAN," *Comput.* **10**, 174–177.

Berra, P., and Oliver E. [1979]. "The Role of Associative Array Processors in Database Machine Architecture," *Comput.* **12**, 53–61.

Brooks, R., and Lua, R. [1985]. "Yes, an SIMD Machine Can Be Used for AI," Proc. 1985 Int. Joint Conf. Artificial Intelligence, pp. 73–79.

Brownston, L., Farrel, R., Kant, E., and Martin, N. [1985]. *Programming Expert Systems in OPS5*, Addision-Wesley, Reading, MA.

Denning, P., Dennis, J., and Qualitz, J. [1976]. *Machines, Languages, and Computation*, Prentice-Hall, Englewood Cliffs, NJ.

Duncan, R. [1990]. "A Survey of Parallel Computer Architectures," *Comput.* **23**, 5–17.

Falkoff, A. [1962]. "Algorithms for Parallel-Search Memories," *J. Assoc. Comput. Mach.* **9**, 488–511.

Feldman, J., and Rovner, P. [1969]. "An ALGOL-Based Associative Language," *Comm. ACM* **12**, 439–449.

Findler, N. [1967]. "On a Computer Language which Simulates Associative Memory and Parallel Processing," *Cybernetica* **10**, 229–254.

Findler, N. V. (ed.) [1979]. *Associative Networks: Representation and Use of Knowledge by Computers*, Academic Press, New York.

Flynn, A., and Harris, J. [1985]. "Recognition Algorithms for the Connection Machine," Proc. 1985 Int. Joint Conf. Artificial Intelligence, pp. 57–60.

Forgy, C. [1981]. "OPS5 User's Manual," Technical Report CMU-CS-81-135, Carnegie-Mellon University.

Forgy, C. [1982]. "RETE: A Fast Algorithm for the Many Pattern/Many Object Pattern Match Problem," *Artificial Intelligence* **19**, 17–37.

Foster, C. [1976]. *Content Addressable Parallel Processors*, Van Nostrand-Reinhold, New York.

Gallopoulos, E. [1985]. "Fluid Dynamics Modeling," in Potter [1985], pp. 85–103.

Ginsburg, S. [1966]. *The Mathematical Theory of Context Free Languages*, McGraw-Hill, New York.

Gupta, A. [1984]. "Implementing OPS5 Production System on DADO," Proc. Int. 1984 Conf. Parallel Processing, pp. 83–91.

Harrison, W., and Padua, D. [1984]. "Representing S-expressions for the Efficient Evaluation of Lisp on Parallel Computers," Proc. 1984 Int. Conf. Parallel Processing, pp. 122–129.

Haston, T. [1987]. "An OPS5 Implementation on a SIMD Computer," M.S. Thesis, Kent State University.

Heaty, L., Lipovski, G., and Doty, K. [1972]. "The Architecture of a Context Addressed Segment-sequential Memory," Proc. AFIPS Fall Joint Computer Conference, pp. 691–701.

Hillis, W., and Steele, G. [1986]. "Data Parallel Algorithms," *Comm. ACM* **29**, 1170–1183.

Hilyer, B., and Shaw, D. [1986]. "Execution of OPS5 Production Systems on a Massively Parallel Machine," *JPDC* **3** pp. 236–268.

Hioe, K. [1986]. "ASPROL," M.S. Thesis, Kent State University.

Hsiao, D. (ed.) [1983]. *Advanced Database Machine Architecture*, Prentice-Hall, Englewood Cliffs, NJ.

Hwang, K., and Briggs, F. [1984]. *Computer Architecture and Parallel Processing*, McGraw-Hill, New York.

Jacks, E. (ed.) [1971]. *Associative Information Techniques*, Elsevier, New York.

Johnsson, S., and Mather, K. [1989]. "Data Structures and Algorithms for the Finite Element Method," Technical Report CS89-1, Thinking Machines Corporation, Cambridge, MA.

Kowalski, R. [1979]. "Algorithm = logic + control," *Comm. ACM* **22**, 424–436.

Kohonen, T. [1978]. *Associative Memory, a System: Theoretical Approach*, Springer-Verlag, Berlin.

Lea, R. [1985]. "Associative Processing," in *Advanced Digital Information Systems*, Prentice-Hall, Englewood Cliffs, NJ, pp. 531–575.

Oliver, E. [1979]. "RELACS, An Associative Computer Architecture to Support a Relational Data Model," Department of Industrial Engineering and Operations Research, Syracuse University.

Pasik, A. [1988]. "A Methodology for Programming Production Systems and Its Implementation on Parallelism," Computer Science Department Technical Report, Columbia University.

Potter, J. [1983]. "Alternative Data Structures for Lists in Parallel Associative Computers," Proc. 1983 Int. Conf. Parallel Processing, pp. 486–491.

Potter, J. [1984]. "A Scene Analysis SIMD Processor," Proc. ICCD, pp. 520–525.

Potter, J. "List Based Processing on the MPP," in Potter [1985b], pp. 124–140.

Potter, J. [1985a]. "Using Hextrees to Model 4 Space," Proc. Topical Meeting Machine Vision, pp. 191–194.

Potter, J. (ed.) [1985b]. *The Massively Parallel Processor*, MIT Press, Cambridge, MA.

Potter, J. [1985c]. "Specialized SIMD Instructions for Associative Processing," Proc. 1985 Int. Conf. Circuit Design, pp. 1138–1141.

Potter, J. [1987a]. "An Associative Model of Computation," Proc. 1987 Int. Conf. Super-Computing.

Potter, J., Rivett, M., and Haston, T. [1987b]. "Rule-based Systems on SIMD Computers," Proc. ROBEXS, pp. 198–204.

Potter, J. and Meilander, W. [1989]. "Array Processor Supercomputers," *Proc. IEEE* **77**, 1896–1914.

Quillian, R. [1968]. "Semantic Memory," in Minsky, M. (ed.), *Semantic Information Processing*, MIT Press, Cambridge, MA.

Reed, B. [1985]. "An Implementation of Lisp on a SIMD Parallel Processor," Proc. Conf. Aerospace Applications of AI, pp. 31–36.

Reed, R. [1985]. "The ASPRO Parallel Inference Engine (P.I.E.)— A Real Time Production Rule System," Proc. Conf. Aerospace, pp. 89–85.

Reeves, A. [1985]. "Parallel Pascal and the Massively Parallel Processor," in Potter, J. (ed.) [1985b], pp. 230–260.

Rich, E. [1983]. *Artificial Intelligence*, McGraw-Hill, New York.

Rose, J., and Steele, G. [1987]. "C*: An Extended C Language for Data Parallel Programming," Technical Report PL87-5, Thinking Machines Corporation, Cambridge, MA.

Savitt, D., Love, H., and Troop, R. [1967]. Proc. 1967 Spring Joint Computer Conf. pp. 87–102.

Schuster, S., Nguyen, H., Ozkarahan, E., and Smith, K. [1979]. "Rap.2: An Associative Processor for Databases and Its Applications," *IEEE Trans. Comput.* **C-28**, 446–458.

Shaw, D. [1982]. "SIMD and MSIMD Variants of the Non-Von Supercomputer," Technical Report, Department of Computer Science, Columbia University.

Shaw, D. [1985]. "Non-Von's Applicability to Three AI Task Areas," Proc. 1985 Int. Joint Conf. Artificial Intelligence, pp. 61–72.

Siegel, H., Siegel, L., Kemmerer, C., Mueller, P., Sinalley, H., and Smith, S. [1981]. "PASM: A Partitionable SIMD/MIMD System for Image Processing and Pattern Recognition," *IEEE Trans. Comput.* **C-30**, 934–947.

Siegel, L., Siegel, H., and Feather, A. [1983]. "Parallel Processing Approaches to Image Correlation," *IEEE Trans. Comput.* **C-31**, 208–218.

Siegel, L., Siegel, H., and Swain, P. [1982]. "Performance Measures for Evaluating Algorithms for SIMD Machines," *IEEE Trans. Software Engrg.* **SE-8**, 319–331.

Simon, H. and Newell, A. [1970]. "Information-Processing in Computers and Man," in Pylshyn, Z. (ed.), *Perspectives on the Computer Revolution*, Prentice-Hall, Englewood Cliffs, NJ.

Steele, G., and Hillis, W. [1986]. "Connection Machine Lisp: Fine-Grained Parallel Symbolic Processing," Technical Report PL86-2, Thinking Machines Corporation, Cambridge, MA.

Stolfo, S. and Miranker, D. [1984]. "DADO: A Parallel Processor for Expert Systems," in Proc. 1984 Int. Conf. Parallel Processing, pp. 74–82.

Stone, H. [1975]. *Introduction to Computer Architecture*, Science Research Associates, Chicago, IL.

Su, S., Nguyen, L., Emam, A., and Ripovski, G. [1979]. "The Architectural Features and Implementation Techniques of the Multicell CASSM," *IEEE Trans. Comput.* **C-28**, 430–445.

Thinking Machines Corporation [1986]. "Introduction to Data Level Parallelism," Thinking Machines Corporation, Technical Report TR86-14.

Thurber, K. [1975]. "Associative and Parallel Processors," *Computing Surveys* **7**, 215–255.

Weems, C. [1985]. "The Content Addressable Array Parallel Process: Architectural Evaluation and Enhancement," Proc. 1985 Int. Conf. Circuit Design, pp. 500–503.

White, R. [1985]. "Inversion of Positive Definite Matrices on the MPP," in Potter, J. (ed.) [1985b], pp. 7–30.

Whorf, B., and Sapir, E. [1956]. *Language, Thought and Reality*, Technology Press, Cambridge, England.

Index